CURIOUSITY, Adventure Travel, Exploration, Trade, War, Murder

PROOF

pictures Wrong

CURIOUSITY, Adventure Travel, Exploration, Trade, War, Murder

THE EUROPEAN EXPANSION, 15TH TO 20TH CENTURY

James B. Read

ISBN-13: 9781539496366
ISBN-10: 1539496368
Library of Congress Control Number: 2016917120
CreateSpace Independent Publishing Platform
North Charleston, South Carolina

Cover illustration of the *Bartolomu Dias* designed by Ann Read

Acknowledgements

———

MY THANKS GO FIRST TO Suratman (Atman) Dahlam whose tour of Ternate provided me the inspiration for this book. Next I thank his mentor Ibraham Umakamea who brought us together. Docent Abdul Rahman of Makassar was also an inspiration. My wife Annie set me up with an old Apple with Scrivner word processor to get this project underway.In addition, Annie did the cover illustration of the *Bartolomu Dias*. Rich Becket very patiently brought me into the 21st century teaching me computer skills after a 15-year withdrawal. Thanks also go to my friend Dr. Steve Petty, who has been published half a dozen times. He put me in touch with Amazon Create Space. My thanks also extend to Devon of Create Space who performed a copy edit and induced me to take a critical look, clean up some things and add more depth and detail.

Introduction

———

IN THE SUMMER OF 1958, I, an eighteen-year-old kid, was exposed to Hawaii, Japan, the Philippines, Hong Kong, Formosa (Taiwan), the East and South China Seas, French Indochina (Laos, Vietnam), the Gulf of Siam (Thailand), Singapore and the equator, all courtesy of the US Navy. A fellow crew member, named Short, had the romantic idea of retiring, purchasing a Chinese Junk, and cruising the South Pacific with a young woman. What a fun idea.

In 1973, while running a mom-and-pop corner store in San Francisco, I had the privilege of meeting a colorful Portuguese customer named Tony. Tony had been a merchant seaman and a policeman in Macau, China, and was very proud of his country's history. He described Prince Henry the Navigator and told me how Henry almost single-handedly initiated the exploration of the world.

In 1982 my twelve-year-old son, Tom, went to a YMCA Ski and Sail camp. On returning, he managed to convince his mom that the family needed a sailboat. Sailing turned out to be a fun and addicting idea, and within a few years Tom and I shared a Ranger 26.

In 1988 Aunt Betty and Uncle Bill invited me to sail down the coast with them in their thirty-six-foot cruiser, from Sausalito to Morro Bay, California. After that I was hooked and knew I had to go cruising on my own sailboat.

In 1993, after my wife passed away, I met my future one, Annie, at a Single Sailors raft-up on San Francisco Bay. Soon we purchased *Camille*, a fixer-upper ex–racing boat, with the idea of converting it into a cruiser. In 2005 we were the first married couple in a hundred years to doublehand the Transpac race from Long Beach to Hawaii. Sadly, while cruising, we lost *Camille* on a reef in Samoa.

As a sailor, a backpacker, an adventure traveler, and an amateur marine historian, I have related my stories of early explorers many times. Like me years earlier, most people have little or no knowledge of Prince Henry. In the summer of 2013, after visiting the island of Ternate, the Spice Island that drew the Portuguese, the Dutch, the British, Columbus, and Magellan, I was inspired to see where Henry came from and to write this book. The second part of this book relates the inspirational trips that motivated me. I was litterally driven to uncover and write the history related in the first part.

Contents

_____

The real voyage of discovery
consists not in seeking new landscapes,
but in having new eyes.

MARCEL PROUST, *1909*

Marco Polo, by Rustichello de Pisa 1256-1324

———

I N 1271 M A R C O P O L O, a curious fifteen-year-old tagalong boy, left his cozy cocoon in the Venice Republic, where everything was warm, comfortable, and predictable. He began a three-year, seven-thousand-mile odyssey to Peking, present-day Beijing, China, to meet the great Mongol emperor Kublai Khan, grandson of Genghis Khan.

Two years earlier, after having served the emperor for three years, Marco's father, Niccolò, and uncle Maffeo, wealthy traders, completed a fifteen-thousand-mile-round trip and returned to Venice. On their return, Niccolò discovered that his wife had died but had left him a son, Marco. If Marco had been older than thirteen or fourteen, Niccolo would have known of his son's existence prior to departing for Asia.

The brothers had originally sailed to Constantinople and crossed the Black Sea, trading jewels. On horseback, they reached Assara, now inside Turkey, where they befriended a Tartar chief named Barka. Barka entertained them for a year, paid them twice the value of the jewels they carried while even giving them expensive gifts. When the Polos decided to return home, Barka, who had recently lost a battle with neighboring Chief Alau, advised them to return via the east, where travel would be safer. They crossed the Tigress River to Bokhara, where they were welcomed by Prince Barak.

After patiently waiting three years for a safe return route home, they befriended one of Chief Alau's ambassadors to the Mongol Empire. The ambassador, enjoying their company and thinking the khan would be pleased to meet them, invited the Polos to join him on his journey back to China. The following year they reached Peking (now Beijing) and were introduced to the Great Khan.

The Polos became conversant in the Tartar language and had long meetings with Kublai Khan, who was very curious about Venice and their trading and travel experiences. The khan trusted the brothers enough to send them back to Venice with a gold tablet and documents and to represent him in meetings with the pope, kings, and princes of Europe. He also requested that they bring him some holy oil from Jerusalem, specifically that which was burned over Christ's sepulcher.

In 1269, the brothers returned to Venice, picked up young Marco and then journeyed on to the Vatican. Pope Gregory responded to the khan's requests with two friars bearing papal letters and gifts of crystal.

Marco, his father, his uncle, and the two friars headed for China via Laiassus. After a short while they learned that Armenia had been overrun by Bundokdari of Babylonia. The friars, fearful for their lives, handed over the gifts and documents to the Polos then returned to the safety of the Vatican.

Three and a half years later, the Polos reached Clemenfu Palace, where Niccolò introduced Marco to Kublai Khan as "your servant and my son." Marco was well received by the khan and soon became proficient in the Tartar language. When Marco returned from a six-month inspection trip, the khan was so impressed with his report that he appointed Marco his inspector general. In this capacity and accompanied by soldiers, scribes, and cooks, Marco traveled to many sections of the empire, making careful note of what he observed.

Over a period of seventeen years, Marco led expeditions inside China, Burma, Ceylon, and India and down the South China Sea to Vietnam, Malaya, and Sumatra. In the book of his travels, he notes gifts of a hundred thousand white horses, parades with five thousand elephants, meals served to forty thousand guests, and a ruby as big as a fist. He also referred to the mythical Prestor John as though this wealthy and powerful Christian king actually existed. Later the Portuguese would spend much effort-all for naught-hoping to locate Prestor John, share his riches, and use his services to kill or convert the Muslim enemy. Other less preposterous stories—describing flesh-eating and tattooed natives, huge crocodiles, and the island of Sumatra, where all the spices in the world grow—are more believable. Marco's tales of spices, jewels, and inexhaustible gold would later arouse the curiosity and greed of both Prince Henry and Columbus.

After seventeen years in China, the Polos wished to return home, but Kublai Khan, who enjoyed their trust, company, and expertise, had no desire to see them leave. By a quirk of fate, Queen Bolgana, wife of Arghun, sovereign of India and close relative of the khan, had recently died. She had willed that her husband re-marries only one of her own relatives, only to be found inside the khan's empire. Arghun selected three nobles to bring back a new queen from Cathay. They selected a beautiful and accomplished seventeen-year-old girl named Kogatin but were unable to complete her passage to India. Upon hearing of Marco's successful return from Sumatra, the three nobles petitioned the khan to have the Polos assist with Kogatin's journey.

With great reluctance and after securing the Polos' promises to return, Kublai Khan allowed them to leave. On reaching India, they found that Arghun had died, and they were redirected to Persia, where Arghun's son was commanding a garrison of sixty thousand men. Upon safely delivering Kogatin, the Polos returned to Venice and reestablished themselves as traders.

In 1298 Marco was captured aboard a Venetian vessel and became a prisoner of war in the Republic of Genoa. By chance, Rustichello, a writer and fellow prisoner from Pisa, was placed in Marco's cell. Marco's tales pushed Rustichello's imagination, but when Marco displayed the gold and jewels sewn in his cuffs, his story seemed much more credible. Rustichello recorded the story in three volumes and it was translated under at least two titles, *Il Millione* and *The Travels of Marco Polo*.

Following his release in 1299, Marco married and fathered three daughters, finally dying in 1324. There is some doubt as to when Marco was born, but there is universal acceptance of when he died. If he left Venice at fifteen and lived to be sixty-eight, he had to have been born in 1256. If he left Venice at nineteen and lived to be seventy-two, he had to have been born in 1252. Due to the shorter average life-spans of the period, 1256 seems more credible.

This saga contains an incredible amount of luck. All three Polos were blessed with extremely durable bodies, and they were never described as having any major health problems. Equally amazing, they were never injured by highwaymen or warriors, natural disasters, or accidents. Niccolò and Maffeo, unable to return home when Chief Barka's territory was rendered unsafe, were escorted directly to Kublai Khan. The khan welcomed them as ambassadors and requested that they represent him to the pope, kings, and princes of Europe, trusting them to deliver his gifts, gold, and documents after receiving their promise to return to him with the rare oil. Happily, the stage was then set for young Marco to impress the khan and become his inspector general. The Polos would have been stuck in Cathay forever but for the need to escort Kogatin. This amazing story would have gone unrecorded but for Marco's chance meeting with Rustichello.

Rustichello was a romantic writer and storyteller and lately has come under criticism. A recent program aired on PBS could find no evidence of the war between the Republics of Venice and Genoa, where Marco allegedly became a prisoner. A final note: Though much of what Marco described was fictional, he did bring back the secrets of gunpowder and the magnetic compass, in addition he described the usage of coal and paper currency.

Prince Henry the Navigator 1394-1460

─────

HENRIQUE O INFANTE WAS BORN in 1394, just seventy years after Marco Polo was laid to rest. He was the third son of King Joao of Portugal and Philippa Lancaster, granddaughter of Edward II of England. His older brothers, Duarte and Pedro, both became kings.

At fourteen Henry became a duke, even owning his own house. He was a recipient of the finest education available in his country. Brother Pedro, a cultured and well-traveled scholar, brought home one day, a copy of Rustichello's *Il Millione*, which enlightened Henry to the treasures and delights of China, India, Arabia, Malaya, Japan, and Sumatra, especially the gold, jewels, and spices.

Henry grew up with two major obsessions: to conquer the coast of Africa to enable acquisition of the gold and spices Marco Polo described, and to rid the world of Muslims. He was still fighting the Crusades with the extreme encouragement of his church and the Pope. He wore a rough hair shirt under his outer clothes as a reminder of his campaign against Muslims. A hair shirt, usually made of woven horsehair, is a rough abrasive garment, typically worn for penance or religious atonement.

In 1414 Henry was involved in the victory of Cueta with a seventy-ship amphibious attack on the Moor city opposite Gibraltar. For several years, he served as governor of the newly conquered territory. During this time, he began organizing seagoing expeditions, one of which resulted in the discovery of the Madeira Islands.

Henry was deeply religious and lived in strict celibacy, very unusual for a man. Possible reasons were: he was gay, he hated women, he had a physical disability, or he considered himself priest like, which is the most likely reason. At age twenty-six he became grand master of the militant Order of Christ, successor to the Knights Templar. The OOC, which had a large treasury, served Henry as a two-edged sword, both to help finance expeditions and to kill, subjugate, or convert Muslims in newly occupied territory. In 1456 Pope Callixtus II granted spiritual jurisdiction to all newly acquired lands, which were to be placed under the guidance of the OOC.

Henry continued to gain power and wealth by gathering to himself a number of rent-seeking positions. These included the following:

- The right to pirate Muslim shipping
- A percentage of income from his monopoly of Portuguese tuna fishing
- A percentage of income from milling cereal and the manufacture of ink and soap
- One-fifth of the value of all captured slaves
- 20 percent of all commodities obtained from his expeditions
- Monopoly on Madeira sugar production (used to break Venice's monopoly on Crete and Cypress sugar)

In addition, he became governor of Algarve, the southernmost province of Portugal. Using his own personal wealth and with help from his brother, the king, Henry erected a fortress on the promontory of Sagres, located in Portugal's southwestern most corner, five kilometers southeast of Cape Saint Vincent.

The Sagres peninsula is beautiful and rugged with a rocky but level surface. Its limestone cliffs rise vertically fifty meters above the Atlantic. It is a thousand meters long and narrows to two hundred meters where it joins the continent. Because of its natural boundaries, only a single wall was required at the narrows to secure the fort's perimeter.

Within this easily defensible space, Henry set up his headquarters and created the first navigation school—or, arguably, at least the first navigational think tank. To staff this operation, he hired the finest available scientists, astronomers, cartographers, ship designers, instrument makers, and other craftsmen, even if they were Muslim.

He also collected the finest instruments available, which included compasses, astrolabes, quadrants, hourglasses, and hanging sundials. These were then modified and improved for accuracy and ease of use in a rolling sea. Under Henry's authority, the quadrant and astrolabe were converted from astronomical land-use instruments into seagoing altitude-measuring devices.

Henry's scientists began work on an ephemeris, an almanac that depicts the noon position and elevation of the sun, plus selected navigational star positions, for each day of the year. The goal was to determine latitude at sea. Though it was not complete during his lifetime, it was in use by Portuguese pilots by 1485 and was published in 1493 following the theft by Columbus, as *Regiment of the Astrolabe and Quadrant.* Had Columbus not stolen this state secret, he never could have found his way to the New World and back to Spain.

At the time, longitude could only be crudely determined by rate, time, and distance calculations. Time was determined by reading a hanging vertical sundial, a medieval chronometer. Boat speed was calculated using the time that a log attached to a line and thrown into the sea passed from the bow to the stern (hence the term "speed log").

At the Columbus museum in Palos de la Fronteria, I observed a ganged hourglass assembly (six small hourglasses), each with slightly more sand than the previous one) all attached to a single strip of wood. I believe this was a Portuguese invention, a MEDIEVAL STOPWATCH, created for easy and accurate timing of boat speed. Couple this with a pre-calculated listing, and log time in seconds can be immediately converted to boat speed.

For example, six nautical miles per hour is very close to 10 ft. /sec. If a nautical mile is rounded down from 6080 to 6000 feet as does the US Navy, where a nm = 2000 yards, it is precisely 10 feet/ second. Six knots = 6 x 6000 = 36,000 ft./hr. One hour = 60 minutes or 3,600 sec. 36,000 divided by 3,600 = 10 / 1 or 10 ft. / sec. A log would pass a 90- foot caravel traveling 6 nm / HR in 9 seconds. 18 seconds = 3nm / HR, 56 seconds = 1 nm / HR, (drifting). The practical range of the instrument is 5.6 seconds for 10 nm / HR and 28 seconds for 2 nm / HR. The unit is inverted for the 56 second timeout. Speed in nautical miles (knots) is usually indicated by K.

	Math logic
1 K = 56 sec.	three x 3K time
2 K = 28 sec.	1/2 x 1K time
3 K = 18 sec.	twice ref time
4 K = 14 sec.	1/2 x 2K time
5 K = 11.2 sec.	twice 10K time
6 K = 9 sec (reference)	
7 K = 7.7 sec.	(7 x 6000) /3600 = 11.66 90/11.66=7.7
8 K = 7 sec.	1/2 x 4K time
9 K = 6 sec.	(9 x 6000) / 3600 = 15 90/15=6
10 K = 5.6 sec.	1/10 x 1K time

If I was determining the six sand timeouts, I would set it up in seconds as follows: 6, 9, 11.2, 14, 18, 28

What clever people these Portuguese, the pilot had exact boat speed as soon as the log cleared the stern.

Charts were continuously updated or redrawn based on the latest observations and measurements from returning ships. Wind velocity and direction patterns based on daily observations and positions were recorded and updated with each returning vessel. Slowly the Atlantic wind patterns became charted and understood.

Henry's ship designers introduced the *caravel* circa 1443. Light and swift with a shallow draught, it incorporated two masts and a stern-mounted rudder. The mastheads each supported a spar from which the sails were hung. To beat or go to weather, one end of each hinged spar was secured forward at deck level to form a triangular sail. The excess sail was then gathered and reefed, parallel to the deck. This triangular sail pattern allowed the ship to return home at a forty-five-degree angle against the wind. To sail downwind the booms were set horizontally, and the unfurled sails became square rigged.

For forty years, Henry organized expeditions south along the African coast. In 1434 Gil Eanes reached Cape Bojador. Afonso Gonçalves reached the Rio de Ouro, returning with hundreds of sea lion skins and becoming the first expedition with a profit. In 1441 Nuno Tristão rounded Cape Blanco. Sadly, 1441 also marked the first-year slaves were captured. Dinis Dias discovered the

Cape Verde islands, which by 1444 had become a base station. In 1456 the Cadamosto and Usidamare expeditions reached the New Guinea coast. In 1449 the first trading fort was established on Arguim Island. By 1460, the year Henry died, they were shipping a thousand slaves per year from Fort Arguim to Lagos. Henry's personal motto, "The desire to do good", seems a little strange considering his profit from buying and selling human beings.

Prince Henry was buried in his hair shirt as a reminder of his hatred of Muslims. At the time of his death, his expeditions still had not been able to cross the equator. For twenty years after his passing, exploration languished and came to a halt.

In 1481 Henry's great-nephew reached the throne as King Joao II. As a prince, he had overseen the African trade. His first order of business was to resume Henry's exploration program. But unifying the royal family required the elimination of two dissenting members. He had one beheaded and personally dispatched the other himself.

Now, with all his ducks in a row and sufficient funds at his disposal, Joao could focus completely on rounding the final African cape. He established the "Cosmographers Convention" with a focus on charting and determining latitude. For security and projection of power, he began outfitting caravels with large-bore cannons, a historical first. There also was much to learn regarding Atlantic wind and current patterns, and all explorers sailing out of Lisbon were slowly expanding the knowledge base: The mysterious equatorial winds circulate clockwise in the Northern Hemisphere and opposite in the south. Currents are stronger near the shore than farther out.

In 1486 Diogo Cão placed a seven-foot-long stone *padrao* marker at Cape Cross, fifty miles north of Walvis Bay and only five hundred miles from the southern cape. These heavy stone markers, engraved with territorial claims were placed vertically, visible from the sea. Two years later came the great moment.

Bartolomeu Dias, after leaving nine men with a store ship, continued south and found safe anchorage in Walvis Bay. A week later and 250 miles farther south, he found shelter in Luderitz Bay, where a strong southerly kept him holed up for five days.

When the wind eased, he continued southward and passed the unseen mouth of the Orange River. Leaving sight of land at Cape Provence, where he encountered a heavy headwind and foul current, he opted to move some unknown distance offshore. Thirteen days later he gave the command to swing east in search of the coast. To everyone's surprise, no land loomed on the eastern horizon. He then swung north and found the coast to be running east-west. They had finally done it: rounded the first southern cape of South Africa and proceeded into the Indian Ocean.

There are actually two southern capes. Dias called the first cape the Cape of Storms, later renamed by King Joao the Cape of Good Hope, 34:21S. The second cape, 90 nautical miles to the east, is named Cape Agulhas. Agulhas at 34:50S is the southernmost tip of Africa. Cape Agulhas splits the Indian Ocean from the Atlantic Ocean.

Continuing east, they planted a stone padrao at Cape Padrone and then came ashore for fresh water and provisions at Mossel Bay. Had the crew not threatened mutiny, Dias would have continued the exploration up the east coast. On the downwind return trip, Dias charted the southern coast and discovered Table Bay flanked by Table Mountain, the future site of Cape Town.

In 1988, in celebration of the five-hundredth anniversary of the Dias Expedition, Portugal sailed a full-sized working replica of a caravel south from Lisbon, down the coast of Africa, around both capes, and into Mossel Bay. The *Bartolomeu Dias* was then raised to the top of a hill overlooking the bay and enclosed inside a museum, where any curious person can walk its decks. Prince Henry would have been elated.

If one covets another's monopoly,
one who does not wish to share,
then he must steal it,
kill the owner,
or both.

An Historical Abstraction

The Portuguese Empire (1515–1615)

WHEN COLUMBUS ARRIVED IN LISBON in 1493, Joao II questioned him regarding the latitude boundaries of the New World, which were approximately eighteen to twenty-two degrees north. In 1480 Joao had negotiated the Alcáçovas Treaty with Spain, which divided the world horizontally along a baseline passing through the Canary Islands—Spanish territory to the north, Portuguese territory to the south, with each country keeping previous possessions. Joao was hoping to claim the New World for Portugal, but the Alcacovas line was too far south for a Portuguese claim.

Following Columbus's discovery of the New World, the Treaty of Tordesillas was negotiated. The result was to divide the world with a vertical line running just east of the Amazon delta and slightly west of Rio de Janeiro. Portugal now could claim part of South America (Brazil and the Guineas), all of Africa, and anything to the south.

The reader may wonder why not keep things in chronological order, Dias 1488 then Columbus 1492? The entire nation of Portugal had become committed to exploration and dominance of world trade. They had done the astronomical research allowing the determination of latitude. They had completed the required engineering with the creation of the caravel. They had established systematic data collection for a wind and current database. In addition to all that they were continuously improving their instruments, equipment and navigational skills. Portugal was clearly number one and had momentum. Columbus sailed on a Portuguese designed Nao (Santa Maria), escorted by two caravels (Nina and Pinta) and carried with him a Portuguese nautical almanac and Portuguese designed astrolabes for latitude determination. Does it seem fair to allow a tiny start up group of ninety Spaniards led by a thieving Italian spy to steal the Portuguese thunder?

King Manuel succeeded his cousin in 1496 with the full commitment of finding a trade route to India and the Spice Islands. In 1487, to insure the success of the next expedition, Joao, before he died, had sent a Portuguese spy named Pêro da Covilhã overland to find trade routes. Disguised as a Mideast trader, he traveled through Egypt and then by boat to Goa and Calicut, India. He then proceeded back south down the East African coast to Mozambique, and finally north to Cairo, where he passed his information to a courier. The courier then assigned him to find the mythical Prestor John. Covilhã spent his final days in Ethiopia, the captive guest of an African king.

In 1497, with the new information acquired from Covilhã and Bartolomeu Dias, King Manuel launched the Vasco da Gama expedition. With two Naos, a caravel, and a store ship, all armed with cannons, they set sail for India. This time traveling in a circle that almost touched Brazil, they reached Saint Helena in only three months, half the time of Dias. Rounding the capes, they landed at Mossel Bay, where they emptied and burned the store ship then restocked with fresh water, fruit, and livestock. They proceeded north to Mozambique after stopping at the Zavora River to deal with scurvy and make mast repairs.

Mozambique was one of a string of independent city-states, a seaport lined with many substantial white buildings, and contained a Muslim palace. Da Gama received a sour welcome from the sultan when he offered only bells, beads, and cheap trinkets for trade. Not wishing to deal with Christians, the sultan even refused them water. Now miffed, da Gama fired a cannon, which killed three men. He then pirated some trading vessels and, taking several prisoners, headed north to Mombasa.

The local sultan sent out a boatload of sheep and fruit as a welcoming gesture, but when some captives who had agreed to act as pilots jumped overboard, da Gama became suspicious. Pouring hot oil on the bellies of the two remaining pilots revealed that an ambush was in progress. Hurriedly departing Mombasa with the "gifts," da Gama continued north to Malindi.

In Malindi, a Hindu port, da Gama encountered a friendly king who considered the Muslim sultans his enemies. He provided the expedition with food, water, and—to their good fortune—a pilot. On April 24, they headed east across the Indian Ocean. With the assistance of the pilot to avoid reefs and with spring monsoon winds filling their sails, they made Calicut, India, by May 20, 1498.

After a very splendid welcome, the Zamoran Hindu king became appalled by the cheap trinkets offered in trade. Things were further exasperated because most traders in India were Christian-hating Muslims. After three frustrating months of trading, da Gama departed India with a paltry mix of spices and precious stones.

Without the aid of a pilot or any knowledge of the strange phenomenon of the reversing monsoon winds of the Indian Ocean, the expedition took three excruciating months to return to Malinda, more than three times as long as the eastward crossing. To make matters worse, thirty crew succumbed to scurvy. Thanks to the friendly king's provisions of meat and oranges, the remaining crew recovered. Now able to crew only two ships, da Gama burned one and began the long journey home. Rounding the Cape of Good Hope on March 20, da Gama returned to Lisbon August 29, 1499. He would have returned much earlier but detoured to the Azores to bury his brother. In his debriefing with King Manuel, da Gama stated that no spices could be obtained without projection of naval power.

King Manuel now knew everything that was required to establish trade with India. Portugal began building an empire in earnest, and there is no empire without sea power. Foundries began working around the clock, casting four to six-hundred-pound bronze cannons, massive for the day. Caravels were beefed up to accept the new ordinance and became frigates. Naos and galleons were designed as combination cargo-cruisers. The strategy was to completely eliminate the Muslim traders, boats, and ships. After this display of power and elimination of competition, the unfriendly sultans would be forced to cooperate just to stay in business. Without Arab competition the price of goods could be pushed way down and as sole suppliers, they could name the price at home. Competing sultans—suspicious, envious, and jealous of one another—could be manipulated, one against the other. The next step would be to construct a network of fortified trading posts complete with garrisons and chapels, each to be located in a safe harbor with easy access to the sea.

Pedro Alvares Cabral led the next expedition, with thirteen ships transporting twelve hundred men. Sailing slightly too far west, downwind in the newly discovered South Atlantic trade route, Cabral managed to set foot on land, claiming Brazil for his country.

Cabral, now in Calicut harbor while negotiating a trade agreement with the same sultan who refused da Gama, managed to capture a three-hundred-man ship with a cargo of half a dozen elephants. Keeping the cargo for his expedition, he presented the pachyderms to the sultan of Calicut. Greatly impressed that this feat was accomplished with a single twenty-five-man caravel, the sultan warmed up to Cabrel and allowed a seventy-man trading depot to be constructed.

Later a mob of three thousand resentful Muslims stormed the depot, killing fifty men. In retaliation Cabral captured ten Muslim ships, killed their five hundred fifty-man crew, and seized their cargo. Thinking the sultan at least partly responsible, he shot up Calicut and then moved south to Cochin, where he found a friendlier sultan to trade with. In Cochin, he installed a combination trading post, storehouse, chapel, and garrison.

Cabral returned to Lisbon in mid-1501 with only seven ships and half his crew but with an estimated three hundred thousand-pounds of valuable cargo. Pepper sold in Venice for twenty-five times its cost in Calicut. Making fast use of the new resources, King Manuel set up a trading post in Antwerp, a marketplace to sell luxury items to all of Europe. Manual became known through-out Europe as the Grocer King.

Da Gama led the next expedition in 1502, practicing diplomacy with cannons, guns, crossbows, and swords. When the Zamoran sultan of Calicut refused get to get rid of Muslim traders, da Gama performed grisly murders of both Hindus and Muslims, blasting the city with pieces of some unlucky victims from cannons. When he returned to Lisbon in 1503, his ships were crammed full of spices, and the Muslim competition was severely fractured.

In 1505, Francisco de Almeida was commissioned to further implement the master plan. On his trip up the East African coast, he sacked and destroyed Mombasa; then proceeded farther north and captured Sofala and then Kilwa. A young noble, Ferdinand Magellan, was placed in charge of the garrison at Kilwa. Almeida then headed east to India, where he began fortifying a series of harbors. Making use of his new facilities, he raided Muslim commerce, looting and burning their ships and terrorizing his victims. When he completed a three-year term as viceroy of India, Almeida was replaced with an equally cruel leader named Affonso de Albuquerque.

Albuquerque seized Goa, establishing a Portuguese colony in 1510 with a population numbering 450. Goa was to become a major hub, continually occupied by Portuguese until their forced eviction in 1967. Also in 1510, Albuquerque's expeditions discovered the Moluccas, the Spice Islands which were the world's sole source of cloves. In 1511 he conquered the city of Malacca. Malacca offered a trading center with a quiet harbor and provided a choke point where shipping in the Straits of Malacca could be easily controlled. Protected from the monsoons, it was the gateway to both the Orient and the Spice Islands. In 1515 he occupied Hormuz, another choke point. By now the Indian Ocean had become the Portuguese Ocean.

The Portuguese Empire continued to expand until 1568. By then they had established trading forts in Kilwa, Hormuz, Goa, Calicut, Cochin, Ceylon, East India, Sumatra, Malacca, Makassar, Timor, Ternate (four forts), Nagasaki, and Macau. In addition, there was a sugar colony near Rio de Janeiro, and African slaves were being imported from Luanda. At the peak of its empire, Portugal employed more than seven hundred ships, with over two hundred in the Indian Ocean alone.

Once-dominant Venice had been completely trumped by Portugal with Lisbon completely dominating the spice trade. Returning cargos contained black and white pepper from Ceylon and India, cinnamon from Cochin, nutmeg from the Banda Islands, and cloves from Ternate and Tidore. Additionally, there were gold, silver, precious stones, porcelain, perfume, dyes, woven fabrics, and more.

It seems that nothing is forever, and the greatly overstretched empire of a country with only one million citizens slowly began to crack and crumble. Almeida had failed in 1513 to conquer Aden, the gateway to the Red Sea. This left the Arabs with access to a tiny corner of the Indian Ocean and the East African coast. The Arabs slowly began to push back. The expansion also had to be adjusted for real-world costs. The trading forts of Kilwa and Malindi, which did not have enough strategic value to justify their defense, were abandoned in 1512. Similar decisions were made to abandon Fort Pacem, Sumatra; Fort Santa Cruz, Agadir; and Fort Alcacar-Ceguer, both in Morocco.

In 1545, the king's treasury began suffering from severe inflation—not a new phenomenon. The monarchy depended heavily on borrowed money. It began issuing treasury bonds, some of which became almost worthless, selling at 5 percent of face value. German banks became the biggest beneficiaries of the prosperity, with some making 150 percent on their investments. The center of banking followed the money and shifted to Seville, where New World gold and silver were flowing in. Following Magellan's discovery of the Philippines, the Treaty of Zaratoga was signed. In order to keep Ternate and the Mollucan archipelago, Portugal had to pay Spain the significant sum of 350,000 cruzados. Still foolishly fighting the Crusades in 1578, King Sebastio lost the battle in the sands of Alcacer Quibir and was killed in the process. The cost of the misadventure incurred an additional 240,000 cruzados of debt.

Making matters worse, the death of Sebastio left a vacuum in the succession, and Phillip II of Spain decided to take advantage of the opportunity and annex Portugal. With an eight-to-one population advantage and with many Portuguese citizens employed in the far corners of the empire, the invaders were only briefly challenged, and then only at the city limits of Lisbon.

Now under control of Spain, Portugal was forced to participate in the 1588 Invincible Armada fiasco at the cost of many men and ships. The financial cost is off the charts because the empire and entire economy were being run by, and for the benefit of Spain. Spain relinquished control years later only after its own economy and structure began to weaken.

There may also have existed a decay in national attitude. Under control of a king, all enterprise was directed from the top down, with the profits flowing up to the crown. This left little incentive for entrepreneurs to flourish and really push the economy. While shipbuilding and commerce helped provide full employment, people didn't feel any particular sense of ownership. Without a piece of the action, citizens may have developed a sense of apathy or, in some cases, arrogance.

On the island of Ternate on February 28, 1570, Jorge de Castro, in a fit of rage, stabbed and killed Sultan Khairun. Ternate was the primary source of cloves for the European luxury market. It is hard to believe that after such a huge investment in exploration, navigational technology, shipbuilding, diplomacy, establishing trade with the sultan, and building infrastructure, including the construction of four forts and a palace, this lack of situational awareness could result in such a stupid and reckless act. Three days after the murder, native Ternatians extracted their revenge, killing Castro and everyone inside Fort Kastela. By December 31, 1575, all Portuguese were evicted from the island under penalty of death.

The Portuguese attitude may also be seen in their attempts at aggressive religious proselytism, the conversion of colonists and associates to Christianity, a policy much pursued by the Jesuits. With the goal of not allowing converts to worship idols, they destroyed Hindu temples and Buddhist relics. This religious attitude and activity created severe problems in the new bases, especially in China and Japan, eventually resulting in the Portuguese eviction from Nagasaki.

It is difficult to maintain a fighting edge for a hundred years. While the world watched, every Portuguese loss was a message of weakness and vulnerability. Due to staffing problems, many ships employed Dutch and German gunners. Some secrets of their operations became known among the foreign crewmen. One Dutch employee published two books describing Portuguese navigation and shipping routes, fort locations, and trading operations.

In 1602 seventeen Dutch companies merged to form the VOC, the Dutch East India Company. Their primary goal was to demolish Portuguese shipping and infrastructure then establish their own unopposed trade in the Indian Ocean. In 1610 they established a trading colony in Batavia (now Jakarta) located near the northwestern corner of Java. In 1641 they conquered Malacca, the key to the spice trade and the doorway to Asia. That same year they sunk six ships at Makassar, Celebes (now Sulawesi). They went ashore at Makassar, captured the fort, then renamed it Fort Rotterdam. The VOC went on to evict the Portuguese and dominate the Indian Ocean, thus capturing the spice trade monopoly for themselves. It then became known as the "Dutch East Indies".

The Portuguese legacy is that they were the world's first international sea power and the first empire based on control of the seas. Tiny Portugal led Spain in the European expansion, and Portuguese is still the dominant language of Brazil.

Christopher Columbus (1451–1506)

––––

CHRISTOPHER COLUMBUS (CRISTÓBAL COLÓN) WAS born in the Genoese Republic, the son of a weaver and oldest of four brothers. Genoa, a busy seaport, aroused his curiosity and lured him to the sea. In a letter to Ferdinand and Isabella, he states, "At a very tender age I entered upon the sea sailing." His duties and adventure travel took him over much of the Mediterranean, south to Ghana and the Canary Islands, and north all the way to Iceland. His knowledge of wind patterns surrounding the Azores Islands would greatly aid him in safely returning home from the new world.

1476 found him at age twenty-five, captain of a ship southbound off the coast of Cape Saint Vincent, Portugal, in the service of the Di Negri shipping family of Genoa. When a Portuguese cannon wounded him, and sunk his ship, he managed to grab an oar and swim six miles, coming ashore at the beach, immediately north of the fortress at Sagres.

Instead of returning to Spain, he headed north to Lisbon, where he joined his brother in a mapmaking enterprise. Becoming an insider in the art of cartography, he somehow was able to acquire (steal) Portugal's secret knowledge of determining "latitude at sea". By this time nobody exceeded Columbus in experience, and he now possessed all the necessary skills to sail the high seas into the unknown.

When he arrived in Lisbon, he was illiterate, but he soon taught himself to read, write, and converse in three languages, namely Portuguese, Castilian, and Latin. With his new language and literacy skills, he began working his way up the social ladder. He made a point of attending Mass at the Convento Dos Santos, where he met and later married Dona Felipa Perestrello y Moniz, daughter of Captain Bartolomeu Perestrello. The deceased captain had colonized and governed Porto Santo in the Madeira Islands and had acquired an impressive library. His books, along with his logs and charts, were given to Columbus by his mother-in-law. Making hasty use of his new language skills, Columbus discovered three books that would change his life forever.

The first was Rustichello's *Il Millione*, on Marco Polo. In chapter 2 Marco describes an island he has never seen, named Zipangu (Japan): "They have gold in the greatest abundance, its sources being inexhaustible." In the palace, "the entire roof is covered with a plating of gold in the same manner we cover houses or more properly churches with lead. The ceilings of the halls are of the same precious metal; many of the apartments have small tables of pure gold etc." Reading this, Columbus became smitten with gold fever, as all of Spain soon would be. Some of the khan's envoys (spies) must have been allowed inside the Imperial Palace. To give the story some credence, on the next page of "Of the Island of Zipangu," Marco describes the khan's attempted 1264 invasion with numerous vessels and over thirty thousand men. This is apparently the losing side of the great kamikaze, or divine wind, incident where a north wind pushing a violent gale (typhoon) drove much of the fleet on the rocks and caused the remainder to flee, thus saving Japan from the invasion.

The second book was Claudius Ptolemy's *Geographia*. Ptolemy was the accepted scientific authority of the time; especially with the benefit of Eratosthenes's calculation of the earth's circumference at 28,900 miles.

Possibly the most classic experiment in history, done completely without benefit of any scientific equipment, it represents the highest-level thought process of the human brain. I am only going to briefly touch on this with-out any diagrams. Very briefly: Eratosthenes knew that on 21JUN of any year, the sun was observed to shine directly to the bottom of a well located in the city of Aswan. This happens to be extremely close to the Tropic of Cancer, 23.5 degrees north of the equator and the limit of the sun's northerly excursion. Eratosthenes lived in Alexandria, almost due south of Aswan. On 21JUN, just outside his laboratory he measured the shadow angle of a vertical rod to be one fiftieth of a circle (7.2 degrees). Reasoning that if he knew the distance between the two cities, 50 times that distance would equal the circumference of the earth. Making use of statistical analysis with rate x time = distance calculations and the average camel caravan rate based on business records plus a single checkout run for confirmation, he determined that distance to be 5,040 stadia. They didn't measure in miles in those days but in stadia, the length of a stadium. There were two different stadia lengths in use, the preferred one, 185 meters gave a product of 5040 x 185 x 50 = 46,620 km or km x .621 = 28,951-miles circumference. The other, 157.5 meters, gave a product of 39,690 km or km x .621 = 25,847 miles. While this would have virtually equaled the actual 25,000-miles circumference, it is not considered the stadia value he chose.

Without benefit of discovery, Ptolemy described the world as a single landmass. He claimed it stretched 180 degrees from the blessed islands (Cape Verdes) to the center of China. The true range of this distance is 235 degrees of longitude. This led Columbus to believe Zipangu was much closer than it actually was.

The third book, *Imago Mundi*, was written by Pierre d'Ailly, chancellor of the College de Navarre, Paris. This book contained a statement, underlined by Columbus, stating, "The Atlantic is not so great that it can cover three quarters of the globe."

Columbus now knew where the gold, jewels, and spices were and reasoned that if he could sail due west across the Atlantic, he would find a shortcut to Japan and India. Working with both Ptolemy's and d'Ailly's information, he somehow concluded that Zipangu was only 2,760 miles from the Canary Islands (the actual value is 12,000). All he needed now was a sponsor for the expedition.

He engaged his brother Bartolomeu to petition Henry VII of England. Henry was busy fighting a war with France and considered the proposal ridiculous.

With an assist from a Portuguese captain he had crewed with, Columbus gained an audience with King Joao II. Joao was in the midst of launching the Diogo Cão expedition as part of his grand scheme to reach India by way of the African coast and Indian Ocean. Though apparently interested, Joao did not have the resources to explore both south and west but did shuffle Columbus to his court chronicler, who wrote that "he was a big talker and full of fancy and imagination."

Not to be defeated and using all the connections he could muster, Columbus wrangled an introduction to Queen Isabella of Spain. She and Ferdinand were completely focused on ridding Spain of Moors and Jews and then populating the country solely with Christians and converts. His sales pitch, now well honed, included converting all people of any newly discovered land to Christianity. Spices, jewels, gold, and converts were a tempting offer and opened the door to a friendly relationship that would last until the queen's death. She introduced Columbus to her advisor and confessor, Bishop Hernando de Talavera.

For six frustrating years Columbus pleaded his case to Talavera and his committee. During this time, he developed a relationship with Luis de Santangel. Santangel was the wealthy treasurer for both Ferdinand and Santa Hermandad, a vigilante group that seized money from outlaws, especially those who robbed the warm bodies of combatants on the battlefield. Aside from his goal of accumulating great wealth, Santangel also planned to use any newly discovered land to satisfy claims of the Hidalgos, noble officers who were serving Spain in the defeat of the Moors. There simply wasn't enough Spanish land available to satisfy potential claims.

Timing is everything, and no difficult task is accomplished without perseverance. It was January 1492, and with the conquest of the Moors just completed, Columbus and Santangel made the crown an offer it could not refuse. Columbus would lead the expedition; both would finance it. The crown's only obligation was to pay the wages of the crew. With virtually nothing ventured and everything to be gained, the crown gave Columbus everything he bargained for:

* Hereditary title of viceroy and governor of new lands
* Rank of admiral of the ocean sea
* 10 percent ownership of any precious metals and stones
* 12.5 percent of trade profits

Now with the support of the church, the crown, and Santangel, the venture developed swiftly. A site in front of the Monasterio de la Rabidia, Palos de la Fonterra (on the outskirts of Huelva, Spain), was chosen. By May the shipping families Pinzon and Nino had each supplied a caravel, the *Pinta* and the *Niña*. The larger flagship vessel, the *Santa Maria*, a Nao, was obtained from Juan de la Cosa, who also captained it. Martin Alonzo Pinzon captained the *Pinta* and his brother Vicente Yanez Pinzon the *Niña*.

The expedition weighed anchor on August 3, 1492, with a total crew of about ninety men, almost all from within a 25-mile radius of Palos. The first destination was the Canary Islands to top off stores in route. On August 6 and again the next day, the *Pinta*'s rudder became unstepped and began leaking, requiring extra crewmen to work the pumps. They managed to reach Gomera in the Canaries by August 12, and successful repairs were made.

On September 6, with a fresh supply of stores and water, they headed due west into a calm sea, looking to avoid Portuguese caravels. Sailing into the unknown, the superstitious sailors feared sea monsters and sailing over the edge of a precipice or waterfall. Columbus convinced everyone the distance was less than three thousand miles and could be done in three or four weeks. Incredibly, it was twenty-eight hundred miles and thirty-three days, and he managed to average 85 miles per day.

Columbus had more faith in his measurements and instruments than in the physical earth and universe. He concluded that Polaris, the North Star, was not in a fixed position but moved in a circle. He also believed the earth was pear shaped with the stem end north, and that he sometimes sailed uphill. Fortunately, none of his misconceptions had any negative effect on the expedition.

By the fourth week there was much anxiety among the crew. No ship had ever been this long in the open sea, out of sight of land. Sargasso weed and the appearance of new seabirds triggered early expectations of land. After many false sightings, Columbus spotted candle-like flames, verified by his steward on the evening of October 11.

At two in the morning, October 12, Juan Rodriguez Bemino (Rodrigo de Triano) spotted land. Triano's reward was never paid by Columbus. The expedition put ashore later that morning on Watling Island in the Bahamas, where they planted a flag and claimed the new territory for Spain. The European expansion had found the islands of a new continent.

Columbus called the unclothed natives "Indians" because he was sure that he had found India. Later, upon discovering Cuba, he believed he had found Japan, and he took these convictions to his deathbed. After some initial timidity, the Indians—who believed the sailors came from the sky—became friendly and began repeating Columbus's words. Based on this, he figured they would be easy to convert.

The Indians traded balls of cotton, thread, spears, parrots, and anything else they owned for glass beads, bells, and small trinkets. Their most important use of cotton was ropes and hammocks. Hammocks were the Indians own invention. But the most important thing on Columbus's mind was gold. Some Indians did have tiny bits of gold attached to their noses, but after exploring the island for three days and finding no significant amount gold, he set off for Zipangu with several Indians as guides.

They explored three more islands, trading for small amounts of gold, and then spotted a large island, which the Indians called Colba (Cuba). Columbus was positive that this could only be Zipangu. On Cuba, he found tobacco, a bark-less dog, parrots, and some additional gold. The Cubans described Hispaniola, an island to the east that contained much gold. On hearing this, Martin Alonzo Pinzon took off on his own with the *Pinta*, not to be seen again for weeks.

On Hispaniola, Columbus befriended the cacique (king), who was invited aboard the *Santa Maria*, entertained, and allowed to choose his own gifts. In return—and having learned Columbus's preference—he gave gold.

At eleven at PM on Christmas Eve, while drifting in calm water and with no mention of drinking, Columbus retired. The watch was left to a helmsman, who placed an inexperienced boy in charge before he too retired. While everyone slept, the *Santa Maria* drifted onto a reef just offshore of Hispaniola. Columbus sent out a party to kedge off (winch toward an anchor), but the boat, instead of assisting, made for the *Niña*. Vincent Yanez Pinzon, the captain—and younger honorable brother—refused to allow the scallywags aboard and sent a boat to assist Columbus. It is noteworthy that Juan de la Cosa, owner-captain of the *Santa Maria*, had overseen the mid-watch and was also in command of the wayward long boat. Meanwhile, the *Santa Maria* had become holed and began breaking up.

By a stroke of good fortune, the cacique took ownership of the problem, sent natives to assist, and provided three houses to contain the stores and salvageable gear. Columbus, in a state of relief and thankful for the assistance, named the site La Navidad. He directed that a settlement be created for both trade and gathering information. He placed thirty-six men of all trades ashore, armed with tools, weapons, and a Lombard cannon, with a promise to defend the king from his enemies, the Caribs.

The *Niña* weighed anchor on January 4, 1493, and headed back toward Spain. Two days later the *Niña* was reunited with the *Pinta*, and a sheepish Martin Pinzon told a lame story. It was later revealed that he had been trading for gold and had made a secret pact with the crew to split fifty-fifty, thus shorting both Columbus and the crown. On encountering foul winds, Columbus decided to anchor and trade while waiting for a change. A bad encounter with arrows caused the site to be named Golfo de las Fletchas.

On January 16, they cleared the eastern tip of Hispaniola, heading for home. Columbus made a great intuitive decision to work his way northeast, skirting the Sargasso Sea with a plan to catch the westerlies that he knew blew through the Azores. They enjoyed an easy return until February 14, southwest of the Azores, where the two ships became separated in a violent storm. When the storm subsided, he anchored off Santa Maria Island, part of the Portuguese Azores group. He sent a party ashore to seek a shrine and pray thanks for their deliverance. The shore party was imprisoned with a plan to capture Columbus by luring him ashore. After two days of the cat-and-mouse game, while never leaving the safety of his ship, Columbus somehow managed to negotiate the return of his crew.

On March 3rd, they encountered the most severe North Atlantic storm of anyone's memory. With sails shredded and sailing under bare poles, they set storm sails to keep off a lee shore. With a severely damaged ship, Columbus reluctantly anchored in the Taugas River four miles below Lisbon. After a two-day standoff in another cat-and-mouse game and having already communicated with a Spanish messenger, he risked a meeting with King Joao II.

King Joao, curious about the New World, entertained him for two days. Joao was especially curious about whether the latitude was below the baseline running through the Canary Islands (Zaratoga Treaty). It was not; therefore, Portugal had no legal claim. Joao offered Columbus anything he wanted, even an audience with Queen Lenore.

Columbus arrived back in Palos on March 14, completing an epic round trip of six thousand nautical miles in the elapsed time of seven months and twenty days. Martin Alonzo Pinzon, who had arrived ahead of him in Galicia, Spain, attempted to present his own story to the sovereigns and steal the thunder. Rebuffed by the crown, he died within a month—possibly, because of his tarnished name and guilty conscience, by his own hand.

Columbus led a procession to Barcelona, accompanied by six Indians and many parrots but only a small amount of gold. He received a hero's welcome when he presented Ferdinand and Isabella the New World. They bestowed on him all the titles and percentages he had requested. The crown commissioned him to raise a new fleet with great haste and return to Hispaniola as governor. They were extremely worried that Portugal might contest, and wanted to quickly establish a colony for insurance.

Returning to La Navidad, Columbus found that all the colonists had been killed. The suspected reason was that sex starved Spaniards had misbehaved and enraged the local population. He established a new outpost slightly to the east of La Navidad, named it Santa Domingo, and appointed his brother Bartolomeu governor. He then set out to continue exploration. On this second voyage, he managed to discover Puerto Rico, plus the Virgin and Leeward Islands.

Returning on a third voyage in 1498, he discovered Trinidad and the mouth of the Orinoco River but apparently never set foot directly on the South American continent. Severe problems festered in Hispaniola: The new colonists (many were convicts) were far more interested in finding gold than working the fields or tending livestock. When the gold didn't pan out as expected, they rebelled and plotted to kill Columbus and his brother. Columbus retaliated by hanging the mutineers. The crown sent a new governor, who sent Columbus home in chains.

Forbidden to return to Hispaniola, he was allowed one more expedition by the sovereigns. With his son, brother, 150 men, and four ships, he returned to the New World, where everything went dreadfully wrong. He encountered severe storms, hostile Indians, foul winds, and foul currents, but in the spring of 1503, his party was the first to make landfall in Panama, Central America. Pounded by another storm and reduced to two leaking and worm-infested vessels, he beached the ships at Saint Anne's Bay, Jamaica.

Columbus sent fourteen men across the 108-mile channel to notify the governor of his desperate situation. Though fully aware of the shipwrecked sailors' plight and only 130 miles distant, the governor of Hispaniola waited seven months to rescue them.

Desperate for food while waiting for rescue, Columbus made use of his magical powers. In possession of a Portuguese almanac that predicted an eclipse, he told the chief that he would take away the moon unless the chief provided rations for his crew. When the predicted eclipse began on February 28, 1504, the horrified chief gladly promised him what he wanted if only Columbus would restore the moon.

Columbus died May 20, 1506, a wealthy but unhappy man who still believed he had discovered India and Japan. His body is entombed in a casket resting upon the statuary shoulders of four heralds who represent the kingdoms of Castile, Leon, Aragon, and Navarre, each holding up a corner of the casket. The elaborate marble display is located inside the Santa Iglesia Catedral of Seville.

Directly across the street from the cathedral is La Casa de las Indies, a huge three-story building erected in the early 1500s to maintain the records from the New World. La Casa is open to visitors who promise not to use their cameras. On a second-floor table is a letter, safely under glass, signed by Balboa. The document describes the first sighting by Europeans of the Pacific Ocean. What a thrill it was for me to feast my eyes on this.

Who really discovered America? It depends on the precise definitions of judges and attorneys. Amerigo Vespucci, an Italian scientist employed by the Medici family, set foot on Brazil in the spring of 1500. Vespucci definitely had the best P.R. campaign. Martin Waldseemuller, a German cartographer, used the feminine version of Vespucci's name on a much-publicized map of the new continents. Pedro Alvares Cabral, leading a Portuguese trading expedition to India, sailed too far west and set foot on what he thought to be Vera Cruz Island in April 1500; it was later found to be mainland Brazil. Columbus discovered the New World in 1492 but didn't set foot on the actual continent until 1503. Did I forget to mention Leif Ericson who may have reached North America centuries earlier? The Norwegians are positive that he did. The jury is still out.

Ferdinand Magellan (1480–1522)

———

Anthony Pigafetta was the chief chronicler of the Magellan expedition. Venice had been severely losing market share to Lisbon and the Portuguese in the spice trade, and he was probably sent as a spy to find out first hand what was really happening. Magellan accepted him as a friend and found a place for him on board the *Trinidad* as a supernumerary, or extra crewman. Fortunately for history, Pigafetta survived the adventure and, along with his manuscripts, managed to return home with Elcano aboard the *Victoria*.

Ferdinand Magellan was born near Lisbon in 1480, the son of a minor nobleman. At age twelve he became a page to Queen Lenore, Spanish wife of King Joao II. While associated with the palace, he became a king's soldier. Unfortunately for Magellan, he became involved in palace politics and backed the wrong candidate for successor to King Joao. The man who became King Manuel never forgave him.

In 1509 Magellan was part of a company of two hundred soldiers spread throughout a five-ship expeditionary fleet under the command of Diogo Lopes de Sequeira. The goal was to establish trading forts for the spice trade. The fleet dropped anchor in Malacca, a sheltered port located at the top center of the strait that bears its name and strategically halfway between the base in Goa, India, and the Molucca Spice Islands.

Unknown to the Portuguese, their reputation as cruel barbarians had preceded them. The sultan, who wanted to maintain the status quo, hatched up a plan to capture and destroy the unwitting fleet. The sultan appeared friendly and allowed the crews ashore with the promise to visit and purchase whatever they chose. While the crew was enjoying liberty, Magellan and the captain of an adjacent ship sensed a trick; they heard armed Muslim traders who had been allowed on board the ships whispering to one another while others paddled ominously alongside.

The two deftly and quietly cleared the decks of the Muslims while Magellan took the only remaining boat to warn Sequeira, who was playing chess with the Muslim chief. Sequeira upended the chessboard, and together he and Magellan dispatched all the Muslims on board.

A raging battle quickly began, with swords clanking and muskets firing. Magellan, with no thought for his own life, managed to rescue forty of the one hundred crewmen ashore. Sequeira spent two days attempting to recover the sixty remaining hostages. Frustrated, he finally threw two captives overboard; they floated in the water with revenge notes secured to their heads by arrows through their skulls.

Magellan displayed his wit and leadership again during the return trip to Lisbon. After leaving Cochin, both Magellan's ship and the accompanying vessel became shipwrecked on a reef. When the leaders decided to go for help, the crews, stranded without boats and fearful of their lives, threatened mutiny. Magellan volunteered to stay aboard with them as a placating hostage until their rescue eight days later.

In 1513 Magellan was sent to Morocco to battle the Moors, where he received a limp-generating lance wound behind his knee. Having just defeated the Moors, the commander left Magellan in charge of the prizes, which included much livestock. Some of the animals mysteriously disappeared, and Magellan was accused of selling them for personal profit. With his honor at stake, he rushed to Lisbon to clear his name with King Manuel. Unknown to Magellan, the king had already received an accusatory letter prior to the requested audience. Not only did Manuel refuse to see him, but he had him sent back to Morocco in dishonor, AWOL, or absent without leave. On completing his tour of duty in Morocco, Magellan finally had an audience with the king, where he asked for a small pension in payment for his service to Portugal. King Manuel refused his request and unappreciatively said, "For all I care, you can sell your services elsewhere." A dejected and broke Magellan had to concoct a new plan for his life.

Magellan possessed a letter from his close friend Francisco Serrao. In 1510, Serrao had led the first expedition to Ternate, the northernmost island of the

Molucca archipelago. Serrao, making the first European contact with the sultan, managed to negotiate the purchase of cloves. To generate goodwill, he presented the sultan with a gift of two sets of shiny Portuguese armor complete with helmets and shields. These can still be seen today, located inside a display case inside the museum next door to the Portuguese-built Sultan's Palace. Serrao's letter described the beauty and allure of Ternate thusly: "I have found here a new world richer and greater than that of Vasco da Gama…I beg you to join me here, that you may sample for yourself the delights that surround me."

Serrao stayed on Ternate and became tight with the sultan. His multiple roles included Ambassador, Chief trader, Project Engineer for Forts, Palace, Docks etc., and unfortunately for him, Admiral of the Ternate navy. Much like Magellan, Serrao involved himself with the battles of others. After enjoying these roles for 20 years, he was poisoned with betel leaves by the angry sultan of neighboring Tidore. His death happened near the time of Magellan's. He left behind a Javanese wife plus a young son and daughter.

Magellan considered Columbus a failure, as the latter had never reached his goal of India, Japan, or the Spice Islands. Inspired by Serrao's letter, and since he himself had been as near the Moluccas as the port of Malacca, Magellan began to formulate a plan, a shortcut route to the Spice Islands. Magellan was fully aware that Amerigo Vespucci had discovered Brazil and that Balboa had discovered the Pacific Ocean. Together with his eccentric scholarly mathematician-astronomer-astrologer friend Ruy Faleiro, he hatched a plan to seek the Spice Islands by sailing south around the American continent, then west across the Pacific. With a firm plan, all he needed now was a sponsor, most likely from Spain, the same country that had backed the Columbus expedition.

Magellan, accompanied by his personal Malaysian slave, Enrique, and his new partner, Faleiro, made off for Seville. Seville was the trade center for any traffic coming in from the New World. Las Casa de los Indies was the center of trade, and inside this very large building was the headquarters of the ruling council, La Casa de Contratación.

In Seville, Magellan's group met Diogo Barbosa, an expat Portuguese mariner who was currently engaged in the Spanish trade. While discussing plans for his shortcut route, Magellan became enraptured with Diogo's daughter Beatriz, and the two were soon married. To secure backing for his journey, Barbosa convinced him to renounce his Portuguese citizenship and become a naturalized Spaniard. Barbosa then arranged a meeting with the board of La Casa de Contratación, where Magellan and Faleiro's presentation was rejected. After the meeting, the board chairman, acting on his own initiative, approached Magellan. Juan de Aranda proposed that for one-eighth of the expedition's profits, he would arrange a meeting with the king's council.

This new group traveled to Valladolid, where Magellan presented his proposal to the king's council. Bishop Fonseca bought into the plan and arranged an audience with King Charles. The eighteen-year-old Habsburg grandson of Ferdinand and Isabella was impressed with Magellan's idea. When Magellan produced Francisco Serrao's letter and Ruy Faleiro claimed the Spice Islands were only four thousand miles from South America and, more importantly, lay inside of Spain's half of the world, per the Tordesillas Treaty, the deal was done. Young King Charles V signed a contract on March 22, 1518, whereby Magellan and Faleiro would co-lead a fully provisioned fleet of five ships. They would become governors of any discovered islands and share one-fifth of any proceeds; fruits of their discoveries would pass to their heirs. They were promised an exclusive that no future expeditions would compete for at least ten years. Magellan's pay was fifty thousand maravedis, with a monthly salary of eight thousand passing directly to Beatriz. Magellan was given the title of Captain General, supreme commander of the expedition.

Unknown to Magellan, his enemy, King Manuel, had employed a spy to keep close watch on his preparations. Sebastio Alvarez watched his every move, even boarding all the vessels to determine their conditions, taking note of the provisions and especially the cannons and other armament. His report to Manuel stated the ships were leaky and dangerous and that their defense was minimal.

In addition to employing a spy, King Manuel also employed his Spanish ambassador to disrupt the expedition in any way possible. Alvaro da Costa first attempted to persuade the two coleaders that their honor lay with Portugal and they must go home. Failing that, he tried to convince King Charles that the expedition would best be led by native Spaniards. In his final attempt to frustrate the expedition, he wrote to King Manuel, claiming the coleaders wished to return home but Charles would not permit it. This false statement reached an enraged King Charles, who bluntly put an end to Costa's meddling and urged the leaders to focus and proceed with Godspeed.

Bishop Fonseca believed that the terms granted to Magellan and Faleiro were much too generous and provided them too much power. This same bishop had done everything possible to frustrate and discredit Columbus. During the voyage preparations, Faleiro's mental state came into question. Faleiro had become irritable and unstable, possibly from depression or bipolar disorder. Fonseca was able to convince King Charles of the problem, and the king deftly had Faleiro removed from the expedition with the promise he could lead his own at a later date. Now with one of the leaders out of the picture, Fonseca plotted to limit Magellan's power and potential financial gain. Using his cunning and influence, he managed to install his illegitimate son, Juan de Cartagena, as a ship's captain even though Cartagena had no blue water sea experience. Cartagena was also granted the additional title of inspector general complete with a salary greater than that of Magellan's. As if that weren't enough, Cartagena was also appointed treasurer and chief financial officer. On top of all that, he was granted final say over all commercial decisions and was to report directly to the king. Fonseca further commissioned him to be the eyes and ears of the king and report on any noncompliance or incorrect behavior; Cartagena was empowered to be Magellan's watchdog. But Fonseca still wasn't finished. Using his great influence, he was able to appoint two close friends as ship captains, Luis de Mendoza and Gaspar de Quesada. All three Spanish captains were jealous and resentful of Magellan's authority, despised having a foreign expedition leader, and most likely entertained the possibility of command for themselves.

Eighteen months passed before the fleet could finally get underway. The ARMADA of the MOLUCCAS composition was as follows:

Trinidad, flagship, Ferdinand Magellan, captain general
Estevao Gomes, pilot major
Francisco Albo, pilot
Antonio Pigafetta, chronicler
Enrique de Malacca, interpreter (personal slave)

Duarte Barbosa, supernumerary (brother-in-law)
Cristovao Rebelo, supernumerary (Magellan's illegitimate son)
Alvara de Mesquita, supernumerary (Magellan's cousin)

San Antonio, Juan de Cartagena, captain, inspector general
Andres de San Martin, pilot and astrologer
Antonio de Coca, fleet accountant

Conception, Gaspar de Quesada, captain
Joao Lopes Carvalho, pilot
Juan Sebastian Elcano, master

Victoria, Luis de Mendoza, captain
Vasco Gomes Gallego, pilot
Antonio Salomón, master

Santiago, Juan Rodriguez Serrano, captain

After departing Seville, the fleet took a week to transit the Guadalquivir River and anchored at its mouth just off Sanlucar de Barramenda in the Gulf of Cádiz. The unhappy crewmen, restricted from mixing with the town's women, were required to attend Mass and confession. Finally, on September 29, 1519, the five ships and 260 sailors were underway into the unknown.

Magellan, with full knowledge of the contempt and jealousy barely concealed by the Spanish captains, did the best he could to project his authority. He insisted his flagship, the *Trinidad*, always be the lead vessel. In addition, he devised a series of signals displayed with flags by day and lanterns from the stern by night. The trip south to the Canary Islands, where they topped off provisions and water, proceeded smoothly.

With the plan to avoid Portuguese caravels, Magellan sailed south west along the African coast. They were subjected to rain and squalls for sixty days, and finally they were treated to a display of Saint Elmo's fire. The eerie electrical display took the form of a torch atop the mainmast of the *Trinidad*. The two-hour display was considered a good-luck symbol to the crew. The storms abated and the ships were becalmed while crossing the equator. Finally, inside the Southern Hemisphere, they found wind and changed course to west-southwest toward Brazil.

Each evening the ships were required, one by one, to come alongside the *Trinidad*, salute, and request night orders. For two nights, the San Antonio refused the salute. On the third day, Magellan came alongside and brought all the captains aboard the *Trinidad*. The first order of business was a court-martial for Antonio Salomón, master of the *Victoria*. He had been observed sodomizing a cabin boy. Magellan, acting as judge and jury, quickly sentenced him to death by strangulation, the execution to take place in twenty days.

The second order of business was to deal with the insolent and conniving Cartagena. Following a brief exchange, in which clueless Cartagena accused Magellan of leading the fleet through storms, then motionless calms, and in addition displaying allegiance to Portugal, Cartagena stated he would no longer take orders from Magellan. Magellan was not about to be caught off guard. He gave a prearranged signal for the quartermaster, his son, and his brother-in-law, Diogo Barbosa, to storm the cabin with swords drawn. Magellan grabbed Cartagena by the collar and said, "This is mutiny. In the name of the king, you are my prisoner." Cartagena shouted to the two Spanish captains, "Stab Magellan with your daggers." The Spanish captains cautiously failed to respond to the prearranged call for mutiny. The master-at-arms placed the insolent Cartagena under arrest and locked him in stocks on deck. With a sounding of trumpets, Magellan gathered the ships together and announced the new captain of the *San Antonio* to be Antonio de Coca. It was within Magellan's power as captain general to execute Cartagena for mutiny, but he chose leniency because of Cartagena's political connections.

On November 29, they arrived at Cape Saint Augustine, the easternmost promontory of South America. Taking on food and water, they made Rio de Janeiro on December 13, 1519. They entered the great harbor and dropped anchor just past Sugarloaf. The Portuguese had established a trading post at Rio, but no one was present during Magellan's visit.

Groups of naked Indian women swam out to meet the ships, eager for contact with the sailors. Orgies and dancing took place ashore every night the fleet was in Rio. Magellan was able to trade cheap trinkets and knives for food and water. During the stay, Antonio Salomón's sentence was carried out, and he was strangled. Two days after Christmas, with casks full of water and stores re-provisioned, the fleet weighed anchor and headed south. The enamored women followed in canoes, attempting to detain the amorous Spaniards.

On March 31, 1520, at 50 degrees south with the southern winter coming on, Magellan anchored the fleet in a small estuary he named Port Saint Julian (Argentina). He called a meeting and informed the cold and unhappy crew that this was to be their new home until southern spring.

The next night Gaspar Quesada, captain of the *Conception*, snuck aboard San Antonio with two officers and thirty men and placed the captain, Alvaro de Mesquita, in irons. When the second officer came to Mesquita's defense, he was murdered by Quesada. Meanwhile, Captain Mendoza of the *Victoria* freed Cartagena, who took command of the *Conception*. With mutinous Spaniards now in control of three ships, Quesada sent a skiff to the *Trinidad* with a letter demanding that they immediately return to Spain. Magellan sent a letter back agreeing to a face-to-face discussion on board the *Trinidad*. Quesada, sensing a trap, sent the skiff back with a letter of refusal.

Magellan had a plan of his own. Receiving the skiff on the concealed side of the ship he took the oarsmen prisoner and replaced them with armed loyalist crewmen, commanded by fleet chief Marshal Espinoza. Also on the hidden side were fifteen armed men on board the *Trinidad*'s pinnace. Espinoza took his skiff to Mendoza's *Victoria* and, on boarding, stabbed Mendoza in the throat, killing him instantly. The distracted crew of the *Victoria* was quickly overcome by the men from Magellan's pinnace bearing muskets and swords and quickly surrendered.

Magellan, now with a three-to-two advantage, placed his ships in a line, trapping the two rebel ships inside the small harbor. Shortly after midnight, Quesada in the *San Antonio* attempted to escape to the open sea while commanding his crew to fire cannons at Magellan. The *San Antonio*'s cannons were silent, but not the *Trinidad*'s. The errant ship was quickly boarded and Quesada placed in chains. The next morning, Cartagena, the last mutineer, surrendered. At long last Magellan's fleet was under the control of loyal Portuguese captains.

Justice was severe: Quesada was decapitated and quartered. The dead Mendoza was also quartered, the fate of traitors. The politically connected

Cartagena was placed under house arrest. Forty men, including Elcano and another junior officer, were convicted of treason and sentenced to die. After being allowed several days to agonize over their fate, the convicts were unchained and given a reprieve. Grateful for receiving a pardon, they all became loyal crewmen.

A few days after the mutiny, Magellan discovered that Cartagena and a French priest with a Spanish name were plotting a third mutiny. Following the court-martial, Magellan was faced with a difficult decision. He could not bring himself to execute either a priest or Cartagena, with political ties to Archbishop Fonseca. Instead, Pero Sanchez de la Reina and Cartagena were sentenced to be marooned ashore when the fleet sailed south.

In late May, Magellan sent the *Santiago* down the coast to explore and find provisions. It was driven ashore and wrecked in heavy weather. Captain Serrano sent two men north for help, reaching Magellan eleven days later. All but one crew member, who had drowned, were rescued. Magellan moved his fleet south to take advantage of the excellent fishing Serrano had discovered, leaving Cartagena and the priest marooned ashore. The two were never heard from again. The expedition anchored at Puerto Santa Cruz until October 18.

Fully provisioned and welcoming the southern spring, the fleet weighed anchor and proceeded south. Three days later they rounded a cape that mounted a high peak and then entered a bay. They named it the Cape of Eleven Thousand Virgins, later called Cape Virgin. Discovering an inlet, Magellan sent two ships through to investigate. When they returned with positive expectations, he was certain this was the passage he had seen on a secret chart. Since this was the first time any European had ever reached this shore, it was a lucky delusion.

The fleet passed through the inlet into a deep strait, so deep that at night they were forced to anchor to branches projecting from the steep cliffs. Eventually they came to a fork; Magellan with two ships took the southwest, and the *Conception* and the *San Antonio* took the southeast. He sent a pinnace to reconnoiter, and three days it later returned with the good news: they had found the Pacific Ocean. But returning to the rendezvous point at the fork, he found one ship missing. Magellan sent the *Victoria* back to the Atlantic to search for the missing *San Antonio*, which was nowhere to be found. Evidently they had deserted.

On November 28, 1520, the *Trinidad*, the *Conception*, and the *Victoria* entered the Pacific Ocean and proceeded north along the coast, making between 120 and 180 miles per day with following winds. On December 22, at approximately twenty-eight degrees south, Magellan left sight of land and headed west-northwest. With the thought that the Pacific was small and the Moluccas were close by, Magellan had neglected to reprovision and fill the water casks. Unable to anchor at Pukapuka in the Tuamotu group, they discovered uninhabited Caroline Island eleven days later. Still finding no food or water, they were able to fish for sharks.

With men dying of scurvy and starvation, they managed to cross the equator and continue west. On March 6, they reached Guam, where they encountered skillful thieves in fast, highly maneuverable canoes equipped with triangular mat sails. Magellan became infuriated when the natives stole his ship's boat, and he ordered crossbow men to retaliate. Storming ashore with forty armored warriors, they burned the village and helped themselves to food and water.

A week later they reached the Philippine archipelago, making landfall at Homonhon Island. Ashore they slaughtered a pig brought from Guam and were met the next day by a boatload of friendly natives. Four days later the natives brought their chief to Homonhon to meet Magellan.

Following a week of recuperating from scurvy and malnutrition with local fruit and coconuts, the fleet anchored off Limasawa, where Magellan began exchanges with the local ruler. He was much assisted by his personal Malay slave, Enrique, who could speak Tagalog. Rajah Calambu was given a tour of *Trinidad* and was very impressed with Magellan's theatrics, where an armored soldier was able to withstand an attack from swords and daggers. Magellan became a blood brother of the rajah, whom he invited to participate in the Easter ceremony. After all the dramatic displays, Magellan inquired where he could reprovision his fleet. The rajah replied that on completion of the rice harvest in two days, he would act as Magellan's pilot and introduce him to the rajah of Cebu.

Rajah Humabon was not as friendly or easy to deal with as Calambu. Before any deal making, he wanted a tribute such as the current Siamese trading party had provided, presenting him with gold and slaves. The Siamese trader had told Humabon mistakenly that Magellan's group was the same that had set up bases in India and had conquered Malacca. He also told Humabon, "It would be well for you to treat them well." On hearing this, Humabon took a softer stance and sent his nephew to negotiate.

Magellan invited the rajah's nephew, the prince, aboard the *Trinidad*, where he was received in a red felt chair. He and Magellan became blood brothers, and the prince was baptized. Magellan went a step further and baptized a sick man, who miraculously became well a few days later. Between displays of weapons, diplomacy, and magical showmanship, the whole island of Cebu became enthralled and converted to Christianity. Magellan was looked upon as a miracle-working prophet.

Zula, a chief from Mactan Island who served under Rajah Humabon, requested help from the great Magellan. He asked that Magellan assist him in removing from power Chief Lapulapu, a chief who did not respect Rajah Humabon. How could such a powerful miracle worker resist such a trivial request?

Early the next morning the fleet dropped anchor off Mactan Island. Magellan led a party of fifty warriors in full armor wading across hundreds of yards of shallow water to Chief Lapulapu's village. When the islanders defended themselves with bamboo lances, Magellan responded by burning their huts. Eventually Magellan's raiders were overwhelmed by fifteen hundred angry defenders and they retreated to the water.

Magellan ordered his men to back slowly toward the ship, but most made great haste, leaving only a small group to screen the retreat. The natives focused on the captain general, hurling rocks, arrows, and lances at his vulnerable arms and legs. When the "invincible" Magellan fell into the water, the remaining soldiers fled to the safety of the ships. Interestingly, no cannons were fired in support of the Captain General. Magellan was clearly the aggressor and the commemorative site statue clearly indicates how the heroic defenders overcame the evil Magellan.

Magellan had already reached the longitude of the Moluccas, and all he needed to have done to reach the designated goal of the mission was proceed directly south to the equator. Ternate is two degrees north, and Tidore lies just above the equator.

On May 6, 1571, five days after Magellan's death, the wayward *San Antonio* docked in Seville. The mutineers, under command of Estevao Gomes and coconspirator Geronimo Guerra, had stabbed and imprisoned Captain Mesquita, who also happened to be Magellan's cousin. The entire crew of fifty-seven, except for Mesquita, told a well-rehearsed story of Magellan's allegiance to Portugal, his mistreatment of Spanish officers—especially Quesada and Cartagena—his failure to proceed directly around South America, and his reckless behavior. Mesquita was imprisoned, and Magellan's name was besmirched.

Meanwhile, back in the Philippines, the ships returned to Cebu to regroup and determine a new leader. When the slave Enrique found that he would not be freed as promised on Magellan's death, he stole ashore and hatched a plan for revenge with Rajah Calambu, whereby the rajah could capture the ships and cargo. The leaders and captains were invited to a feast ashore, where they were to be murdered.

Joao Serrano and Duarte Barbosa, the expedition's new leaders, accompanied by twenty-seven crew, unsuspectingly went ashore to attend the feast. Pilot Joao Lopez Carvalho and chief marshal Gonzalo Gomez de Espinosa sensed something was wrong and returned to the ship. All in the shore party but Enrique were massacred. In retaliation, the ships fired cannons at the village then sadly departed.

By now the expedition was reduced to eighty men, insufficient crew to man three ships. The *Conception* was stripped and burned, with all stores and useful items split between the *Victoria* and *Trinidad*. Joao Carvello took command of the *Trinidad* and Juan Sebastian Elcano the *Victoria*. The ships needed food, but if the trade goods were spent for stores, what would be left to trade in the Spice Islands? Indecisively, they meandered through the Philippine archipelago for six months as depleted stores approached zero.

Their luck changed when they discovered Palawan Island—in Pigafetta's words, "A veritable Land of Promise." Here the islanders grew rice, ginger, swine, goats, poultry, figs half a cubit long (bananas), coconuts, sweet potatoes, sugar canes and turnips." The jubilant crew befriended the natives, filled their holds, then proceeded southeast, passing far to the east of the Moluccas' meridian.

When they reached Brunei, Borneo, Carvello did a shameful thing. With crewmen inside the village trading with the natives, a fleet of outrigger sailboats began returning to the harbor. Thinking the boats were hostile, he abandoned the five crewmen on shore then kidnapped the crew members of a large junk. Unable to ransom them to the enraged local rajah, he sold them elsewhere as slaves, keeping the gold and three women for his private harem. The stranded crewmen were never recovered.

Carvello died on 14 FEB with no one very upset about it. Command of the Trinidad passed to Espinosa. Finished with careening the ships, they sailed southeast, guided by a captured pilot. Following the grueling two year ordeal, they finally reached Tidore Island, the destination of their dreams.

Tidore is two miles south of Ternate, where the Portuguese had established their trading forts. Knowing full well that he Portuguese would consider any Spaniards as trespassers, subject to death or imprisonment was the reason for picking Tidore. They were welcomed by the rajah sultan, who just happened to be in competition with the sultan of Ternate. The trading went smoothly. The three women were presented to the sultan, who responded with a large additional supply of cloves. On December 18, just as they were ready to depart, the *Trinidad* sprung a huge leak. After patiently waiting for three days, Elcano decided he could wait no longer. Leaving the damaged *Trinidad* to her fate he headed back to Spain.

Seeking a quick trip to avoid starvation, scurvy, and the Portuguese, he took *Victoria* south to Ambon Island before heading west, reaching Timor on January 25, 1522. By May 19 they rounded the Cape of Good Hope after having beat into west winds for thirty-five hundred miles. They never stopped for supplies but continued north to the Portuguese Cape Verde islands. They almost managed to convince the authorities that they had been blown south in a storm while returning from the Caribbean, but someone produced a bag of cloves. Since only Magellan's expedition could have been carrying cloves, the thirteen boatmen were arrested, and Elcano was ordered to surrender. Instead, he quickly weighed anchor and continued toward Spain.

On September 6, 1522, the *Victoria* reached Barra de San Lucar and arrived in Seville two days later. The eighteen gaunt and emaciated survivors of the sixty-man crew managed to fire a few cannons in celebration before parading to the cathedral for prayers of thanks. The twenty-six-ton cargo of cloves did barely cover the cost of the expedition. Elcano was awarded a medal and small pension. Magellan's name was finally cleared.

The *Trinidad* took three months to repair, finally sailing north and west for fifteen weeks attempting to re-cross the Pacific. A typhoon caused the foremast, the forecastle, and the poop to be wrecked. Espinosa spent three long months returning to the Moluccas. The nineteen survivors were taken prisoner by the Portuguese and enslaved to construct a fort on Ternate. Espinosa and three crewmen survived. They were released in Lisbon, finally reaching Seville, where each was granted a small pension.

The Magellan expedition's circumnavigation was by far the greatest feat the world had ever seen, comparable to landing a man on the moon. It finally proved beyond all doubt that the world was round. Spain acquired possession of Guam and the Philippine Islands. Based on the Treaty of Tordesillas, the Moluccas were deemed inside Spanish territory. In the new treaty of Saragossa, Portugal paid 350,000 ducats to retain possession. Interestingly this is the exact amount cash strapped Spanish King Charles had borrowed from Portuguese King Joao III. Let's just call it even!

An interesting mystery became evident when the ships logs were studied. Though no errors could be found with the dates of the daily entries, the number of days did not coincide with the calendar in Seville. Somehow the expedition had gained an extra day. They had crossed the yet to be understood "International Date Line" and had NEGLECTED to subtract a day when crossing from east to west. Had they crossed from west to east they would have lost a day.

This is a difficult concept to grasp, even for me. Try considering this: As the earth rotates in relation to the sun, a person experiences a sunrise and sunset to mark each day. For most of us this occurs 365.25 (365.242) times per year because we stay in the same approximate location day to day. Over a period of three years while constantly moving in the OPPOSITE direction of the revolving earth, members of the Magellan expedition experienced an extra sunrise and sunset compared to us static folks.

The Spanish Empire 1500 to 1793

———

FERDINAND AND ISABELLA, WHO'S WEDDING respectively connected Aragon and Castile, managed to unite Spain. They then arranged the marriages of three daughters to neighboring empires. Spain would continue to increase its power and dominance in Europe through a progression of marriage and inheritance.

In 1490 Isabel, their oldest daughter, was betrothed to Afonso, eldest son of King Joao II of Portugal. With some sense of court intrigue, the prince mysteriously died in a horseback accident the following year. King Joao went into a state of depression, only to be shocked back into reality by the Columbus expedition's discovery of the new world.

In 1496 Joan was wed to Phillip I, which led to the unity between Spain and the Austrian Habsburg Empire.

In 1501 Catherine was wed to Henry VII's son Arthur, Prince of Wales. There would be no King Arthur. Arthur died a year later, and with permission of the pope, the widowed Catherine was wed to his younger brother Henry, thus becoming the first wife of Henry VIII.

The monarchy sent Columbus back to the New World in 1493 with a fleet of ten ships to establish colonies with solid claims that would be uncontestable by Portugal. Simultaneously, it engaged Pope Gregory to negotiate a treaty with Joao II dividing the New World with a vertical line whereby all territory to the west would belong to Spain. Portugal would keep the Azores, Madeira, Cape Verdes, and Africa. In the Treaty of Tordesillas, the line, after extended negotiation by Portugal, was placed near the Amazon River delta, giving the eastern bulge of South America and south to the Plat River (Brazil) to Portugal. An earlier agreement, the Treaty of Zaratoga, with a baseline running through the Canary Islands, gave Spain all new territory north of the line and Portugal to the south but with each country keeping previous territory.

Spain immediately began developing the Caribbean, which included Hispaniola and Cuba, while always searching for gold. By 1500 Mexico was discovered, and shortly thereafter Balboa, leading a group of eighty men, crossed the Isthmus of Panama. They became the first Europeans to view the Pacific Ocean.

In 1519 Hernán Cortés (Hernando Cortez) arrived in Mexico with a small band of four hundred armored conquistadores, some on horseback, to confront the native Aztec inhabitants. Emperor Montezuma II, cautious and fearful of the armored aliens astride powerful creatures never before seen, supplied Cortez with a mistress/interpreter named Malinchi, gifts of gold, and provisions for the men. Cortez, after graciously accepting Montezuma's gifts, cunningly used Malinchi for his personal gratification while gleaning from her all the critical intelligence he needed for his attack plan. In good time Cortez captured Montezuma. Then, using Montezuma's enemies against him and with the shock and awe of armored cavalry bearing muskets, swords, and crossbows—and conveniently aided by massive die-offs from smallpox— he defeated the once-powerful Aztecs. By 1521 the Aztecs were relegated to a cheap labor source for the Spaniards. Simultaneously, Francisco Pizarro, another conquistador, managed to conquer and subjugate the Inca Empire, located between the Pacific coast and the Andes Mountains and between the cities of Quito, Ecuador, and Cusco, Peru. In the final battle, Cusco fell to the Spaniards in 1536.

The Spaniards built ports and trading cities in the conquered land using African slaves and cheap Indian labor. Soon they were farming the newly dis-covered corn, sugarcane, and tobacco while developing large plantations. The potato, capable of being virtually a complete single nutritional food source, was introduced to Europe from high up in the Andes. All the while, the Spaniards continued their relentless quest for gold.

In 1545, to their great luck, an enormous silver strike was made at Potesi, Peru, over 13,000 feet high in the Andes. Equally lucky, a massive source of mercury was discovered a short while later, 800 miles to the north. Spanish metallurgists rediscovered a Chinese process whereby the two metals are mixed, forming an amalgam, then heated to over 700 degrees Fahrenheit. The poisonous mercury vapor is boiled off (retorted), condensed, then recollected, leaving pure silver. The silver was then melted and cast into 65 pound ingots for easy shipping. This massive operation begun in the 1550s eventually grew Potesi to a population of over 150,000 and financed Spanish wars for over six decades.

There is little information available regarding the secret sources of the Spanish gold. Immediately following World War II, an American colonel named Leonard F. Clark purchased for $1,000, a map allegedly locating the Seven Cities of Cibola, the famed Seven Cities of Gold. In his book, *The Rivers Ran East*, he claims to have personally located six of them, the deposits mostly placers. After an incredible jungle adventure, wherein he posed as a naturalist, he managed to collect and smuggle $16,000 of gold (at $35 per ounce) from Peru and Ecuador.

By 1575 the Spanish trade emporium stretched all the way to China by way of the Philippines, swapping silver for silk and porcelain. Silver would leave Potesi on the backs of llamas and be transferred to more-powerful mules at lower altitudes, eventually arriving at Lima. Pacific silver was shipped from Lima to Acapulco, to Manila, and finally to China. Silk and porcelain would be shipped back to Acapulco and then taken overland by mule to Vera Cruz, then on to Havana. Spanish silver was shipped to Panama, across the isthmus to Portobello, on to Havana, and eventually to Cádiz, then by smaller boats upriver to Seville. Ships leaving Cádiz contained wine, tools, manufactured household and luxury trade goods. The returning galleons carried gold, silver, tobacco, sugar, spices, cotton, silk, and porcelain.

Meanwhile, on the continent, the Spanish–Habsburg Austrian Empire was continuing its expansion by means of marriage and inheritance. In 1477 Emperor Maximillian, had married the queen of the Netherlands, uniting both empires. As previously mentioned, his son Prince Phillip wed Joan of Aragon, uniting Spain with the Hapsburg Empire. Phillip I's son Prince Charles, who became Charles V, married and brought Germany into the empire.

In Germany, a religious revolt to be known as the Reformation began taking place. Martin Luther, a Catholic monk and professor of theology, became enraged when he encountered a Dominican friar selling "papal indulgences" to finance a new church in Rome (Saint Peter's Basilica). Indulgences grant absolution for previous sins; therefore, purchasing one could place an errant worshiper back in God's good graces (sin now, pay later). In 1517 Luther nailed a document listing the indulgences along with ninety-four other criticisms of the papacy to the church door in Wittenberg, Germany. This single act would initiate religious wars, lead to the establishment of the Lutheran Church, and split up the Christian world between Catholics and Protestants. By 1530 Lutheranism had spread throughout much of Germany. As far as the pope and the Holy Roman emperor, Charles V—who coincidently was also king of Spain—were concerned, this was heresy, punishable by torture and death. The ensuing Counter-Reformation became known as the Spanish Inquisition.

Phillip, oldest son of Charles V, wed his second cousin Queen Mary, the half-Spanish daughter of Henry VIII and Catherine of Aragon. He temporarily became king of England but had no direct power. During his short reign, he made improvements to the Royal Navy, convinced his wife to burn over three hundred heretics at the stake and declare war against France. After Queen Mary died and he lost all royal power, he returned home to Spain and in 1556 became King Phillip II.

Phillip never had a moment of peace during his entire reign. His European empire stretched from the Netherlands to Belgium, Germany, Austria, Poland, Czechoslovak, and the Balkans, including part of Italy. His American empire included all South America (excluding Brazil), Nicaragua, Panama, Honduras, Mexico, North America, south, east, and west from California to Florida, and of course, the Caribbean. Add to this the Magellan discoveries of Guam and the Philippines, and Spain dominated a third of the entire world.

A devout Catholic, Phillip felt compelled to defend this vast territory from heresy as well as from invaders and pirates. He coveted England and truly wanted to rule the whole world as Catholic from the lavish headquarters he personally commissioned, the Royal Monastery of San Lorenzo de El Escorial, just north of Madrid.

By 1580 the vast sums of American silver were not providing sufficient collateral to back the loans needed to finance constant wars in defense of his empire. Not only did he have to defend against English pirates, France, and the Ottoman Empire, but he also had to deal with internal religious uprisings in Germany and the Netherlands.

When Sebastio I died, still foolishly fighting the Crusades in the sands of North Africa, he left a vacuum in the Portuguese succession. With no strong leadership present, Spain invaded and easily conquered Portugal, encountering major resistance only in the streets of Lisbon. The fruits of Phillip's new acquisition included ten new ships in Lisbon harbor, the royal treasury, and, of course, the empire of trading forts from Africa to Brazil, India, and Indonesia. The Portuguese royal family fled to Brazil.

Phillip hated the heretic Protestant Queen Elizabeth, who sacked and sold the Catholic churches and monastery property formerly belonging to the pope for the benefit of her own treasury. Making matters worse, she was providing naval and financial support to Protestant factions in the Netherlands and France. To add insult to injury, she commissioned pirates like John Hawkins and Frances Drake to steal his much-needed silver and gold. To Phillip, the most powerful leader of the Catholic Empire, this was intolerable heresy.

In 1588, making much use of his new Portuguese assets, he launched the ill-fated Spanish Armada in an attempted invasion against England (details in the chapter on the British Empire). Following its catastrophic failure, he attempted to organize several more invasions, none successful. Phillip died in 1598, leaving a bankrupt economy in his wake.

The Spanish Empire slowly began eroding. The Spanish Navy, now decimated, couldn't impede ingress to the Caribbean by the English and Dutch. Rampant piracy cut deeply into imports and much-needed silver. England began annexing Caribbean island colonies. On the continent, the Ottoman Empire nibbled away from the east. The Dutch won independence physically and religiously, built up a strong fleet, and raised havoc against Spain. Exercising new freedom and financial muscle, they campaigned to steal Portugal's trade on their way to becoming the next dominant empire. Portugal finally regained its independence from Spain in 1640 but was unable to hold onto its southeast asia territory.

By 1700 the Habsburg Empire was gone. After a series of weak monarchs, Phillips III and IV, mentally retarded Charles II inherited the throne. As a result of the War of Spanish Succession, Charles willed the monarchy to Frenchman Phillip of Anjou, the Spanish Bourbon who became Phillip IV. The new leader brought renewed prosperity to the now-smaller, and cheaper-to-defend, Spanish Empire. Spain did manage to stand off British invasion attempts against Cartagena and Santiago, Cuba, in 1741 and during the American Revolutionary War, Spain retook the Bahamas from a much-distracted England.

On the negative side, Spain began having its own colonial problems. Tupac Amaru II, a well-educated descendant of the last Inca emperor, Tupac Amaru, led a revolution to end the brutal system of forced labor. He was captured and killed near Cusco in 1781. Though the revolution was eventually unsuccessful, its legacy would spark future ones both in South America and Mexico.

After the French Revolution of 1786, Napoleon seized power. His first order of business was to annex Spain and the remaining pieces of the old Habsburg Empire. Spain came under French control after the war of 1793. Napoleon incorporated the Spanish Navy to supplement his own forces but after the catastrophic losses in the Battle of the Nile and later Cape Trafalgar, the combined French/Spanish fleet became practically a joke.

The Louisiana Territory, a vast area extending from the mouth of the Mississippi River to the Canadian border, ceded by France to Spain in 1763, was retaken and sold to the new United States as the Louisiana Purchase. The proceeds were needed to finance Napoleon's expensive military expeditions. With help from England, Spain was finally liberated in 1815. Napoleon was captured and exiled to the island of Saint Helena.

Ideas of revolution and freedom from colonial oppression are difficult for a despotic regime to control. Led by Simon Bolivar and others, South America won its freedom from the war-weary Spanish cavalry in 1824. That same year Mexico gained its independence under the leadership of a priest named Hidalgo.

In 1898, the American battleship USS *Maine* mysteriously exploded in the harbor of Havana, Cuba. The exact reason has never been determined, but it generated a huge reaction from the American people (much influenced by the press). As a result, the United States declared war against Spain. By the end of the Spanish-American War, Spain had lost Cuba, Puerto Rico, Guam, and the Philippines. Following World War II, Spain lost its African colonies, and the great Spanish Empire, where "the sun never sets," faded away to a distant dream.

In 1492 Elio Antonio de Nebrija, the light of Salamanca, published his *Art of the Castilian Language*, the first grammar of a European language. When he presented a copy to Queen Isabella, she inquired for what purpose the grammar might be used. One of her courtiers replied, "Your Royal Majesty, language has always been the companion of empire."

Spain left a huge legacy. Listed here are just a few of its accomplishments: Over four hundred million people speak Spanish throughout the world. Spanish music and architectural influence is everywhere. And in California, Spain left a string of twenty-one beautiful missions, stretched one day's ride apart from San Diego north to Sonoma.

The Dutch Empire (1630–1780)

It was 1592 when the British, still at war with Spain and its reluctant ally Portugal, captured the magnificent carrack *Madre de Deus* in a bloody six-against-one high sea engagement. After it was safely docked and unloaded in Portsmouth, its full cargo was revealed: gold and silver coins, pearls, amber, musk, tapestries, calico, 425 tons' pepper, 45 tons' cloves, 35 tons' cinnamon, 25 tons' cochineal dye, 3 tons' mace, 3 tons' nutmeg, 2.5 tons' Benjamin perfume base, and 15 tons' ebony. Portugal had a really good thing going, and the British and Dutch each wanted a piece of the action. It turned out that the Dutch were in the best position to profit.

Portugal, with a total population of only one million, was always short-handed and opted to employ both Dutch and German gunners to defend its huge vessels. Based on personal observations, Dutch "spies" began reporting details of Portugal's confidential South Seas trading operations to eager-eared businessmen in the Netherlands. Jan Huygen van Linschoten published two books based on his experience, noting details of wind, current, and trade routes plus a list of most trading forts complete with locations and descriptions. Equally important was his observation that the forts were "tolerated by the sultans".

In 1602, following a long war with Spain, the Netherlands won their independence. They then pioneered the world's first banking system, which included the world's first stock market. This new market provided them the resources and ability to form holding companies, raise capital, and finance expensive expeditions.

Using engineering drawings, precision measurement tools, templates, plus wind- and water-powered sawmills that facilitated precision cuts, skilled Dutch craftsmen were able to construct ships four times faster than the competition. In other words, ships were assembled with precision parts, which required minimum tedious and labor-intensive hand fitting, almost snapping together like Lego blocks. Since production also incorporated economy of scale, many hulls were identical. The average construction time was a mere four months.

Also in 1602, seventeen private Dutch shipping companies agreed to stop competing and merged to form the Verenigde Oost-Indische Compagnie (VOC), or the Dutch East India Company. The company creators were known as the Heeren XVII, or the Lords Seventeen. Their charter had two main objectives: open up trade in the South Seas and eliminate Portuguese competition. Moving quickly, they sent out an expedition in 1603 with the primary purpose of locating a site and setting up a trading base for their factors (traders). The first site they chose for their fort, trading post, or factory (different names, same thing) was Bantam, Java, the same port city used by the English. Bantam is located in the northwest corner of Java near the north end of the Sunda Strait, which separates it from Sumatra.

The VOC charter, approved by the Netherland's States General, gave Dutch company leaders the power to wage war and a mandate to set up factories, or trading forts. In a response letter from Jan Pieterszoon Coen, the governor general, sent to VOC headquarters, he stated, "We cannot carry on trade without war nor war without trade." The general plan was hegemony, the absolute monopoly of the spice trade in India, Ceylon, the Moluccas, and the Banda Islands. This meant eliminating any foreign presence or competition, allowing the company to enjoy low noncompetitive purchase prices and become the exclusive world supplier of cloves, nutmeg, mace, and pepper, thus maximizing profit.

In 1604 they drove the Portuguese out of Tidore and captured their fort at Ambon. By 1606 the VOC had forts or factories at Bantam, Jakarta, Ternate, Tidore, Ambon, and Niera, Banda Islands. Cloves were sourced from Ternate and Tidore in the Moluccas plus Ceram and Ambon farther south. Nutmeg was to be found only on five of the Banda Islands: Great Banda, Niera, Rosengain, Pulao Ai, and Pulao Rhun (Run). The remaining central Banda Island, Gunung Api, harbors an active volcano that destroys vegetation and sometimes becomes a nuisance to its neighbors.

In 1609 Admiral Verhoeven, newly in the employ of the VOC, was ambushed and murdered along with forty-one comrades while attempting to obtain a signed (coerced) exclusive trade agreement with the Banda natives. The natives were upset because the Dutch had invaded and built a fort on Niera without receiving or even asking permission from them. In addition, the Dutch had forced the native chieftains to sign exclusive trade agreements against their will and without any understanding of the legalese. The Bandanese chiefs had no central leader; how could only a few chiefs sign for the many? Worse yet, after they had signed the agreement, violating the contract and selling nutmeg to the English or Portuguese was a treasonable offense, and treason was punishable by death in Holland. In retaliation to the massacre, the Dutch made a formal declaration of war against Niera, which allowed them to destroy vessels, burn villages, and kill any problem natives.

The English, constantly harassed by the Dutch, desperately needed an exclusive nutmeg factory free from Dutch interference. At that time their only other source factory was a small post at Luthu, Ceram, where they obtained cloves.

British commander Nathaniel Courthope, with two ships, was ordered to set up a nutmeg factory on Pulao Rhun (Run Island), located west of Niera. The English desperately needed a secure island of their own away from the feisty Dutch. After having been unable to defend Pulo Ai, Run was the nutmeg island of last resort. The native Bandanese—who by now despised the Dutch—welcomed a friendly trading partner and happily surrendered their island to the English, ceding it to the dominion of King James. Outside of trade, all they wanted in exchange was protection from the Dutch. With the newly signed document, the English had accomplished their first and only East Indies territorial acquisition.

The natives provided eager assistance, moving cannons ashore and constructing a small fort, which enabled Courthope to successfully repel the Dutch in January 1617. In February, the *Swan* was captured while performing interisland trade. A month later the cowardly crew of the *Attendant* silently cut the anchor cables and surrendered their ship to the Dutch on Niera. In March 1618, the British sent two ships to relieve Courthope, but both were captured by the Dutch. Courthope, now aware that he was on his own, was forced to fend for himself. Somehow, with great resolve, patriotism, and sheer guts, he was able to maintain possession of Run Island for four years in spite of Dutch blockades. He was finally killed while attempting to obtain supplies in Niera, his presence revealed by a spy. The Dutch retook Run, but to their greedy dismay, the English retained legal possession.

In March 1618 Jan Pieterszoon Coen became the fourth governor general of the VOC, at age 31. In November 1618 John Jourdain, aged 46, arrived at Bantam to assume presidency of the English East India Company. Both men despised one another; Jourdain had been warned off by Coen while attempting to purchase cloves in Ceram five years earlier. In a heated discussion that would later cost him his life, Jourdain commented on the 26-year-old Coen's peach-fuzz beard. Jourdain was able to purchase cloves nearby, but when Coen found out, he intimidated that supplier and dried up the source.

Jourdain called a meeting shortly after his arrival in Bantam "to redeem the disgraces and losses to our Kinge and country." Three days later the Brits captured a Dutch ship and anchored it off their Bantam factory. While searching for liquor, someone accidently dropped a candle, setting the ship ablaze and destroying a cargo valued at £14,000.

Now the war shifted into high gear. Coen burned down the British factory in Jakarta. In January 1619 Sir Thomas Dale took a fleet of eleven ships to Port Sunda Kalapa, Jakarta, leaving four ships to defend Bantam. In a lackadaisical confrontation against seven Dutch ships where over three thousand cannons were fired, no ships were actually sunk, but the Dutch fleet did suffer the most damage. When three more ships from Bantam arrived to swell the opposition to fourteen, Coen wisely managed to escape with three ships and headed to the Moluccas to regroup and obtain reinforcements.

As soon as Coen was safely gone, the king of Jakarta attacked the factory fort. The Brits eagerly assisted the king, but with the factory ready to surrender, the Pangram who claimed sovereignty over both Bantam and Jakarta arrived with a large army. He threatened to destroy the English factory at Bantam unless the fort was turned over to him rather than the Jakarta king. Instead of wiping out the Dutch fort when he had them on the ropes, Dale, lacking the Dutch killer instinct, withdrew and shortly thereafter took his fleet to India.

Jourdain took two ships east, planning on reinforcing Courthope on Run Island, but foolishly left Bantam unguarded.

Coen returned with his reinforcements, laid siege to Jakarta, and regained the fort. In celebration of his victory over both kings, he named his operation Batavia, meaning "old Holland." His next order of business was to destroy the unguarded English factory at Bantam. Completing that, he then sent three ships to hunt down Jourdain. With a three-to-two advantage, the Dutch found and overpowered Jourdan's tiny fleet, which was lying at anchor. Unable to bring his cannons to bear, Jourdain surrendered. When he raised the white flag, he was shot and killed. Three years after establishing a fort on Run Island, the Brits had lost eleven ships, either captured or destroyed; the Dutch, only one.

An English squadron was dispatched from India to avenge and patch up the Indonesian operations. In the Sunda Strait on July 1619, just before entering Bantam harbor, the squadron encountered an English ship bearing news. The directors of the two companies had agreed to end hostilities, return captured vessels, and exchange prisoners. The Dutch lucked out; there would be no retribution from the English.

The new terms dictated the English share to be one-third of the Molucca spice trade and one-half of the Java pepper trade. In addition, the English were required to share one-third of the expenses and team together with the VOC against the Spaniards and Portuguese. Extremely resentful of any form of sharing, Coen muttered cynically, "It must be nice to be an Englishman." Coen did allow the English a tiny area inside his Batavia factory, but he made certain that the Brits, with very limited resources in comparison to the VOC's, were never able to pay their "fair share" of his impossible terms.

Having directed the English ships to other pursuits and acting on his own, Coen took two thousand company troops and thirteen ships to Fort Nassau on Great Banda Island. The reason for his invasion was revenge for the 1609 uprising and to completely dominate the native Muslim Orang Kaya, who seemed to enjoy the company of and trading with the English. Over a period of three months, he murdered, tortured, and enslaved the Orangs, reducing the population of the Bandas from approximately fifteen thousand down to one thousand. This was still not enough; in violation of the company's "agreement," he captured all the English, took them prisoner, tortured some, and destroyed their facilities. The company gave Coen a mild scolding for his heavy-handed tactics, but as a reward for securing a complete monopoly for the VOC, he was awarded three thousand guilders.

Coen returned to the Netherlands to enjoy the rewards of his toils, purchased land, and married the daughter of a VOC director.

Just prior to leaving for Holland, Coen had made a final tour of the outlying islands. During his instructional visit to Fort Victoria, Amboyna Island (Ambon), rich in cloves and located halfway between the Moluccas and the Bandas, Coen warned Herman van Speult, the governor and his cold-blooded admirer, to "beware of suspicious English activity."

With Fort Victoria now on alert, a night guard became suspicious of a Japanese worker supposedly making strange inquiries regarding security. Van Speult had the man tortured until he admitted to an implausible plot whereby 12 Englishmen from a ramshackle factory nearby would storm and occupy the 200 man fort he commanded. This would be treasonous; the English were there by treaty, and treason was punishable by death in Holland. Van Spuelt suspected treasonous activity because the English on Run had trained the locals on the use of fortifications and firearms. The English enjoyed much better rapport with the natives because they treated them with dignity and respect and paid them a fair price for spices. It was paranoid to think a dozen men could overpower two hundred.

Using a combination of bribes and torture, van Speult extracted confessions from the workers as proof of the suspected treasonous activity. One evening the unsuspecting English, who frequently dined with the Dutch, were kidnapped and taken prisoner inside the fort. For a week, they were interrogated and tortured, shot, stabbed, mutilated, and finally beheaded.

News of this heinous massacre caused an outrage both in England and Holland. Eventually the VOC paid a heavy fine in retribution. Coen, who had contracted for another term as governor general, snuck back to Batavia with his new bride three years later, delayed by the outraged atmosphere from the massacre.

Arriving back at Batavia, he found his 12 old foster daughter, Saartje Specx, daughter of a VOC official and left under his protection, in a naked embrace with a 15 old soldier. In a fit of rage, he had Saartje publicly whipped; the luckless boy was beheaded. The cold-blooded, vengeful, tyrannical Coen died of dysentery at age 41 with a legacy of complete VOC control of East Indies spice trade and the essential enslavement of all its citizens. There is a positive side: his Batavia factory became Jakarta, the capital of modern Indonesia.

Port Sunda Kalapa, located fifty miles east of Bantam at the mouth of the Cilwung River, was first considered for a trading site by a Portuguese named Alva. Sultan King Surawisesia, aware of Portugal's conquests in Goa and Malacca, was looking for an ally to assist him in defense against his Muslim enemy in nearby Cimanuk harbor. The king signed a treaty guaranteeing the Portuguese a thousand free sacks of pepper per year if they would construct a fort and defend him against his neighbor. The Portuguese placed a padrao on the site in 1527 to mark their newly acquired territory. When Sultan Fatahila Balatehan realized the Portuguese intentions, he seized Sunda Kalapa from Surawisesia and renamed it Jayakarta (Jakarta).

In 1619, when Coen returned from Molucca with reinforcements, he was surprised that Dale and Jourdain had left Jakarta's fate to the dueling kings and that his garrison was still just able to resist. Now back with force, he took control, overpowered the Muslim town of Jayakarta, and renamed it Batavia, meaning "new Holland." In the form of private enterprise, Coen built a break-water on both sides of the mouth of the Cilwung River, creating a sheltered harbor at the entrance to his trading fort. He then had huge warehouses con-structed along with all the necessary infrastructure required to support his operation. Thus, began a vast colony that would morph into the megalopolis Jakarta, with a population now exceeding ten million.

The Dutch Empire was not limited to the VOC and East Indies though for sure it was their greatest legacy. They controlled the pepper industry in Ceylon and seized control of Malacca and Makassar. They set up colonies in India, Cape Town, Brazil, and the Caribbean and up both sides of the African coast. For a period, they were the most aggressive and successful slavers.

Perhaps the biggest jewel of the Dutch Empire was New Amsterdam. In 1609 the VOC, in another attempt to suppress competition, financed Henry Hudson's third expedition seeking a Northeast Passage shortcut to the Spice

Islands. The English captain's first two attempts were foiled when he encountered pack ice off eastern Newfoundland. Afraid that the passage might actually exist, the VOC certainly did not want the route ownership in the hands of the English. Sponsored for a third attempt and again encountering a wall of ice, Hudson proceeded south down the American coast in his search. Having heard an Indian tale of the existence of a great water flowing from the northwest, he continued his search south, finally discovering his namesake river, and anchored near the present-day site of Coney Island. He discovered a land with trees, grass, and beavers inhabited by native Lenape and Mahican Indians who smoked tabacca. Completing his initial survey, he sailed up the river to the present site of Albany, where it became too shallow to navigate. After retracing his route, the crew, with suggestions of mutiny, forced the expedition to return home.

In 1621 the Dutch West India Company was chartered to both trade and support pirate operations against the Spanish. They erected a fort on Mata Hatta (Manhattan) strictly for that purpose. Present-day Wall Street is located at the site of one of the fort's walls. Pirate operations yielded eleven million guilders in 1628, and within the next ten years another forty million was made selling prizes (Spanish ships) and their cargo. Beaver pelts were a big hit on the continent; by 1630 fur was a twenty-seven-thousand-guilder business.

There was always a conflict between the demands of a for-profit company and the rights of the individual colonists who came from a liberal country that espoused freedom. Colonists were actually required to pay taxes to the company. Most colonists engaged in black market fur trade to augment their meager income.

In 1647 Peter Stuyvesant was selected to be the new governor to bring peace and accord to a colony in turmoil and to replace a warrior governor who had murdered sixteen hundred Indians. Stuyvesant, a one-legged war hero, turned out to be a rational though dedicated company man. His job was to create order from chaos, thus returning the colony to peace and profitability. Adrian Van der Donck preceded the governor, coming to New Amsterdam in 1641. A skilled lawyer, he fought for human rights for its citizens. Van der Donck was able to convince the new governor to create a council of nine advisors, of which he was president. Though officially on the inside, he continued to collect a list of grievances from distraught colonists until he was arrested for treason in 1648. Jailing Van der Donck caused a public outcry, and the governor was forced to release him.

On his release, Van der Donck immediately got back to work, creating an eighty-three-page document, known as *The Remonstrance.* In it he described the unlawful behavior of the company and a list of fixes that included schoolhouses, churches, and orphanages. Primarily, his petition was to remove company control and make the colony independent under then-current Dutch laws. Accompanied by several petition signers, he sailed back to the Netherlands and presented his case before the States General at The Hague. Thus, in 1652 the States General ordered the company to set up a municipal government. Just as Van der Donck was set to return, the first Anglo-Dutch trade war broke out, with cannons firing in the English Channel. Now with the company's focus on defense against the English, it dropped the new mandates. The war was a short one and never reached New Amsterdam. The company made a few improvements, and Van der Donck was allowed to return home but was stripped of any official power. The colonists continued to resent the repressive company.

In 1664 King Charles II sent four frigates across the Atlantic to annex New Amsterdam and thus give England complete control of the North American east coast. Colonel Richard Nicolls arrived at Fort Amsterdam with two thousand troops and demanded that the governor surrender the colony. Stuyvesant was a rational man, knowing full well that his defenses were insufficient to repel the aggressors. He also knew that the colonists lacked a unified will to fight. It was like a Mexican standoff; if no cannons were fired, there would be no bloodshed. He was between a rock and a hard place, but his job was to defend the company's property. Nicolls adroitly sent a negotiator to meet with Stuyvesant in a tavern to discuss terms. On reading the surrender document, Stuyvesant became enraged and ripped it to shreds. Under pressure from the concerned onlookers, Stuyvesant collected the scraps, left them on the table, and stalked out. It was as good as over when the document was pieced together and its terms were revealed—religious freedom, property rights, and so on—all the things that had gone missing. The next morning, with a petition in his hand signed by his own son and ninety-two leading citizens, Stuyvesant surrendered New Amsterdam to the British. Colonel Nicolls proclaimed New Amsterdam be renamed New York.

Following the end of the Second Anglo-Dutch War, both sides signed the 1674 Breda Treaty, whereby England gave up recently acquired Dutch Guinea and title to Run Island but retained the title to New Amsterdam. New York morphed into the largest city in the United States. The Indonesian book in the Lonely Planet series cites this as "the inauspicious land swap."

Holland lost colonies in Africa, Cape Town, Ceylon, India, Brazil, the East Indies, and the Caribbean during the Napoleonic Wars. Following World War II, it attempted to regain its old East Indies colonies after the Japanese were evicted. The citizens revolted and in 1947 formed a new country renaming it Indonesia. Batavia was renamed Jakarta and became its capital.

The French Empire, 0000-0000

There was no French Empire based on exploration or projection of naval power. France only gets an honorable mention in the European Expansion.

THE RELATIVE POPULATION COMPARISON OF 16th century Europe reads like a binary progression:

Portugal	1 million
Netherlands	2 million
Britain	4 million
Spain	8 million
France	16 million

France was always second with her colonies seeming to always follow Britain's lead. Britain was in North America before Quebec and Nova Scotia were established. Samuel Wallis discovered Tahiti, Bougainville for whom the beautiful flowery vine was named was the second. Spain was first in the Caribbean and South America. English and Dutch traders preceded French activity in India.

French Indochina began with settlements of Catholic missionaries in Laos, Cambodia, and Vietnam. The Vietnamese emperor attempted to drive them out. With the concept of increasing French Influence throughout the world, Napoleon III sent 14 ships and 2,500 troops in defense of the missionaries. By 1859 they occupied the ports of Da Nang and Saigon. The coerced emperor ceded three provinces to France. When he didn't live up to the treaty, the French navy returned. The result was that Cochin china became French territory.

In 1863 Cambodian King Norodom rebelled against his Siamese sponsors and opted for French alliance. In 1867, to convince the King of Siam to accept the French Cambodian protectorate, they secured his approval by ceding to him, two provinces of Laos. The result became known as French Indochina.

Following WWII France attempted to re-establish the colonies but the world had changed and no one wanted to live under colonialism. The push back resulted in a war and the French were driven out in 1954. The United States foolishly became involved based on the "Domino Theory" in suppression of communism. The tragic result was the Vietnam war.

French Polynesia is considered by France to be an Overseas Protectorate. It consists of six island groups, namely: Society, Tuamoto Archipelago, Gambier, Marquesa, and Austral. These have been under control by France since 1842.

France took possession of New Caledonia in 1853. Originally established as a penal colony, at one time it contained 22,000 criminals. Today the main use is mining.

France loaned the Mexican government 135 million French francs. In 1861 Benito Juarez overthrew the conservative Mexican government and refused to honor the French debt. With the U.S. involved in a civil war and unable to enforce the Monroe Doctrine, 7000 French troops marched on Mexico City. They were defeated May 5th, 1862. This is the background of the Cinco de Mayo holiday. France made a successful attack the next year with 22,000 troops and installed Maximilian I as Emperor. In 1867, Juarez again defeated the French controlled government, Maximilian was captured and shot Jun 19th, 1867.

Today French territory includes: Reunion, Guadeloupe, Martinique, Polynesia, French Guiana, Mayotte, New Caledonia, Saint Pierre and Miquelon.

The British Empire 1760-1947

———

Welshman Henry Tudor defeated King Richard III in the bloody 1485 battle of Bosworth Field and became King Henry VII. This feat united Wales and England. To improve relations with Scotland, he prompted his daughter Margaret to marry James Stuart, James IV of Scotland. To cement relations with Spain and counter a growing threat from France, he prompted his son Arthur, Prince of Wales, to marry Princess Catherine of Aragon, daughter of Ferdinand and Isabella. There would be no King Arthur; he died soon after the wedding. With some convincing of the pope to a rearranged marriage, Princess Catherine was wed to his second son, Henry. Upon the death of his father in 1509, the new Prince of Wales became Henry VIII.

Henry, an indulgent and impatient monarch, wanted it all, and he wanted it now. His reign inspired William Shakespeare to create the legendary play *The Six Wives of Henry the Eighth*. Only the first three wives would have a serious effect on England. After tiring of the Spanish princess whom he couldn't divorce (they were both Catholic) and aware of Martin Luther's break with the church and the Reformation of 1517, Henry created the Protestant Church of England and divorced his first wife. Soon after, he married his new sweetheart, Anne Boleyn.

Catherine had produced a Catholic daughter, who would become Queen Mary. Anne Boleyn produced a Protestant daughter, who would become Queen Elizabeth. After being unable to produce a male heir in three years, Anne was accused of adultery, a treasonous offense, and beheaded. Jayne Seymour, Henry's third wife, produced a sickly male heir, who would become King Edward. She died of complications in childbirth. Henry's marriage to his fourth wife, a mail-order bride selected on the basis of a flattering portrait, was quickly annulled, and she was quietly pensioned off. Anne of Cleves evidently did not resemble her portrait; Henry hissed, "a Flanders mare, I like her not." Bride number five fared no better than Anne Boleyn. A gorgeous 18 old, Catherine Howard found it difficult being betrothed to a corpulent, non-ambulatory fifty-year-old tyrant king. She actually did consort with others and was subsequently beheaded. Henry finally got it right on his sixth attempt at matrimony. Catherine Parr was much closer to Henry's age and performed duties as a nurse and caregiver to wheelchair-stricken Henry. She was a kind and benevolent stepmother to his three children, kept her head, and managed to outlive him.

Unable to afford a large standing army and with a need to defend a long coastline, Henry decided to do the obvious: he built up the Royal Navy. First he created the Navy Board to oversee shipbuilding, docks and facilities, planning, maintenance, and personnel. Next he increased the capital ship count from twelve to eighty-four, just in time to repel a Scottish uprising. Almost simultaneously he had to defend against a thirty-thousand-man invasion from France. In 1545 the Royal Navy defeated the French in the Battle of Portsmouth.

Upon Henry's death in 1547, his son became Edward VI, who, with a bankrupt treasury, made a hasty peace with France. Soon contracting TB, Edward died after a very short reign, leaving the kingdom to his Catholic and half-Spanish half-sister.

Queen Mary took the throne with a mission to make things right again. Known as Bloody Mary, she attempted to reinstall the Catholic Church to dominance. In the process, she had the archbishop of Canterbury and many others burned at the stake for heresy. She married her cousin, Prince Phillip of Spain, who was later to become King Phillip II. Phillip was unsuccessful in gaining the ruling power in England he desperately sought, but as king he did manage to increase the size of the Royal Navy and its facilities. At Phillip's urging, Mary entered into a new war with France. In 1558 France retook Calais, the last English fort on the continent, and a short while later, a heartbroken Mary was dead. The throne now passed to her Protestant half-sister.

Queen Elizabeth's first order of business was to "repair the damage" Queen Mary had caused. She burned and sacked Catholic churches and monasteries then transferred their treasures into her own. Her campaign was supported by John Foxe, who had fled the country to avoid being burned at the stake himself. He published *The Acts and Monuments of the English Church*, complete with drawings depicting the atrocities committed under Mary. His *Foxe's Book of Martyrs* became the most widely read book in England.

With a much depleted treasury, Elizabeth embarked on an undeclared cold war with Phillip II, the former king of England and now king of Spain. By issuing a letter of marque to a privateer, she could enable a pirate to capture an enemy ship, steal its treasure, and share one-fifth with England. With no capital ventured, she was essentially waging for-profit economic war whereby her treasury was fattened while Phillip's was depleted.

John Hawkins was a second-generation privateer. His operation was partially financed by investors inside the queen's Privy Council. The queen had even loaned him a ship from her Royal Navy, the *Jesus of Lubeck*. With a marque and five ships under his command, he carried four hundred slaves for sale to the Caribbean. While customers were usually eager to purchase slaves at a discount from the English, Phillip II had recently mandated "no trading with the enemy." After some difficult transactions in three different ports but with a huge load of gold, jewels, and silver to show for it, he began heading home. Slammed with two severe storms in rapid succession, and with the vessels in urgent need of repair, they snuck into the safe harbor of San Juan de Ulloa, fifteen miles south of the Mexican capital of Vera Cruz. Entering without flags, they were accepted as Spanish vessels and actually received a cannon salute. Soon someone correctly identified them as English and shouted, "Lutherans," which cleared the beach of everyone but the port captain. Finding himself alone and defenseless, he had little choice but to allow them to stay. The next day the viceroy of Mexico arrived at the mouth of San Juan harbor with a fleet carrying one thousand soldiers. Hawkins, in anticipation of trouble, had stationed some of his men at the fortress cannons, thus preventing the fleet's entry. Delgadillo, the port captain, went back and forth with each side's demands, acting as negotiator. Finally, with a signed agreement and each side holding ten hostages, the Spanish were allowed into their own harbor. For two days, the fleets coexisted with Hawkins nervously attempting repairs. At dawn on the third morning, the Spanish, in an act of treachery, attacked the English. Hawkins managed to destroy two ships, including the Spanish flagship, but the *Jesus* lost two masts from the shore fire and began taking on water. Hawkins managed to transfer part of his treasure to the *Minion* and escaped in the company of his 20 year old cousin and the captain of the *Judith*, Francis Drake. The two cousins now had a personal vendetta against the Spanish viceroy but even more so against Phillip II. Hawkins returned to England with twenty-five thousand gold pesos and, in 1569, filed a damage claim against the Spanish for £28,000. He had lost a hundred men at San Juan; most of the captives would succumb to the tortures of the Spanish Inquisition.

Francis Drake, harboring a personal vendetta and armed with a letter of marque, was wounded in a failed attempt to steal from the Spanish treasury at Noviembre de Dias in Panama. After his escape but remaining in Panama, he hatched up a plan to capture a mule train hauling vast sums of silver. With the help of Cimmeroons, escaped slaves he had befriended, and a French privateer, he found his mule train. After the melee, he discovered enough silver to sink his ship several times over, requiring him to order most of it buried. In 1573 he arrived in Plymouth with a treasure valued at over £20,000.

In 1576 Martin Frobisher, in a search for the Northeast Passage, made landfall on Resolution Island near Baffin Island in what is now part of Canada. He did manage to trade with the native Inuit Eskimos but was stopped from going farther north by snow and ice. When he returned to England with a large stone bearing specks of gold-like reflective particles, the search for the elusive passage was abandoned. He was sponsored for two more treasure trips before the shiny gold was found to be pyrite (fool's gold).

England's first attempt at colonization was made in Ireland. There were three considerations driving this. The pesky Irish, who didn't want to give up their Catholicism, seemed always to be in revolt. They were considered savages, needing to be "educated" to English standards and trained to obedience. Second, the Scots and Spanish needed to be kept away from the island lest the Irish pick up allies. Third, colonization seemed a profitable idea, and investment companies were formed to finance them. Colonies were established in the area surrounding Dublin, the only area under English control. Establishing colonies required driving out the existing property owners by whatever means necessary. The colonization produced farms, produce, livestock, and, of course, wool. The first uprising was led by James Fitzgerald in 1569 and resulted in a bloody massacre with many burned buildings. Elizabeth's lord deputy, Sir Henry Sidney, authorized Humphry Gilbert, military governor in charge, to respond with any means necessary. On eventually crushing the revolt, Gilbert forced the survivors to crawl between two rows of severed heads to beg him for forgiveness. The long lines of heads, consisting of men, women, and children, had all been taken from the losers' families and neighbors.

As a follow-up, a plan was made to take the Scottish fortress on Rathlin Island, located three miles from Ireland and thirteen from Scotland. In 1575 Francis Drake was commissioned to supply three ships to ferry three hundred troops for the invasion. After the Scots inside the fort surrendered, Sorely Boy MacDonnell, the commander and the son of a Scottish lord, along with his family, were allowed to live. All others and everyone else on the island, almost six hundred victims, were murdered. There is no record of Drake's part in the action.

In 1577 Drake departed England with five ships, a commission, and the full support of the queen and Royal Navy. His secret orders were to access the South Sea (Pacific) and continue northward up the South American coast, looking to trade and to obtain "special commodities". Also, if the situation was amenable, he would lay claim to any unclaimed land for England. In the Cape Verde islands, he managed to capture a Portuguese vessel and acquired the services of master pilot Nuno de Silva along with charts of the Brazilian coast.

In Brazil, a serious problem cropped up. While there can be only one leader of an expedition, his friend Thomas Doughty, with a company of "gentlemen", began to claim authority. Eventually Drake had to put an end to it. With all ships anchored, he sent everyone ashore and conducted a kangaroo court. Doughty was convicted of mutiny and sedition and subsequently beheaded. This moment forever established the captain of a ship as the final authority. Drake then asked that he must "have the gentlemen to haul and draw with the mariner and the mariner with the gentlemen."

Down to three ships, the fleet traversed the recently discovered Straits of Magellan. Encountering a storm on the Pacific side, Drake became separated from the *Elizabeth*, and the other ship, the *Marigold*, was never to be seen again. After attempting a reunion for two weeks, the *Elizabeth* returned home. Down to a single ship, Drake headed north with the *Golden Hind*.

For three months, Drake, virtually unopposed, raided the small towns and ports of the South American coast with the help of the captured pilot and local charts. He didn't obtain much loot but did manage to damage many churches and justified his actions by showing the frightened victims pictures from *Foxe's Book of Martyrs*.

On March 1, 1578, just north of Lima, Drake captured the undefended treasure ship *Nuestra Señora de la Conception*. It took almost a week to transfer the twenty-five tons of gold, silver, and jewels to the *Golden Hind*. After entertaining the captain aboard his ship, Drake bid the crew farewell, generously returning to them some of the captured gifts. Wisely deciding that it would be dangerous to retrace his route, Drake continued north, missing the entrance to San Francisco Bay (Golden Gate) which probably was shrouded in a fog bank. It could also have been during the night. Only about 20 miles farther north, inside the protective heel of Point Reyes and very visible to a northbound vessel, the sheltered waters of his namesake Drake's Bay beckoned him in. There is some speculation about the location, but the coast apparently does resemble the cliffs of Dover, and he called the location where he last careened, Nova Albion. In addition, his description of the native Indians provides some further substantiation. Although some historians including Samuel Bawlf, author of the Drake book in my bibliography discount his landing at Drake's Bay, the US National Park system, the citizens of California, and particularly the people of Marin County are absolutely positive. After careening the bottom, he continued north, possibly to Puget Sound, in search of an easy Northwest Passage.

One thing is certain: Drake did not want to risk his treasure with excessive exploration. In July 1579, he headed due west and arrived at the Molucca Spice Islands in November. The sultan was curious as to why Drake purchased only a small quantity of spices, not knowing his holds were already chock-full of treasure. Because of the extreme secrecy and lost or destroyed records, there is little detail of his circumnavigation beyond the American coast.

By September 1580, Drake was home in Plymouth. His first question was, "Is the queen alive and well?" He was testing the waters; not sure he was still welcome and nervous about having killed Doughty. With the queen's share of the treasure valued at £160,000, all was so OK that Queen Elizabeth actually came down to his ship where he was knighted. He became Sir Francis Drake.

In 1578 Portuguese King Sebastio was killed in combat in North Africa. In 1580, Portugal, with a weak selection of king prospects, was annexed by Phillip II. Spanish troops advanced virtually unopposed except for some street fighting inside Lisbon. The Spanish Empire now included Austria; parts of Germany, Africa, and Italy, the Netherlands, the Americas, the Philippines, and now Portugal, with all its ships and holdings in India and the East Indies. But this world was still not enough; Phillip wanted England too. Phillip conceived a plan to invade England with a thirty-thousand-man armada. In 1587 he foolishly published a fleet list of the armada. In response Elizabeth dispatched a preemptive strike with sixteen ships led by Drake, resulting in the destruction of thirty anchored ships inside Cádiz harbor. Drake then spent a month attacking commerce in the shipping lane, even coming ashore to raid the Portuguese fort at Sagres. To cap it off, he proceeded to the Azores and captured yet another treasure ship.

In 1588, just as the invasion was getting underway, Admiral Santa Cruz died. His replacement, Medina Sidonia, was cautious and lacked Santa Cruz's self-confidence and initiative. The element of surprise was lost when fishermen spotted the armada forming up near Plymouth while waiting for the slower vessels to arrive. The English were quickly alerted, and the plan was to follow the armada up the channel, with the advantage of being upwind. The defenders consisted of four groups, led respectively by Lord Admiral Howard, naval treasurer John Hawkins, Drake, and Frobisher.

After four days of very cautious maneuvering and losing only two ships, Sidonia sent a boat into Calais, where the Duke of Parma's invasion group was supposedly massed. To Sidonia's dismay, they were nowhere to be found. Sidonia's luck began quickly changing. Dodging fire ships, his squadron became disorganized, enabling the English to become much more aggressive. Now under heavy fire, Sidonia lost four ships in rapid succession. With the thought of just salvaging his fleet, he decided to return to Spain by way of Ireland. It proved to be a fatal mistake. With no charts or local knowledge and in the teeth of a storm with massive waves higher than any of them had ever seen before, he lost half the fleet. Phillip made three more attempts at invasion, but none ever reached England.

Phillip died in 1599, and Elizabeth followed in 1603. With no Tudor heirs, the throne passed to her cousin, James Stuart, King James VI of Scotland and now King James I of England and son of beheaded Mary, Queen of Scots. A scholar and theologian with a desire to reunite Catholics and Protestants, he wrote the King James Version of the Bible, signed a peace treaty with Spain and disallowed all Marques.

The first American colony, Roanoke, established in 1585, was a failure due to the colonists' lack of frontier skills, their inability to coexist with native Indians, and lack of support by the stockholder company. In 1606 King James appointed a board of private investors and government officials to establish a royal colony in America. In 1607 the London Company set up a colony on Chesapeake Bay called Jamestown. It succeeded due to the strong leadership of John Smith, its military governor. In 1620 they set up a second colony at Plymouth consisting of a religious group called the Puritans. Soon there were colonies stretching from Bermuda to Boston. The colonies quickly became a profitable business shipping cotton, tobacco, and sugar back to England.

Protestant public sentiment was for war with Catholic Spain. James finally agreed if Parliament would finance it. Parliament was for the war but refused the funding. In 1625 James died, passing the throne to his son King Charles I. At the urging of his friend Lord Admiral Buckingham and with £140,000 from Parliament, Charles agreed to attack Cádiz. With a hundred vessels, some borrowed from the Dutch. The expedition, led by an admiral who had never even had sea duty, was a complete failure. Ships refused to fight, typhus infection was rampant, and the few soldiers that were landed became drunk on captured wine. The Royal Navy was now at the lowest point in its history. Parliament voted to impeach Buckingham. Charles, in defense of his friend, dissolved Parliament. In a misdirected attempt to restore his lost confidence, Buckingham took the ill-managed fleet to La Rochelle to aid French Protestants against a siege from King

Louis XIII. When that failed, expedition returned to Plymouth with droves of wounded and typhus-stricken sailors, Buckingham was stabbed to death by angry survivors.

With a nonexistent Parliament, Charles and his council decided that a tax was needed to restore the long-neglected navy to fighting shape. In 1634 he imposed the ship money tax. Though highly unpopular, it did enable some restoration of the navy and increase morale. The new navy was comprised of professional officers, surgeons, and chaplains, all receiving increased pay. But five years later the Royal Navy lost respect when it allowed the newly power-ful Dutch fleet to destroy the Spanish fleet inside its home waters. While the Protestants were happy that Spain had lost forty ships and seven thousand men, the "impotent" Royal Navy lost face because it had allowed the action to take place inside British waters.

With a civil war being fought in Scotland, Charles decided to form a new Parliament, but he quickly dissolved it when he found they wanted to restrict his royal powers. When the Spanish ambassador requested Charles provide a Royal Navy escort to enable his remaining ships to transit the channel and return home for four million ducats, the opposition leaders of Parliament objected. Charles responded by imprisoning them. Public outrage forced Charles to release his prisoners and reopen Parliament, whereupon their first act was to repeal the ship money tax.

Two years later, in 1642, the English Civil War broke out, with Parliament in complete control of the Royal Navy. Under Parliament's control, the navy managed to ensure that trade continued and that no foreign monarchs could become involved. In 1643 Parliament imposed an excise tax on salt and meat to cover the expense of the military. By the close of the war in 1648, the excise and customs tax was supporting a combined army and navy of a hun-dred thousand men. The result of the civil war was that the Royalists lost, Charles was tried and convicted of treasonous behavior and was subsequently beheaded. Oliver Cromwell became lord protector and leader of the country.

England was declared to be a commonwealth. The monarchy was abol-ished. Both Scotland and Ireland had thrown off English rule. Son Charles, Prince of Wales, went into exile. Cromwell, England's greatest soldier, pro-ceeded to Ireland and laid siege to the largest royalist garrisons there. After three months' fighting, the Irish were subdued and the conquered land redistributed to Cromwell's soldiers. The exiled Prince of Wales became Charles II of Scotland. Cromwell managed to defeat Charles at Worcester and regained rule over both Scotland and Ireland. The defeated Charles fled to France.

When Lord Protector Cromwell died in 1658, the title passed to his son Richard, whose protectorate lasted only eight months. A free Parliament was convened (free because no royal person had summoned it). It was decreed that Parliament would decide all issues of importance but that England should be governed by a king. Charles II was welcomed back and reigned for the next twenty-five years.

Anne, the last of the Stuarts, became queen in 1702. Louis XIV's troops were poised to overrun Holland and currently occupied the Spanish Netherlands to the south. The fear was that if Holland were defeated, Louis would invade England and place Catholic James III on the throne. To make the situation more desperate, the elector of Bavaria came in on the side of France and began allowing French troops to mass there.

Anne's friend John Marlborough became commander of the Anglo-Dutch army on the death of King William. With a secret and well-executed plan, marching 250 miles at night, he rendezvoused with Prince Eugene's troops. In the ensuing battle, the French were defeated, twenty-three thousand French soldiers were killed, and another fifteen thousand were taken prisoner. The threat of a French invasion was completely negated.

This victory aided in coercing the Scots to unite with England. With the promise of unity and free trade, they agreed to the Act of Union and a united Parliament. Taxation and coinage would be the same for both countries. The Scots received forty-five seats in the House of Commons and sixteen seats in the House of Lords. After 1707, England, Scotland, and Wales became Great Britain, also to be known as the United Kingdom or the UK.

As the American colonies grew and began to thrive, Parliament wanted more control. They passed the Navigation Act, which required all colonial shipping, including any shipping between colonies, be done with English ships. This restriction, which eliminated Dutch competition, also enabled easy collection of custom duties. Year by year, the American colonists became more self-sufficient and resentful of English control. When Parliament passed the

Stamp Act, which imposed a direct tax on the Americans, the latter claimed it was "taxation without representation" and revolted. In 1776 leaders from all thirteen colonies gathered in Philadelphia and declared their independence from England. The result was the bloody American Revolutionary War.

Sustaining heavy early losses against an organized redcoat army, in 1779 the colonists finally enjoyed winning a battle with the Royal Navy. Ambassador to France, Ben Franklin, managed to obtain an old merchant vessel that was converted into a warship. The *Bonhomme Richard* under command of John Paul Jones attacked several seaports in the south and west of England causing them to consider their lack of coastal defense.

In the northern channel near Flamborough head a huge convoy came into Jones's view. It was under the escort of a 50-gun ship of the line and four smaller vessels. The *Serapis* immediately began firing on the *Richard*. Aware that he was in an impossible situation, Jones managed to grapple on to the *Serapis*. In the ensuing battle the inside of the *Richard* was blown away but the Marine sharp shooters in the rigging managed to keep the British below deck while setting the *Serapis* on fire. In the melee, the captain of the *Serapis* asked Jones if he would strike his colors? Jones famously replied: "I have just begun to fight". The result of the battle was that *Serapis* surrendered, *Richard's* hulk was cut loose and Jones sailed the prize into Holland. Jones became the hero symbol of the U.S. Navy and his remains are entombed inside the chapel of the Naval Academy in Annapolis.

By 1787 the colonists were winning. Under sustained attack, General Cornwallis had retreated down Virginia to the fort at the mouth of the James River. The French Navy managed to maintain a blockade, thus preventing his resupply and reinforcement. The colonists under General Washington finally overran the fort at Yorktown, and Cornwallis was forced to surrender. The Americans continued to win the skirmishes, and in 1783 the thirteen colonies became the United States of America. Cornwallis went on to have a successful career in India.

Captain James Cook, with a knowledge of astronomy and a history of precision mapmaking, was commissioned by the Royal Society and the Royal Navy to explore and chart the southern oceans. He commanded three expeditions into the South Seas. The iconic role model for Captain James Kirk in the Star Trek series, Cook proclaimed: "I had ambition not only to go farther than any man has been before me, but as far as I think it is possible for man to go". Star Trek's knock-off statement, more elegantly phrased was "To boldly go where no man has gone before".

On Cook's first expedition, he was equipped with a Hadley sextant, which allowed him to determine latitude to within one-sixtieth of a degree (one nautical mile). To determine longitude, he was given the Royal Society's lunar tables, not nearly as accurate. His first mission was to set up an observatory on Tahiti to measure the transit of Venus across the sun. Accompanying Cook were scientists Sir Joseph Banks and Daniel Solendar, plus naturalist painter Sidney Parkinson. While Cook was charting the shoreline, the three naturalists were busy collecting specimens and documenting the flora and fauna. This was the world's first scientific expedition and was the precursor to Darwin's.

Completing the transit measurements, Cook's next assignment was to search for the existence of Terra Australis Incognita, a suspected island or southern continent. While searching for it, he circumnavigated and charted both islands of New Zealand, discovered earlier by Abel Tasman. He then proceeded west to New South Wales, the first sighting of Australia's east coast (the west coast had been charted seventy years earlier by William Dampier). Cook discovered Botany Bay near Sydney, and within ten years it was populated by convicts working off their sentences in return for a promised pardon. Cook continued charting north through the barrier reef, around Cape York, then west to Batavia before returning home. During this expedition, Cook proved his theory that consumption of pickled cabbage (sauerkraut) would prevent scurvy. Later the British would carry limes for this, hence the nickname "limeys".

For Cook's second expedition in search of a southern continent, he proceeded east around the capes of Africa and then through the Southern Ocean back to New Zealand from the other direction. He disproved the incognita theory and demonstrated that at seventy degrees south there was only Antarctica. For this voyage, he was equipped with a brand-new chronometer, a compact copy of John Harrison's invention. This extremely accurate timepiece, which employed a spiral mainspring, was unaffected by a ship's motion, mounted on gimbals, and was compensated for temperature variation. Instead of lunar tables, he was provided with an ephemeris from the Royal Greenwich Observatory, with tables of sun and star positions for every day of the year. Equipped with these new tools, he became the first person able to accurately determine longitude on land or at sea.

Cook's assignment for his third expedition was to search for a Northwest Passage above the North American continent. This proved impossible due to ice in the Bering Sea. (With the "benefit" of global warming, several small sailboats have actually been able to complete this passage in the twenty-first century.) Cook then sailed south and managed to discover Hawaii, which he named the Sandwich Islands in honor of Lord Sandwich, first lord of the Admiralty. He also discovered Fiji, the Cooks, New Hebrides, and many others. He was killed in Hawaii on February 14, 1779, while attempting to recover a stolen longboat.

The English East India Company was formed to compete with the ruthless Dutch VOC. In the process of ousting the Portuguese by any means possible, the VOC were absolutely intolerant of any English competition. In 1623 the trading fort at Ambon, southeast of the Moluccas in present-day Indonesia, was attacked by the VOC, its occupants tortured and murdered.

Wisely deciding not to compete with the much stronger Dutch, the company decided to concentrate its resources in India, leaving only a small outpost at Run Island to collect nutmeg. The personnel at Bantam, Java, were transferred to Surat, India, on the northwest coast. The other main operations were Madras, on the east central coast, and Calcutta, in the northeast. Initially the stockholder company wanted to set up trade in India where they could obtain silk, pepper, spices, textiles, indigo dye, and most important of all, saltpeter. Saltpeter (potassium nitrate), the primary ingredient of gunpowder, occurred naturally near Calcutta in Bengal.

By 1657 profits were down due to increased competition, especially from the French government–controlled Compagnie des Indes Orientales, which set up a trading fort 130 kilometers south of Madras in Pondicherry. With the specter of possible insolvency, the British government, not wanting to lose the income and the strategic India connection, agreed to help insure the company's monopoly. In 1660 the new monarch, Charles II, issued a royal charter giving the trading company many of the powers of a nation. The new charter allowed the company the power to "Wage War, Administer Justice, engage in Diplomacy, Acquire Territory, Raise Armies and Capture Ships."

In 1705 the Mughal emperor, who was descended from invading Mongols, died, leaving India without any centralized control. The local leaders, suddenly empowered to do their own thing, began exercising political interaction with the trading companies. The French company, virtually an extension of its own government, began to engage in military operations, which allowed the local ruler to increase his territory at the expense of his neighbors and the English. The English responded in kind, with both sides engaging the service of their respective navies. The 1744 War of Austrian Succession officially pitted both mother countries against each other, and in 1745 the Royal Navy captured two French ships just offshore of Madras. In 1746 the French responded, attacking and capturing the Pondicherry outpost.

A young company clerk, Robert Clive, leading a small party, managed to escape and travel 150 kilometers south to trading post Fort Saint David. When the French attacked the alerted fort, they were repelled, assisted by both local native troops and the Royal Navy. For his courage and bravery, Clive was awarded an ensign's commission and promoted to company steward, which allowed him to collect sales commissions on provisions for regional employees.

After 1748, even when their respective nations were at peace, the two companies continued to joust. The French company managed to gain the support of Raza, the Carnatic ruler, who managed to oust Mohammed Ali, a friend of the English. Clive, now a captain, led a group 100 kilometers to the capital city of Argo, where they managed to capture and defend it in the name of Ali. Against great odds, Clive and Ali prevailed, and after four months of battle, Raza and the French were defeated.

Clive, with a new wife and now becoming rich and famous, was appointed governor of Fort Saint David. Meanwhile, the French were down but not out. In Bengal, Siraj ud-Dowlah came to power on the death of his Nawab grandfather. With French backing, he captured the English forts at Kasimbazar and Calcutta, placing the captives in the infamous Black Hole of Calcutta. Clive led a force consisting of five Royal Navy vessels, three company ships, two hundred soldiers, and a thousand local troops. They managed to retake Calcutta in 1757 and secure a peace treaty with Siraj.

The Seven Years' War, begun in 1756, renewed the conflict between the two companies and their respective countries. Clive, now on the offensive and with an assist from the Royal Navy, captured the French fort at Chandernagore. Three months after his defeat at Chandernagore, Siraj, with fifty thousand troops and the support and guidance of the French, positioned his group to attack the English at Plassey Field, twelve kilometers north of Calcutta. Clive, now acting with the authority of a general and with mixed troops of less than four thousand, attacked Siraj. In the melee, a great portion of the Nawab's army fled. Unknown to Siraj, Clive had made promises of power and glory to Mir Jafar, the leader of the group that fled; he had won the battle at Plassey using bluff and treachery.

In the aftermath of the battle, Clive became the most powerful man in all of India. Inside one of Siraj's former palaces, Clive appointed Mir Jafar the new Nawab. In return, Mir Jafar granted Clive a grant of land surrounding Calcutta that included annual revenues of £27,000. In addition, Clive received over £300,000 in personal gifts. Additional gifts were also presented to his troops. In 1758 Clive was appointed governor of Bengal by the directors.

What had begun as a series of company trading forts had morphed into a private company with the power to collect taxes and govern a country. The distinction of a private English company was blurred due to the assistance of English troops and the Royal Navy. Clive returned to England in 1760 an immensely wealthy man. He was elected to the House of Commons but was required to face a moral question: How can an individual profit so greatly from an operation supported both by his company and the English military? Though the question was never resolved, Clive managed to keep his wealth, and he eventually returned to India.

Following the success of the American Revolutionary War, which bankrupted the French economy in the process of their eager assistance, the citizens of France, with the rallying cry "Liberty, Equality, Fraternity", decided to overthrow the king and establish a democracy.

Due to the unintended consequences of not having qualified leaders, the aftermath was a revolutionary dictatorship. Napoleon Bonaparte emerged from the melee and assumed the role of general and emperor. Not satisfied with destroying the opposition within France, he set about to conquer all of

Europe. Within a short while, he won against Spain and the Netherlands, Austria, and most of Italy. Now as powerful as Phillip II had once been, he also wanted "the world," which again would require defeating England. But first he wanted the riches and income from India that England enjoyed. His goal was to march through Egypt on the way to India.

The English knew that their only defense to protect England and prevent an invasion was the might of the Royal Navy. By the close of the eighteenth century, it was the most formidable navy in the world. Its ships were faster than any others owing to the attachment of copper plates below the waterline, preventing marine growth, barnacles, and *Terredo navalis* worms. They constantly practiced and managed to fire their cannons two to three times faster than any enemy. They practiced maneuvers in close formation with the use of rapidly changing signal flags. In addition to the superior training of their crews, they had the most capable and aggressive leader.

Horatio Nelson proved to be the ablest and most aggressive admiral England had ever employed. He entered service at age twelve, and with some help from his family connections and battle success, he rose rapidly, becoming a captain and commodore by age thirty. In 1797 a fifteen-ship squadron of Royal Navy vessels engaged a twenty-seven-ship Spanish fleet off Cape Saint Vincent, Portugal. At the time Spain was operating under control of Napoleon. Captain Nelson managed to disable and board the 80-gun *San Nicolas*, and when the 120-gun *San Josef* came to its aid, Nelson captured it also. For his skill and daring, Nelson was awarded the rank of admiral.

In 1798, Nelson, now directing fifteen ships, managed to locate Napoleon's invasion fleet at Abukir Bay in the Nile delta. Napoleon was ashore twenty-three miles away, having just stormed the city of Alexandria. Discussing the battle plan earlier with his Band of Brothers, he encouraged the captains to take initiative if the opportunity were to arise. Captain Thomas Foley, with the only chart of the bay, took the initiative and determined that there was enough depth to attack from the shore side of the anchored French fleet. In the ensuing melee, the entire fleet—except for two ships, which escaped—was either captured or destroyed. Many English ships were damaged, but all were repairable. The French had lost more than seventeen hundred men; the English, just over two hundred. Napoleon abandoned his thirty-four-thousand-man invasion force in Egypt, leaving them to die or be captured, but he himself managed to return to France.

Trying a new approach, Napoleon instituted a League of Armed Neutrality with all the Baltic states. The goal was to exclude England from any trade whatsoever with the region.

The English diplomatic response was to present the Danish king with an ultimatum: drop out of the neutrality pact or risk the destruction of Copenhagen. After the king chose to favor the pact with Napoleon, Nelson engaged the anchored Danish fleet, anchoring alongside at point-blank range. With the Royal Navy's three-times-faster firepower, the adjacent enemy ships were quickly destroyed. Having heavily damaged the Danes, Nelson defied an order from his superior to withdraw and instead met with the Danish leader. Nelson informed him that if they did not surrender, the many captured hulks would be set afire, with the crews left to die on board. Regardless of whether Nelson would have followed through with the cruel threat, the Danes presumed he would, signed a truce, and dropped out of the Neutrality League. In 1802, with the League broken, Napoleon requested peace, but only with England.

Due to Napoleon's continuing military expeditions, England still feared an invasion and fourteen months later declared war against France. While the English were blockading the French fleet at Toulon, foul weather enabled Napoleon to escape out into the Atlantic. Reaching Cádiz, and dropping off Napoleon, the French picked up seven Spanish ships and retreated to the Caribbean with a total of eighteen ships of the line. Nelson chased them to the Caribbean then back to Cádiz, where he managed to keep them blockaded.

Finally, the combined French and Spanish fleet emerged, carrying reinforcements for Napoleon's Mediterranean campaign. Admiral Villanueva brought his fleet out in a line to the north off nearby Cape Trafalgar. Nelson attacked with two columns, his to the center and Rear Admiral Collingwood's to split the rear. Nelson raised his favorite flag signals: "engage the enemy" and then "engage the enemy more closely." The attack plan wreaked havoc on the defenders. After two hours, four of their ships were out of action, dead in the water. The French ship, *Redoubtable* managed to grapple with the flagship *Victory*, which allowed a sharpshooter to kill Nelson. He was an easy target to spot, a tiny 135 pound man with a huge double-pointed blue hat, one arm, one eye, and shiny medals on his chest.

In the aftermath of the battle, all ships suffered damage, but the combined French-Spanish fleet was completely destroyed. The emperor's invasion plans were wrecked, and the Royal Navy became the undisputed master of the seas.

Nelson received a huge state funeral in January 1806 and was enshrined with the creation of Trafalgar Square. In the square front stands an enormous fifty-foot pedestal with the conquering hero standing on top, surveying Whitehall, London. The legacy that best described Nelson's worth was uttered by the captured admiral. Even though Nelson had died only four hours into the great battle, Villanueva stated that "all the captains were Nelsons".

Meanwhile, Napoleon attempted to restrict trade with England from all the seaports that he controlled. England responded by blockading those ports from any trade, including ports in the new United States. The blockade was a great success but gave cause for the United States to declare the War of 1812. This was in response to both the blockade, which included seizure of "contraband cargo", and the kidnapping of American citizens, who were then pressed into Royal Navy service. During the war, the British managed to set fire to the White House, probably a little dig to avenge their defeat in the Revolutionary War.

England finally decided that if it were to have any security at all, it would have to invade France and completely destroy Napoleon's army. In 1815 General Wellington severely crushed and defeated Napoleon's army at Waterloo, Belgium. Instead of being killed, Napoleon was allowed to spend the rest of his life imprisoned on the island of Saint Helena.

The aftermath of the Napoleonic Wars was almost a hundred years of peace—Pax Britannia—between England and Europe, a truce in the 1812 war with the new United States, and the annexation of the African cape colonies, Ceylon, Dutch Guiana, South America and Mauritius from the Dutch.

Following Trafalgar, the Royal Navy received a new assignment: eliminating slavery. Britain had abolished its own slave trade in 1807. By 1833 it was abolished in all British possessions. The Royal Navy was assigned to eliminate slavery in Africa, South America, and the southern shores of the Mediterranean. For this, the Royal Navy acquired an altruistic humanitarian gloss. Interestingly, many slavers flew the Stars and Stripes knowing that US flagged vessels would not be searched (as per the treaty ending the War of 1812). Lincoln finally put an end to that in 1862, allowing slave searches on US flagged vessels.

In 1662 the Royal Society was chartered by recently restored King Charles II, who cherished scientific methods. Charter and early members included Christopher Wren, Robert Boyle, Frances Bacon, Robert Hooke, and Isaac Newton. This elite group helped spark the Industrial Revolution.

The Industrial Revolution could never have evolved without individual freedom combined with the concept and security of intellectual property rights. Why this concept first took root in England has been the subject of much thought and discussion, but the record shows that it had the right stuff. The second requirement is a need to produce something. The third requirement is a stock of educated, inventive, and creative people. The list is long, but near the top is having a market that will justify the effort required to produce the invention or product in the first place.

England, like adjacent countries, had a metal industry and rivers to power mill rotation. Its chief industry, though, was wool production. The biggest mechanical need was pumps to dewater its many mines. In 1702, engineer Thomas Savery, making use of facilities of the Royal Office of Ordnance, produced the first working steam pump for that very purpose.

By 1712, Thomas Newcomen and John Cally, in communication with Robert Hooke for consultation, produced a much improved steam-driven pump that used both pressure and vacuum to drive a piston, producing motion with a seesaw-like pivoting beam. Savery and his heirs were able, under the newly protective patent system, to extract royalty payments from Newcomen's very successful engine. James Watt's further improvements increased the steam engine's efficiency 60 percent over Newcomen's. The Boulton and Watt Company was also able to mass-produce their pump and make it portable so that factories could be set up anywhere, especially near urban areas able to supply a ready labor pool.

Richard Arkwright's cotton-spinning machines and Edmund Cartwright's looms revolutionized the cotton industry. India, the original source of cheap cotton textiles, became one of the largest markets. The father-and-son team of George and Robert Stephenson produced the first reliable steam locomotive, which was replicated and placed on standard-gauge steel rails transporting cotton and cloth between Manchester factories and the seaport of Liverpool. Invention begets invention, and the process never stops. The British standard of living increased approximately threefold between 1780 and 1830 while the empire provided a hungry market for the mass-produced products.

The Irish potato famine was a strange and sad phenomenon. Potatoes, first cultivated by the Inca Indians, included a wide variety of tubers. A few varieties were brought to Europe by the Spaniards, most notably *S. Tuberosom*. The Irish cultivated this single variety, which worked well for many years, providing most bodily nutritional requirements for its consumers. It is now believed that the potatoes' enemy also came from Inca land, transported through the distribution of the miracle fertilizer discovery, Peruvian bird guano. The blight first showed up in Belgium in 1854. By 1845 it was all over Europe, including Ireland. *P. Infestans* destroyed 30 percent of the Irish crop the first year. The next year was worse. Forty percent of the population ate nothing else, with the rest of the country heavily dependent on potatoes. Ironically, Ireland exported 430,000 tons of grain in 1846 and 1847. The result of the famine was mass migration to the United States and Canada, with heavy die-offs aboard the death ships.

Other substantial migration was encouraged by the government. Prisoners were sent to Botany Bay near Sydney, Australia, with the possibility of working off their sentences after six to ten years and then becoming free men. New Zealand needed young healthy workers, especially tradesmen and farmers. If you were under thirty, you were eligible for free, indentured, or subsidized transportation.

In 1833 the English East India Company lost its Parliament-granted monopoly to trade with China. Now with England completely addicted to tea, drastic measures were required. Opium from India and Ceylon (40 percent of Indian exports) was exchanged for English manufactured goods and then smuggled inside China by eager Chinese in fast boats who paid in silver. Each transaction provided a highly profitable uplift; the silver was redeemed for tea, which was shipped home immediately on speedy clipper ships. Duties on tea provided 10 percent of the national revenue, half the cost of the Royal Navy.

The Opium Wars followed; Chinese officials attempted to stop the immoral trade but were essentially powerless to do so against heavily armed company gunboats. Losing the war, China was strong-armed into giving the company rights to trade from Hong Kong in an 1842 settlement. Eventually, British citizens with a conscience managed to force an end to the opium trade, but Hong Kong evolved into a prosperous trading port for both countries and a critical Royal Navy base. Tea was eventually planted in India, and the tea trade with China became much less critical.

By 1858 the English East India Company was in bankruptcy. They had been paying out more to investors and managers than was coming in, owing mostly to greed and the costly maintenance of a company army, which was required to insure tax collection and put down revolts. Queen Victoria agreed to nationalize the operation in exchange for all company assets, which included forts, property, ships, inventory, and tax-collection rights. The investors received 10 percent per year for ten years against their original outlays, an extremely generous agreement for creditors of an insolvent company.

India then became a possession of England, which had the right to collect taxes but also the responsibility to govern and defend it. Outside of the fact that tax collection was not much more than expenses, possession included a huge market outlet for manufactured cloth and trading goods, plus the services of a 130,000-man standing army at no additional cost (paid for by taxes). India remained a major source of pepper, tea, and saltpeter, plus many other items.

England annexed the African cape colonies from the Dutch in 1815 while the latter were locked in a war with Napoleon. The mostly Dutch migrants who initially came as workers for the Dutch East India Company were known as Boers. As the colonists became acclimatized and more secure, they moved inland to farm and raise livestock independent of the colonial company. Always displacing the native blacks, they enjoyed the use of black labor both as slaves and as paid workers. The British outlawed slavery in 1807, and enforcement of this policy against the Boers would eventually lead to war. By 1852 European South Africa consisted of three colonies: The British Cape Colony, the Dutch Orange Free State, and the Dutch Transvaal.

In 1861 diamonds were discovered in Kimberly, and that area was quickly annexed by the British. Sixteen-year-old Cecil Rhodes journeyed to South Africa in 1871 to meet his brother and seek his fortune. Initially he farmed cotton and made improvements to his brother's land; then he partnered with him in a mining claim at Kimberly. With the single-minded purpose of acquiring great wealth, Rhodes began accumulating shares in the mine. Within a few years, he bought out his brother's stake and, with a new partner, began purchasing shares in the De Beers mine. Continuing to increase their stake he and his partner formed the De Beers Company, which eventually owned both mines and cornered the diamond market with the power to limit production and maintain premium prices.

Not satisfied just with wealth, Rhodes also sought power both for himself and, with a sense of pride and nationalism, the British Empire. He managed to become prime minister of the Cape Colony, and with political power on his side, he managed to build roads, railroads, dams, and general infrastructure, in many cases to the benefit of his companies. Gold was discovered in Transvaal, leading to the creation of the city of Johannesburg. Rhodes speculated that he could go into the gold business himself and, using his wealth and political power, formed the Consolidated Gold Company and eventually the British South Africa Company.

While no vast goldfields were discovered, his company, with the ability to form a large standing army, carved out a massive region to the north, which he "allowed" to be named the colony of Rhodesia. In response to a query from Queen Victoria asking, "What have you done since our last meeting?" Rhodes replied, "Madam, I have added two new provinces to your possessions."

Rhodes's legacy was twofold. His racist influence disallowed the native blacks to have any vote or power; they were used only to supply cheap labor. He established the Rhodes scholarship program to provide three years of college education for qualified students. Rhodes himself would never have been able to meet the high-minded requirements for his scholarships. The British Empire continued to expand throughout Africa and Egypt.

Germany, feeling strengthened by its own very successful industrial revolution and with thoughts of many years' domination by Napoleon, fought and won the Franco- Prussian war in 1875 against France. In commemoration, it erected a 225-step tower that supports a golden angel called the Winged Victory. This monument is located inside Tiergarten Park in central Berlin and is only a few hundred meters from the iconic Brandenburg Gate

Now with a new nationalistic pride, it continued to arm itself and seek a position of power in Europe. In 1914, using as an excuse the assassination of Archduke Ferdinand, Germany initiated World War I.

Britain, feeling subjected to defense treaties with Belgium and France, entered the war on the side of the two defender countries. It was a long, grueling, bloody affair with much stupid waste of lives in muddy trench warfare on both sides. Eventually the United States came to the Allies' assistance in 1917. The war ended at the eleventh hour of the eleventh month of the eleventh day of 1918 at a cost of ten million dead. Britain, which had originally been a powerful lender country, swapped roles with the United States and became a debtor nation. The British Empire, still controlling over three hundred million people and a quarter of the world's land surface, continued to expand ever so slightly until Italy, Germany, and the new Empire of the Rising Sun began to contest it.

Benito Mussolini began building up the Italian naval fleet and in 1935 sent ships through the British-controlled Suez Canal to invade and seize Ethiopia. In 1931 Japan invaded Manchuria and then in 1937 bombed Shanghai and began controlling China itself. Adolph Hitler forced his way to power in Germany, becoming Reich Chancellor in 1933. Germany had never recovered from its defeat in World War I. The combination of a worldwide depression and punitive treatment from France attempting to collect retribution for its war debt left Germany's economy in a shamble; a wheelbarrow full of worthless marks could barely purchase a loaf of bread. With the full backing of the banking and munitions industries, Hitler began a rapid buildup of war material and conscripted thousands of young men into military service. With full employment, a new national pride, and the largest standing army in Europe, Hitler began to flex his muscles. He established his Nazi headquarters within a hundred meters of the Brandenburg Gate and a short walk from the Winged Victory.

On September 1, 1939, Hitler invaded Poland. Two days later, in honor of a treaty to come to Poland's aid, Britain and France declared war against Germany, thus beginning World War II. Using a blitzkrieg of tanks and bombers, Hitler quickly overran Poland, Holland, and Belgium and then, bypassing the "impenetrable" Maginot Line, crossed over the border north of it into France. In May 1940, the British Expeditionary Force and the French army were overwhelmed and retreated to Dunkirk near the border of France and Belgium. 240,000 Brits and 95,000 Frenchmen were evacuated with the aid of weather, the Royal Air Force, the Royal Navy, hundreds of small private and commercial vessels, and the incredible luck that Hitler's forces didn't press for the kill. By June, Germany was in Paris and France was completely occupied.

Construction began immediately, establishing U-boat bases in Brittany, submarine pens with virtually impenetrable ten-meter-thick reinforced concrete ceilings. In addition, large heavy duty concrete gun emplacements were located at strategic points along the coast to defend against Allied invasion. In the space of six months, Hitler, leading a population of only sixty million, had created Fortress Europe.

In May, the passive UK prime minister, Nevil Chamberlin, was replaced by the feisty and charismatic Winston Churchill. He quickly increased war production and generated a national pride and fighting spirit. England, all alone, was the only major European country not under Hitler's domination; Spain, Portugal, and Switzerland had managed to maintain neutrality. Hitler's plan was to invade England but first to soften it up with bombing.

The Battle of Britain began on August 13, when Hitler's Luftwaffe sent almost fifteen hundred planes over Kent and Sussex. With the help of England's invention of radar, its fighter planes had early warning and were able to concentrate their efforts on the attackers. After fifty-seven continuous night raids over London, Hitler gave up the air raids. The Royal Air Force had finally won the air battle. Germany had lost twenty-two hundred aircraft; England, six hundred. In his famous victory speech, Churchill stated, "Never have so many owed so much to so few." What Hitler had failed to understand was that the bombings, rather than demoralizing the citizens, cemented the British together actually making them a much tougher foe.

Britain sent fifty thousand troops to North Africa to counter Mussolini's Italian forces, who were now allied with Hitler's. The unity of the aggressor nations of Germany, Italy and Japan was coined "the Axis". When Italy began the invasion of Greece, the British force was diverted to assist them. Germany came to Italy's aid, and together they occupied Greece and Yugoslavia. The British withdrew to Crete but did manage to free Ethiopia and capture two hundred thousand Italians in May 1941. Meanwhile, to the happy relief of

England, Hitler decided to invade Russia, temporarily postponing the nightmare of English invasion.

Cut off from most trade—meaning income, war material, food, and precious fuel—Britain, isolated and with its back to the wall, desperately needed help from America. The response from the still-isolationist United States was the lend-lease of fifty old destroyers in return for naval access to Caribbean bases plus financial loans of food and war material supplied by convoys.

On December 7, 1941, the Japanese attacked Pearl Harbor, bringing America into the war. Four days later, Germany declared war against the United States. Now with a partner and co-defender, England was being supplied by massive convoys from the United States. In addition, America established air bases in England and sent hundreds of B-17 bombers to destroy German cities and war production.

U-boats feasted on the convoys, sinking three hundred thousand tons per month until the summer of 1943 while operating from the safety of bombproof bunkers. Assembled at five different locations, a single yard, Blom & Voss in Hamburg had the capacity to mass-produce one Type VII-C submarine every week using the system of pre-staged hulls, each one closer to completion than the latter one. Bombing and parts shortages reduced the B & V output to a maximum of forty-three U-boats a year.

To counteract this menace required a comprehensive plan. Code breakers had secretly captured an Enigma decryption machine from U-110 in 1941. This machine employed three code wheels. Making use of it and the accompanying code books, the Allies were able to read Hitler's mail for a short while. Later, a fourth wheel was added to the Enigma to increase its security and confound code breakers. Thousands of code breakers were secretly employed at Bletchley Park and Washington, DC. They, assisted with mechanical computers, were often able to read the intercepts and obtain exact U-boat positions and, of course, read Hitler's mail. Additionally, radio direction finders were employed to triangulate U-boat radio transmission locations.

Aided by interpreting concentrated statistical data, the following schemes were incorporated: Small escort carriers were employed to provide convoy air cover. Sonar techniques and equipment were constantly improved. Methods for launching multiple hedgehog and depth charge arrays were developed.

Long-range patrol planes began continuously flying missions over the shallow Biscay Bay routes to and from the impenetrable bunkers. To increase their effectiveness, they employed radar and carbon arc Leigh Lights at night. Huge convoys of fifty or more ships were formed losing an average of two or three ships per transit, the same numbers lost with much smaller convoys.

Making use of the above mentioned anti-submarine warfare techniques, the tide of battle quickly began to change and Hitler began losing the Battle of the Atlantic. 34 U-boats were sunk in April 1943 alone, 530 by war's end. Two of Admiral Doenitz's own sons lost their lives in submarines. Suddenly confronted with huge losses, Doenitz temporarily shut down Atlantic U-boat operations in a futile attempt to regroup.

A combined Allied effort pushed the Germans out of North Africa, and in 1943 the force managed to get a toehold in Italy by way of Sicily. Finally, the same month of the invasion, there was some good news: Mussolini was killed by his own people. Italy surrendered, and with Italian assistance, the Allies began driving out the Germans. Then there was more good news: The Russian invasion was repulsed, with Hitler's defeat at Stalingrad. Germany now had three opponents all beginning to close in on her.

On June 6, 1944, 156,000 American, Canadian, and British troops landed on the shores of Normandy, France, against Fortress Europe. After twenty-four hours of fighting, they managed to secure the three beachheads at a cost of ten thousand men killed; over six thousand were Americans. The Germans, now on the run, were steadily being pushed out of France. Hitler ordered a huge stand in the Ardennes Forest of Belgium. The resulting Battle of the Bulge caused thousands of unnecessary casualties. By May 1945, with Russians inside Berlin, Hitler committed suicide. Germany unconditionally surrendered May 8, 1945.

The Pacific War began with everything going Japan's way. The battle-ship *Prince of Wales* and the cruiser *Repulse* were attacked and sunk in the Gulf of Siam on December 10, 1941, by planes from occupied Saigon. In February 1942, the Royal Naval bases at Singapore and Hong Kong were captured. Darwin, Australia, was bombed; Burma and part of New Guinea were occupied. When the Japanese showed up on the Burmese border with India, the Indian Congress Party offered Britain a choice: Britain could grant India independence after the war or India would be "liberated" by the Japanese. White colonial rule was over in both the Pacific and Indian Oceans. The Japanese Empire occupied the Dutch East Indies, French Indochina, Malaya, Burma, the Philippine Islands, and China.

When Admiral Yamamoto was retrieving the planes aboard his flagship aircraft carrier, which had just attacked Pearl Harbor, he said prophetically, "We may have just awakened a sleeping giant". The isolationist United States, in a war it did not wish for, was driven to become the most powerful nation (empire) that the world had ever seen. With feelings of hatred, revenge, and national pride, the entire country was mobilized for war and war production. Women were liberated to perform industrial jobs, transformed into "Rosie the Riveters". Stay-at-home moms planted victory gardens while their brothers, sons, and husbands went off to fight a war on two oceans. Even movie actress Marilyn Monroe was building warplanes.

To make a long story short, the Pacific War was highlighted by victories of submarines, aircraft carriers, and vicious island combat. By war's end, targets for patrolling US submarines were either extremely hard to find or nonexistent. Attrition had reduced Japanese shipping to a mere trickle. Carrier battles went from breakeven at the Coral Sea to US dominance at Midway Island, an operation much aided by cryptanalysts. US Marine Corps and US Army personnel captured key Pacific islands to secure sites for construction of airfields, which enabled long-range B-29 bombing of the Japanese homeland. With the fear that the Japanese would fight to the death, as they had done defending their Pacific islands, potentially risking the deaths of over one million US soldiers, President Truman decided to use atomic bombs. On August 6, 1945, the first bomb was dropped on Hiroshima. When it failed to produce a surrender, a second was dropped on Nagasaki, three days later. Completely overwhelmed, Japan agreed to unconditional surrender, signed on August 15, 1945.

The Hiroshima bomb consisted of expensive enriched uranium processed using centrifuges and electromagnetic cyclotrons. The two halves of the critical mass were brought together inside a modified five-inch naval gun. The Uranium bomb had never been tested but nuclear theory and twisting the dragons tail experiments all but guaranteed its success. The bomb was designed to explode at 1800 feet above ground, but had the barometric and radar controlled trigger mechanism failed, the sudden stop of the impact would have would have successfully brought the two uranium hemispheres inside the vertically oriented cannon together anyway.

The Nagasaki bomb configuration required imploding and compressing a critical mass of plutonium. This was accomplished by enclosing the plutonium inside a spherical array of explosive charges, all detonated simultaneously. Prior to its introduction in Japan, it was successfully tested at a remote site in New Mexico. This may sound a little diabolical, Hiroshima and Nagasaki were both kept off limits from any form of bombing before August 1945 so that the full effects of the new weapons could be evaluated.

The plutonium bomb has become the nuclear holocaust weapon of choice, cheaply mass produced inside a reactor. For over 60 years the major powers have focused on mass production, increasing yields, throw weights and miniaturization for more efficient delivery.

Following the war, Great Britain, now known as the UK, began losing its former colonies. India, as promised, became the first. Things are never as simple as planned, especially where religious divisions are concerned. The majority of India's citizens are Hindu, but large pockets of Muslims were located in the east, north of Bengal, and in the west. To reduce religious tension and allow people to concentrate themselves by religious groups, Viceroy Lord Mountbatten divided the country into three parts. The large central part, India, was to remain Hindu. The outer Muslim parts were named East and West Pakistan. The new borders were kept open for three months to allow people the opportunity to relocate. East Pakistan renamed itself Bangladesh; West Pakistan became simply Pakistan. Heavy tensions continue into the twenty-first century, driving both India and Pakistan to develop nuclear weapons and rockets for their "defense".

Palestine also became a problem area. Six million Jews had been murdered inside Hitler's Nazi Germany, generating a worldwide feeling of guilt for not having been able to prevent it and compassion for the thousands of displaced Jewish refugees left inside war-torn Europe. Palestine contained four hundred thousand Jews prior to World War II. In a negotiation to placate the Arabs— who just happened to own much of the world's oil—Britain attempted to limit refugees to seventy-five thousand and to partition Palestine, separating both inside its border. Neither side could agree to the terms. Both during and after the war, Jewish refugees continued pouring into Palestine, to the great consternation of the surrounding Arabs. The British, under extreme Arab pressure, decided to blockade the swarming Jewish refugees. Back in 1944, Jewish terrorists had murdered the British minister in charge; in 1946 they bombed British army headquarters; and in 1947 they kidnapped and hanged two British sergeants. Britain, no longer willing or able to afford the role of "world's policeman", referred the problem to the newly formed United Nations, which voted for the partition. Britain pulled out of Palestine on May 14, 1948. That same day, the Jews declared the independent state of Israel to be located inside Palestine. The fighting has never ceased.

In 1953, upon the death of her father, King George VI, Queen Elizabeth II became the new monarch. Her inheritance of royalty was through Henry VII, his daughter Margaret, (Mary, Queen of Scots), and King James Stuart. Elizabeth subscribed to the time-honored system of preserving the royal bloodline; she married her distant cousin, Prince Phillip Mountbatten. Her first offspring, Charles, Prince of Wales, was born in 1948. In 1951 Winston Churchill again became prime minister, but he and Elizabeth together were unable to preserve the old empire; the colonies continued to slip away.

Singapore and Malaya each became independent states in 1957 but for a while remained inside the Commonwealth. Other colonies becoming independent were Ghana in 1957, Nigeria in 1958, Sierra Leone in 1961, South Africa, Jamaica, Trinidad, Tobago, Fiji, and so on.

By 1992 the realm of the British Commonwealth had dwindled to sixteen nations with a combined population of just over 130 million. Their element of commonality is that though each nation maintains its own independent government, they all share the same monarch, namely Queen Elizabeth. All but two million people reside in the six most populous nations, which are the UK, Canada, Australia, Papua New Guinea, New Zealand, and Jamaica. The remainders are Antigua and Barbados, the Bahamas, Belize, Grenada, Saint Kitts and Nevis, Saint Vincent and the Grenadines, the Solomon Islands, and finally the Monarchy of Tuvalu.

The legacy of the British Empire is obvious: World commerce is negotiated in English. The empire of the British Commonwealth still exists but only with the continuing approval of all current members.

The Noon Sight

———

IN THE MODERN WORLD, COMMERCIAL ships report their noon positions to headquarters. This is a tradition evolved from the noon sight. I will now attempt a brief discourse on locating a ship's position at sea without benefit of GPS or modern technology. Note that this is only a brief discussion, not a how-to manual.

For navigational purposes, the earth stands still while the sun revolves around it once every 24 hours. Therefore, every 24 hours, the sun makes a 360-degree rotation around the earth, moving 15 degrees per hour. Because England became the world's mightiest maritime power, it placed a navigational reference line and observatory at the "center of the world," the Greenwich district of London. The reference line is the zero meridian, or Greenwich Meridian, which is also a longitude that stretches from the North to the South Pole. The Greenwich Observatory houses a transit telescope with trunnions located on an east-west axis so that it can swing only in a rigid north-south direction. This north-south vertical swing of the telescope enables the observatory to measure the transit, or crossing time, of any celestial object, such as the sun or stars, at the zero meridian. The definition of a meridian crossing is when an object passes from east to west and is momentarily directly overhead, or at the zenith. Making use of repeated daily transit measurements, the observatory creates and publishes *The Nautical Almanac*.

Because the sun rotates 24 hours per day or 15 degrees per hour, the earth is segmented into 24 equal time zones. Political time zones vary; navigational time zones do not, nor do they allow for political daylight saving time. With regard to the noon position of the sun in London, the Greenwich Meridian was designated to be hour 0. Therefore, hour 0 is located exactly on zero longitude. Exactly halfway around world (180 is half of 360) is the 180th meridian, or longitude 180. Hour 12 is located on the 180th meridian. The navigational day begins at midnight UT (Universal Time) in Greenwich. At that same time, it is noon, 12:00 hours in Tonga, exactly on the 180th meridian—the International Date Line. Crossing the line from east to west deletes a day. When I flew from San Francisco to Auckland, Friday, May 21, 2013, was subtracted from my calendar. The time was the same, but the day became Saturday, May 22. I got the twenty-four hours back, one hour at a time, by continuing west. The calendar date there is one day ahead of Greenwich.

Now I must define GHA or Greenwich Hour Angle. GHA is the position of the constantly moving SUN always directly over the center of the earth. Think of it as the instantaneous longitude of the SUN but referenced as an angle measured west from the 0 Greenwich meridian. Noon in London happens exactly at 12:00 UT. The GHA of the SUN where it crosses the 0 meridian may happen up to 16 minutes BEFORE or AFTER 12:00 UT noon in London. Just prior to reaching the zenith, at or near the 0 meridian, the GHA is 359:59.9. When directly overhead at zenith it becomes 000:00.0 then continues increasing toward 359:59.9 at noon the next day.

As anyone who has experimented with a sundial knows the sun crosses the local meridian at high noon only four times a year. At all other times of the year, the meridian crossing will be up to sixteen minutes early or late. I actually own a small hanging sundial that can be compensated for this variation. This is an early version of a marine chronometer. The name for this instrument is THE EQUATORIAL RING DIAL which is discussed next.

The Greenwich Observatory in co-operation with the U.S. Naval Observatory, produces an ephemeris titled *The Nautical Almanac*. Inside this booklet can be found the GHA, which is the Greenwich hour angle. GHA 0 is the time of the Greenwich Meridian crossing of the sun. BY COMPARING THE EXACT TIME, THE SUN CROSSES MY MERIDIAN WITH THE ALMANAC LISTED GHA OF THE SUN, I CAN DETERMINE MY LONGITUDE.

On March 20, the sun leaves the Southern Hemisphere, crossing the equator northbound. This marks the start of spring, the vernal equinox, and the first point of Aries the Ram, the reference that star positions are measured from. At the moment, the sun is on the meridian of the equator, its Dec, or declination, is 00:00.0 degrees. The sun continues moving northward until it reaches latitude 23 degrees, 26 minutes north, the June 21 summer solstice. At this time, the Dec is 23:26 N. Continuing this yearly cycle, the sun then reverses and heads south. On reaching the equator September 22, which terminates summer, it continues south to the winter solstice on December 21 at Dec 23:26 S and then reverses northward to complete the cycle.

Latitude is measured in degrees from the equator (00:00) to the North Pole (90:00 N) and from the equator (00:00 to –90 or (90:00 S), the South Pole. All latitude measurements are equal in distance; that is, 1 degree, which measures 60 nm, or nautical miles, near the equator is the same near either pole.

Longitude is also measured in degrees east (E) or west (W). At the equator, 1 degree equals 60 nm. At the North or South Pole, all meridians converge to measure 0 miles. All distances between the equator and the poles are reduced by the cosine of the latitude. Charts produced with a Mercator projection are compensated to provide a measurable solution.

Distance is measured in nm, nautical miles, where, as stated above, 1 degree equals 60 nm and 1 nm equals 1 minute. The diameter of the earth is approximately 25,000 statute miles at 5,280 feet per mile. The circumference of the earth in nm is 60 x 360 nm, which equals 21,600 nm. One nm, 1/21,600, equals 6,080 feet. As a matter of interest, the US Navy rounds a nautical mile down to 2,000 yards for targeting purpose.

Note: The earth is not a perfect sphere but is considered an "oblate spheroid". The bulge at the equator is caused because centrifugal force is attempting to spin mass out but gravity is counteracting this, attempting to keep the earth spherical. I have read different listings for a nautical mile, some at 6082,

6084 or even 6086 feet. These different values may be an attempt to account for the bulge. To me this is just a nit.

On January 1, 2016, the first day listed in my new 2016 Nautical Almanac, I attempted to perform a noon sight with supposedly ideal conditions at Drake's Beach on the Point Reyes National Seashore, twenty-five miles north of San Francisco. The exact location as displayed on a GPS is 38:01.6 N, 122:57.4 W. The sun was low in the sky and was producing a wide band of reflections. My sextant incorporates a pair of rotating polarized filters. The filter to reduce the blinding effects of the sun was OK. The filter to reduce horizontal glare was frozen and refused to rotate. The result was frustrating; my measurements were all over the place because the horizon was not sharp. I threw away my notes, but I still could have determined latitude.

On January 1, the Dec of the sun was 23:00 S. My latitude was virtually 38:00 N. Working backward, the sextant reading had to be 29 degrees. The simple math for this problem with the sun south of the equator is this: 90 – (23 + sextant reading) equals latitude. Thus, 90 – (23 + 29) = 38.

Many days later I managed to free the stuck filter and prepared for a new attempt.

On Friday, May 27, I returned to the exact same location, halfway between the parking lot and the surf, a hundred yards from the museum. This time I had truly ideal conditions: the sun was now high in the sky, allowing a sharp crisp horizon, so crisp that I didn't use the filter. My friend and assistant, Finn, had a clipboard plus my wife's iPhone, which displayed the exact time in minutes and seconds in large digital numbers. Instead of taking measurements from a rocking boat and timing the readings for an average eye height, I was standing on terra firma. The plan was to take a careful reading, bringing the lower edge of the sun (lower limb) down to the horizon, and shout ready, then mark when I had what I considered a good reading. He would subtract one second and then record the time. I would then read and call out the sextant angle in degrees, minutes, and sometimes tenths of minutes. The process was repeated until the sun reached maximum height and then began descending.

Before going into the readings and corrections, let me discuss some details: The sextant measures an angle noted as Hs. The sextant always has an instrument error, caused mostly by expansion and contraction from temperature variation, and is noted as Ie. My sextant read +4 minutes when the reflected image and actual horizon were aligned together. Many navigators would consider this sloppy, and when I was actively using the instrument, I kept it adjusted to keep the error under 2 minutes. To correct for this, I must subtract 4 minutes from Hs. The sun and moon both have a diameter of approximately half a degree, or 30 minutes. The center of the sun is 15 minutes above the lower limb. The atmosphere acts as a refracting lens, maximizing apparent height at low altitudes, with nearly true readings higher than 70 degrees. When you observe a sunset and the upper limb just disappears, it is already far below the horizon. The altitude correction for the sun center at this elevation and this time of year is +15.7 minutes. The height of my eye while standing safely behind the surf line was approximately 8 feet above the level of the water. I disregarded the tide height, which also happens to equally affect and balance the surf with the horizon. My horizon was about 2 miles distant. The eye height is called DIP; 8 feet of DIP correction listed in a table is –2.8 minutes. The result after all corrections is height observed, or Ho. The following are the actual *measurements and corrections:*

Now for the actual readings:

11:48:21 72:39.5
12:00:05 73:11.5
12:05:22 73:13.2
12:06:22 73:17.5*
12:07:23 73:14.5
12:08:08 73:16.0
12:09:15 73:16.0
12:11:05 73:19.0*
12:12:21 73:15.0

12:13:11 73:13.5
12:14:09 73:13.0
12:29:46 72:39.5

Both measurements denoted by an asterisk (*) were obviously wrong and were ignored. After determining that the sun was descending, I set the instrument to match the 72:39.5 height and timed the re-occurrence. The mid-time of the two 72:39.5 readings is 12:09:15, which agrees with the position and spacing of my highest reading. THE SUN CROSSED MY MERIDIAN AT 12:09:15 AT A HEIGHT OF 73:16.0 DEGREES.

Hs 73:16.0
Ac   +15.7
Ie   −04.0
DIP −02.8
Ho 73:24.9 …round to 73:25

Now from *The Nautical Almanac*, Friday, May 27, 2016:

UT	GHA	DEC
11:00	345:42.2	N 21:24.6
12:00	000:42.1	N 21:24.6
20:00	120:41.5	N 21:27.9
21:00	135:41.4	N 21:28.3

As you can see in the table, the sun crossed the Greenwich Meridian some-time between 11:00 and 12:00 noon UT, reaching a GHA of 359:59.9, then becoming 000:00.0 at transit. We do not need to interpolate the time of GHA 000:00.0; I showed it only for clarity and to help the reader understand what is represented. Note that the sun crossed early.

San Francisco (my closest major city), is located in time zone 8, 8 hours west of Greenwich, one-third of the way around the world. Because we are inside zone 8, we add 8 hours; my UT begins with hour 20.

UT	GHA	DEC
20:00	120:41.5	N 21:27.9
00:09:15	002:18.8	N 00:00.1
20:09:15	123:00.3	N 21:28.0

The 002:18.8 came from a table that gives a between-the-hour GHA reading for each minute and second. The 00:00.1 was determined as follows. Between UT 20:00 and UT 21:00, the sun moved north 00.4 minutes, or 0.1 minute every 15 minutes of time. I interpolated 09:15 to be closer to 0.1 than 0.

Our longitude is 123:00 W.

Our latitude is 90 – (73:25 + 21:28) = 38:03 N.

The GPS indicated 38:01.6 N and 122:57.4 W. Rounding the GPS figures gives 38:02 N and 122:57 W.

When taking a noon sight at sea on a bouncing rolling vessel, I expect to be within three miles of latitude and twenty miles of longitude. Naturally, early seafarers could do only latitude before the invention of the chronometer. My guess is that latitude could be determined within a thirty-mile range using an astrolabe, a quadrant or a cross staff and crude almanac. The Portuguese almanac would have only listed the DEC of the sun for a given day. What strikes me as amazing is that Columbus knew the exact time and date of an eclipse from the Portuguese almanac.

Some notes of interest:

I picked Drakes Beach because it is only 15 miles from my home, it faces south, and is an easy ride over the hill. What I will now discuss is that it also provided some obstacles to my measurements. Initially as the sun was rising I had a clear horizon. As the sun, heading west, was reaching zenith, Chimney Rock at the heel of Point Reyes got in the way of a clear horizon. This was responsible for the 73:17.5 DEC that I had to reject. All the data shown is exactly what I read off to my assistant, Finn, the figures are all honest. If I had taken the measurements from Limintour beach 10 miles to the south, I would have had a clear horizon and possibly could have measured the altitude slightly higher resulting in a smaller latitude error, say from 8,000 Ft. down to 2 or 3,000 ft. As the sun progressed west the horizon reference moved into Drakes Bay. As this was happening, I made comparisons of the sea horizon with the far edge of the bay. With my eye height of 8 ft. I was unable to detect any difference between the two different horizons.

Regarding the LONGITUDE, my measurement of 123:00 W is 2.6 nm different from the GPS reading of 122:57.4 W. Using the cosine of 38 degrees times the 2.6 nm error the result is 0.788 x 2.6 = 2.1 statute miles or about 11,000 ft.

Some further notes regarding sextant navigation:
Most sailors are happy to be within a couple of miles of their exact position, most islands show up when within seven to ten miles distant. Most use a publication called HO 249 also called the Airman's Sight Reduction tables. The US Navy uses a six volume set that provides a higher level of accuracy. Navy Ensigns, Lieutenants and occasionally Quartermasters are held to a higher standard even taking into account the barometric pressure in their calculations. The Navy uses the finest sextants available, nominally Weems and Plath, made in Germany. Mine is a Japanese make that cost me $175 from a fellow sailor and he picked it up from a thrift shop in Houston, Texas. Lyn Silva, a good friend of mine who races and does boat deliveries once used a Weems and Plath with a 500 series U-boat number stamped on it, say U573 for instance, she couldn't remember the exact number. Anyway, a US Navy navigator was expected to locate his ship within a tenth of a mile (600 ft.) always knowing the captain might want to review things. In this fast moving world with instantaneous GPS locations at hand, sextant navigation is becoming a lost art. Some years ago, the Annapolis Naval Academy was being petitioned to drop it from the curriculum. My guess is that it is already gone.

Equatorial Ring Dial (hanging sundial)

————

THIS IS PORTABLE VERSION OF the Armillary Sphere. Invented circa 1600, it folds flat but opens into double rings, 90 degrees apart. The instrument hangs from a cord and the mount is adjustable for the user's latitude. With correct latitude, the bar in the center is aligned with the poles.

An adjustable style slides inside the bar and is set for the user's date. With the correct date, unit aligned N/S, bar rotated to allow sunshine through slit, the time is displayed on the inside of the ring.

With the unit displaying time on the inside ring, the outer ring is aligned N/S and can be used to compare variation on a magnetic compass. My sundial is five inches in diameter. A larger unit, say nine inches in diameter could be calibrated to read within five minutes of U.T. at the time of transit.

Maps:

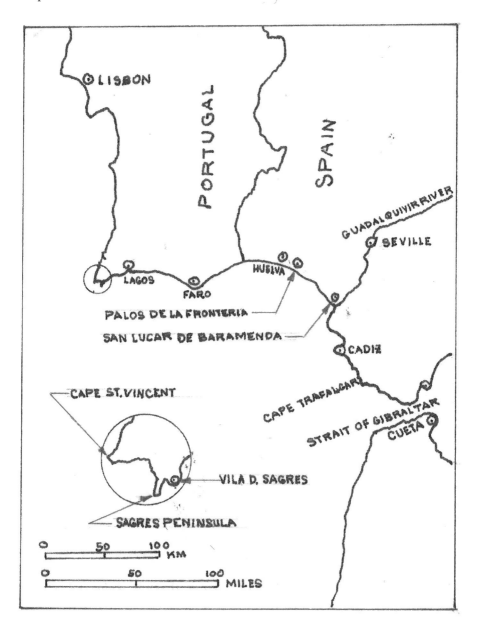

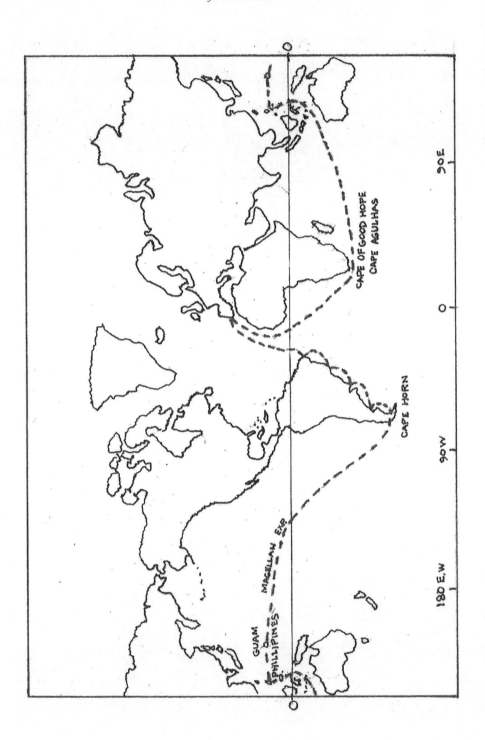

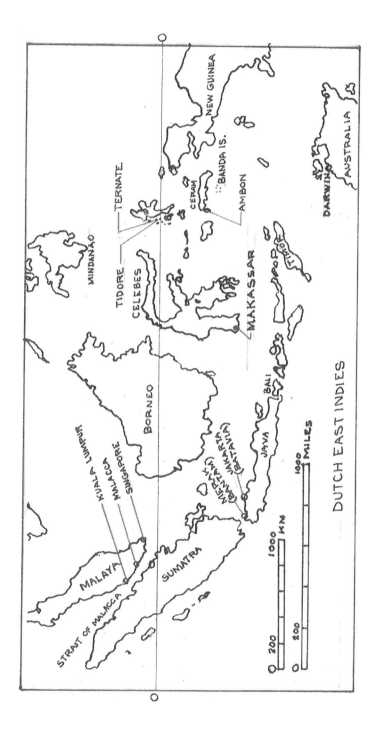

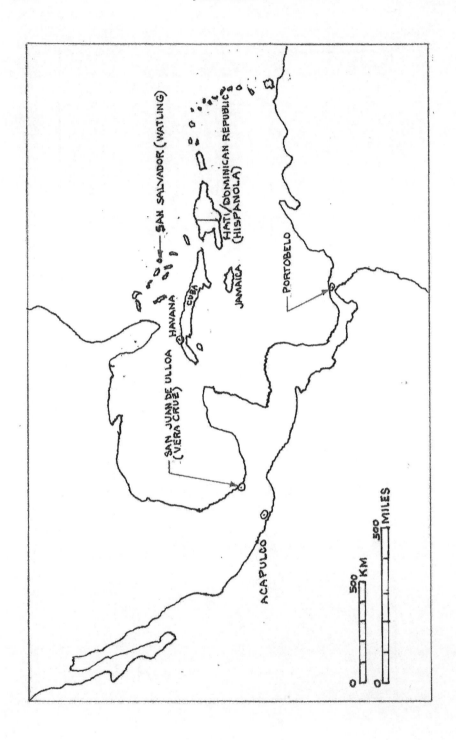

DUTCH SHIP CONSTRUCTION

Akmal, Author, Mohammed Muyazdlala (Lala), Hasrulla Salam, Juliandri Saputra

Jean on Tropicbird

Final day aboard Tropicbird, Captain Julian, Author, Jean, Darwin, Australia

1995 America's Cup winner, NZ-32, Black Magic, Auckland
Note: WINGED KEEL

Tropicbird

Waterfall in Litchfield Park, Australia

Hendy on buffalo

Abdul, Fort Rotterdam, Makassar

Atman, Author, Ibraham, Ternate

Author picking cloves, Ternate

Atman with nutmeg nurseryman, Anwar, Ternate

Mace covering nutmeg nut, Ternate

Memorial to natives killed in volcanic eruption, Ternate

Portuguese armor, Ternate

Monument to murdered Sultan, Ternate

Old Batavia at Sunda Kalapa, Jakarta

VOC symbol on shipping container, museum, Jakarta

Giant ship replica housing museum, Malacca

Replica of caravel Nina at Columbus museum, Palos de la Fronteria, Spain

Henrique D Infante, Prince Henry the Navigator, Sagres, Portugal

Sagres promontory, Sagres, Portugal

Beach, immediately north of fort, accessed by Columbus and Drake

Fort entrance, Sagres Portugal

Guard station, Sagres fort - Identical design at Malacca fort

Columbus tomb held aloft by four heralds, Seville

Royal Greenwich Observatory, London

GARUDA, 2 headed eagle, symbol of Sultanate of Ternate

unknown relative, Author, Crown Prince Hidayat Mudaffar Syah, Rusdi Karim

Equatorial Ring sundial, author collection

Adventure Travel, 2013

———

IN THE SPRING OF 2013, I set out to get a little salt air and pick a clove from a tree in Ternate in the Molucca Spice Islands. As an amateur marine historian, I was curious to see for myself the tropical island that attracted the Portuguese, the Dutch, the British, Columbus, and Magellan. The previous summer I had sailed with Julian Roe on *Tropicbird* between Tahiti and Fiji and managed to relink with him on the Internet. Julian was in Noumea, New Caledonia, preparing for a passage to Darwin. When one is setting off into the unknown, it is comforting to begin with a known starting point.

The flight to Noumea required a change in Auckland, so I decided to take a few days and explore the local delights. The eleven-hour flight from San Francisco crossed the 180th meridian, which is both twelve hours east and twelve hours west of Greenwich, England. Crossing in a westerly direction subtracts an entire day, so Friday, May 31, never existed on my calendar. By continuing west around the world, I was later able to recover the 24-hour gap one hour at a time.

Always drawn to the waterfront, I made a thorough survey of the Te Papa National Maritime Museum. New Zealand was discovered by the Dutch explorer Tasman, who also discovered his namesake Tasmania but left the discovery of Australia to Englishmen. England laid claim to New Zealand and promoted settlement with free passage for qualified tradesmen, farmers, and workers under thirty. Several rooms are devoted to the emigrants' lives aboard the ships.

The museum centerpiece is the winner of the 1995 America's Cup race, NZL-32 Black Magic, sporting its innovation, the secret winged keel.

Campaigned by Sir Peter Blake, a national hero, captained by Russel Coutts, and with the support of the entire country, they beat the US defender, Dennis Connors, in San Diego, five races to zero.

There is a shrine to another national hero on the top floor of the War Memorial Museum: Sir Edmund Hillary and his conquest of Mount Everest, featuring tools, clothing, and a large tabletop diorama depicting the day-by-day climb with his Sherpa guide, Tenzing Norgay. This momentous event can be studied in great detail.

Just southeast of Auckland is the Coromandel peninsula. I rented a car for 39 dollars a day and set off through the countryside. The scenery was clean, green, and gorgeous; all the people I met were both friendly and helpful. The road was slow and winding up to a 2,500 foot ridge, but at the crest was a spectacular view of the eastern shore filled with many small islands. The forest was partially composed of many tall, straight kauri trees and a several access trails. The early settlers built homes and barns with kauri, but as the number of trees began dwindling, the government restricted their use to boatbuilding. The wood contains a very aromatic pitch, which discourages the *Terredo navalis* worm, and it seems to love salt water, making it probably the world's most durable natural product for boat construction. Sadly, the only trees left are in national forests and are closely protected. I had a personal connection to the kauri tree. In 2009 I lost a magnificent forty-two-foot cold-molded (three-layer) kauri sloop on a reef in Samoa.

The perimeter road drops down to sea level, giving access to beaches. One beach is a hot beach. With the tide out and a rented shovel, you can dig a body-sized hole about ten inches deep, which fills with warm water. The area is volcanic, and it provides a natural warm sauna. Continuing counterclockwise around the peninsula, you pass through fishing and tourist villages. One town sports a miniature railway offering rides to kiddies and adults alike.

That night, on returning to Auckland, I filled the tank, placed the car in a secure parking garage, and dropped the keys in a slot where I rented the car. Big mistake. I should have personally brought the car back to the company myself so I could be present for the inspection. They called my wife in California, informing her that the edge of the left-side rearview mirror was damaged. They removed NZ$135 dollars from my Visa card to cover the alleged damage. The car had been washed and re-rented for six days before I could return that afternoon. The only proof they had was a picture on a digital camera of a mirror with some minor damage. I asked to see the latest rental agreement, which they reluctantly and partially revealed (privacy). There was no mention of the damage on that contract. The $39 rental price had ballooned to $174.

Early the next morning at the Air New Zealand ticket counter, I was advised that no boarding was permitted unless I purchased a return ticket to Auckland from Noumea. New Caledonia, like Tahiti, is a French possession. French immigration is paranoid in its resolve to keep homeless people from the United States and Canada away from its territory. Persons holding European passports are exempt. Because I could show no hard evidence that I would be leaving the island on a small boat, Air New Zealand, with the purpose of avoiding a huge fine, forced me to purchase a refundable (more expensive) return ticket.

The flight to Noumea was about two and a half hours, which included a nice breakfast and two small bottles of wine. The first view through the clouds showed gorgeous reefs with all the tropical colors, pale blue, light to dark green, and finally the dark blue of deep water. The countryside we overflew was reddish and somewhat barren. At the airport, I began the long ordeal of recovering a refund, unfortunately not to be had until I returned home.

I contacted Julian on *Tropicbird*, channel 16 and 67. He picked me up in a small dinghy, and we discussed old times and fellow shipmates. Julian, a Brit, had bought *Tropicbird in the Caribbean*, a fifty-foot ketch capable of hosting eight. For US$35 a day, room and board, he will take you on his passage. I met Barry "Baz" Dewson, who had crewed from NZ over some mean seas. Barry was a big, young, friendly guy, also British, who was traveling the world by land and sea, no aircraft. He was trained as a chef and performed much volunteer work.

The next day was spent exploring Noumea by foot. I visited a small museum to pick up on local history. The island lies at forty-five degrees across the Tropic of Capricorn. It is between 350 and 400 miles long and about 50 miles wide. The natives mostly occupy the northeast; the French, the southwest. The main industry is mining and is the source of 25 percent of world's known nickel deposits. The 2009 recession was felt quite strongly as mining is 30 percent of the economy. During World War II, with the French occupied by Germany, the United States, Australia, and New Zealand used New Caledonia as a supply base during the campaigns in the Solomon Islands and the Pacific in general. This presence also kept out the Japanese.

I spent two frustrating days and two international phone cards trying to secure a refund, all to no avail. We picked up a fourth crew member, Jean Pierron, a thirty-year-old Frenchman, actually born to French parents on the island. Jean is a professional adventure traveler until his money runs out and he needs work. He has been to India, the Himalayas, Malaysia, and many other exotic places. When he heard of my two "wasted days," he happily described the delights I could have seen. On our last night in port, Baz made a chocolate cake to celebrate Julian's birthday.

We weighed anchor Saturday, topped off fuel and water, and were through the passage by noon. Steering 270T, we were accompanied by four dolphins swimming our bow wave. It was great to be back on the water to get my salt fix. We were sailing downwind, wing on wing, the first two days, heading for Cairns, Australia. With the failure of the autopilot, Julian chose entry at Mackay. It was an easy, uneventful trip, with four men steering three hours on and nine off. It was the good life; we swapped stories, read, played cards, fished, ate, and slept, all the while breathing the fresh, warm tropic air.

At noon on Sunday, June 16, we entered the Great Barrier Reef with calm seas and a light breeze. We arrived Mackay harbor Monday, June 17, at eleven thirty and then circled until tie up for a one o'clock appointment with customs.

We were greeted by three officials: an unarmed man representing agriculture and quarantine, plus a man and a young married woman, each packing an automatic sidearm. They represented both customs and border patrol. These people turned out to be the nicest, friendliest representatives of their country you could ever meet, just like next-door neighbors. We all had Australian visas and valid passports and I guess, didn't look like druggies. The paperwork was cleared within forty-five minutes.

We were allowed to take free hot showers, a real treat, and explore the port but had to check back with Julian in an hour. The harbor was very industrial, set up for coal and sugarcane, but was surprisingly clean. The town was seven kilometers away, but close by I found a nice public park with plenty of kiddy fixtures, including a crawl-through crocodile which could eat willing children. Julian was unable to obtain parts for motor repair, so we headed for Cairns but without Baz. He needed to find work and was seeking an old girlfriend.

Leaving Mackay, we headed north, following the shipping channel inside the Great Barrier Reef. That night we watched the half-moon set amid the Whitsunday Islands. The next morning, we had dolphins riding the bow wave again. I just love this mode of travel. There was nothing spectacular about the barrier reef, at least not from the surface, though it is reported to have great diving. The water is shallow, 60 to 400 feet deep, the channel typically 80 to 120. The islands are mostly smooth, small, and colorless though some have interesting rock formations and beaches. Vessel traffic sometimes consists of three or more ships per hour. Navigation would be extremely difficult without electronic charts as the channel direction changes often. For safety, we always stayed on the outside edge of the channel, right-hand side. All traffic passes port to port (left side to left side), the same as highway traffic in the United States.

Three days after leaving Mackay, we passed through a narrow and very shallow channel and entered Cairns harbor. Julian, never one to hang out in marinas, found a nice quiet anchorage near some mangrove trees.

Cairns is a very modern city and attracts many tourists. It sports a large mall, many US franchises, and a railhead stretching south to Sydney. A delightful feature is the Esplanade, a two-kilometer shoreline walkway extending from the main pier west to the hotels, passing through many green parks. Several storyboards describe the city history and wildlife. Near the pier and adjacent to downtown is a large green park, which features a huge swimming and wading pool that is only one meter deep. Warmed by the tropical sun, it is a safe and comfortable place for both adults and kiddies.

On the southern winter solstice, June 21, I took an eleven-dollar city bus ride to Palm Cove, passing the airport, the zoo, the university, and sugarcane fields serviced by a narrow-gauge railway. Palm Cove is a resort town thirty miles north of Cairns. It sports parks, sandy beaches, and a long fishing pier.

The pier marked the north end of the road and edge of town. A large sign warned "Beware of Crocodiles." A dirt path beyond the sign led to a Y in the trail. Taking the left fork and passing a large vertical rock formation resembling a miniature version of Devil's Postpile National Monument in California soon revealed a tree-covered swamp. After a very cautious survey, it appeared to be croc-free. The right fork led to a rocky point overlooking a nearby island with ships traversing the barrier reef beyond. A lone kite boarder was swishing back and forth between the point and the island, really picturesque.

The next day I caught a $106 ride on the Cairns/Kuranda Scenic Railway. The line runs along the flatland past cane fields until it begins a long and twisty climb following the Barron River gorge. After stopping on a cantilever bridge at a waterfall for photo ops, it continues to the tourist town of Kuranda.

Inside the town limits are two very beautiful three-quarter-mile nature walks along a creek inside the rain forest. Once inside, the town disappears and you are literally back to nature. Countless birds sing overhead, and there are many curious twisted-vine formations. Other than providing a well-maintained trail, the town and civilization evaporate inside the rain forest. Boat rides are available on the river.

For the return trip, I chose a seven-mile overhead tram ride. The tram provides breathtaking views of the park, river, railroad, and magnificent waterfalls. At the halfway point, riders are set down and given the opportunity of visiting a nature museum and signing up for a guided nature tour. I was the only guest for the three o'clock tour and had Ranger Fuda all to myself for a twenty-five-minute walking lecture. He explained how much of the park had been logged but restoration was bringing it back. From the air there hadn't appeared to be any damage. One of the stops was a five-foot-diameter kauri tree rising absolutely vertically over a hundred feet to the canopy. He explained that the bark sheds quickly to provide a smooth surface, lowering its resistance to high winds. One kauri tree had a beautiful orchid growing on its side. He pointed out an evil nettle plant and described how a macho athlete had ignored advice and run straight through a nettle grove, causing poisonous stings to 70 percent of his body. He nearly died and was put into a coma for pain relief during his treatment. A bus provided us tram riders transport back to Cairns.

The next day, still unable to repair the autopilot, we departed Cairns for Darwin. Four uneventful days later, we rounded Cape York. Cape York is the northernmost point of Australia and is within a hundred miles of New Guinea. Heading due west in the Torres Strait with the barrier reef behind, we sailed in the Timor Sea with New Guinea just to the north. Twice a day we were overflown and contacted by an Australian patrol plane evidently searching for smuggling operations or illegal refugees. One night we had two small dolphins playing in the bow wave and a pair of hitchhiking seabirds; in the morning, we found an ugly mess. For the most part, the passage from Cape York was smooth and sunny, but that can be deceptive. Early one morning I was literally ejected out of my bunk by a sneaker wave. We dropped anchor in Darwin harbor on July 4 after a passage of 2,847 nautical miles, just three hundred yards from a marina and one and a half miles from downtown.

Darwin is a modern city with a shopping mall, fast-food restaurants, Internet cafés, and museums. I explored Darwin in the company of Jean, pronounced "zzhohn," a thirty-year-old French adventure traveler and fellow crewman. After we reviewed the material in the tourist info building, we made a plan to visit three national parks together. I rented a camper van, and he agreed to buy fuel. After bidding good-bye to Julian and *Tropicbird*, we headed south to the closest park.

It took only about four hours to reach the entrance to Litchfield Park. The ride was pretty much boring and unstimulating, the land flat but with small hills. One thing that seemed unusual was the constant smoke and roadside fires that were purposely set by the native Aborigines. While we in the United States would consider this air pollution, it is part of their heritage and allowed by the government.

The first attraction was a giant termite mound, five feet in diameter and over twenty feet high. Close by was a large semicircle kiosk with four storyboards describing the local flora and fauna, mostly termites. The strangest description was about magnetic termites. These insects build mounds shaped like tombstones about ten inches thick, three feet wide, and six feet high. The thin sides are always aligned north-south so that one side is always in the shadow of the tropical sun. The latitude here is fourteen degrees south, well within the tropics. Sure enough, within a short walk there were over thirty "tombstones" in a field, all aligned north-south.

The country was bone dry with skinny, thinly spaced aspen-like trees, but the two main attractions were swimming holes in the creek. One was at the foot of a fifty-foot waterfall. A few brave souls were violating the signs and jumping from the top. The water was about seventy degrees Fahrenheit, really refreshing. The park trails were made of poured concrete or embedded flagstones and led through tall trees shading the creek. Overhead were many bats hanging upside down from the shady treetops. The camping fee was thirteen dollars, but the campground was full. We stayed in a parking lot and never even saw a ranger in Litchfield. Our general feeling about Australia was freedom; there was virtually no sign of Big Brother constantly watching. Thinking back and reviewing the trip, we couldn't remember ever even seeing a highway patrol car.

The next morning, we left the "free" park, and I drove forty kilometers to the main highway. Jean seemed very unhappy with my driving and being in control. It turned out that Jean was a control freak. When we reached the highway, I turned the keys over to him. His mood changed, he became happy, and I could either scan the countryside, nap, or write in my log. A great solution for both of us. We drove three or four hours south to Katherine, a very small city but the only one for hundreds of miles. It is located about seven hundred miles north of Alice Springs, the center of the continent. Katherine was the first place we saw any police vehicles. In front of the police station were two pickup trucks with cages mounted in the rear. Apparently, they were used to control drunk or wayward Aborigines. This was our first contact with the natives. They appeared to be living in poverty as viewed from the street. They have their own bars where whites are excluded. I attempted to purchase a box of table wine in the early afternoon, but boxes were unavailable until later in the day.

Nitmiluk National Park was less than an hour east of Katherine. Along the road were many dead wallabies. These small marsupial members of the kangaroo family wander the roads at night and don't seem to respect cars. The park headquarters contained a hotel, restaurant, and museum. Located on the Roper River, the main attraction is a gorgeous river-carved red sandstone canyon. It was two o'clock, and the river cruises were fully booked. The only thing to do was hike the scenic trails. Jean and I started out on a well-constructed trail with carved steps and railings that climbed steeply toward a canyon overlook. Jean would zoom ahead and then wait for me to catch up; remember he is thirty, and I'm seventy-three. After a kilometer, I reached the top with a beautiful panoramic view of the canyon. We decided to continue the hike five kilometers to another overlook and a swimming hole. Hiking one and a half kilometers, we met at a fork with a small water tank in the center. After topping off our containers, I told him to go ahead and I would meet him at my own pace.

That night, as we recreated the strange events of the rest of the day, Jean dubbed it "the French Connection." I was carrying the van keys in the shallow left front pocket of my swimming shorts. Unbeknownst to me, they fell out onto the trail. Two French women with several small children passed me on their way back to the headquarters. I continued toward the next overlook, completely unaware that I had lost the keys. Almost there, I met Jean, who was just returning from the overlook. He wanted to reach the swimming hole half a kilometer below from where we stood, and I promised to meet him there after catching the view.

Unlike the trails at our first park, these trails were skimpy, marked only by an occasional aluminum tag hanging from a tree. After enjoying the gorgeous view, I headed down toward the swimming hole. Near the bottom, the trail became very dangerous where it crossed a field of boulders. I proceeded through the boulders very carefully, not wanting to break an ankle or a leg, and reached a dry stream bed at the foot of a dry waterfall. By now it was four o'clock, and I was getting nervous about the time. Just then three young Frenchman appeared; they were coming across the boulders, heading for the swimming hole. I asked them to notify Jean that I was returning. At that moment Jean came around a corner fifty feet away, returning from the river. One of the Frenchmen asked Jean whether he had lost his keys. He said no but asked me whether I still had mine. My shocked reply was no. The guys had found them on the trail and passed them to the two women with children who were headed back to headquarters. By this time, it was four fifteen, and the HQ closed at five thirty. Jean, with a light knapsack, ran the five kilometers back to HQ, arriving just as they were locking the door. Luckily for us, they gave him the key.

Meanwhile, I carefully traversed the boulders and began working my way back. Somehow I lost the poorly marked trail, and instead of returning to the last marker, I mistakenly thought I could reconnect by working to the left. Amazingly, blazing my own trail wasn't much different from hiking the "constructed" one that I had lost.

One thought that went through my mind was snakes. The claim is that Australia has more varieties of snakes than any other country, most of them being poisonous. Using the setting sun for direction, I finally came to a 4WD road, which I knew had to be the other trail of the fork. Now with the small dangling aluminum trail markers for confirmation, I returned to the fork and refilled my water bottle. The sun sets vertically in the tropics and especially early near the time of winter solstice. By now it was six thirty, and darkness was closing fast. I hurried as quickly as I could over a loop trail that I was unfamiliar with

It was pitch dark when I finally reached a road near the campground. Surprisingly a van pulled up alongside with somebody calling me Jim. It was the three French hikers out on a search party looking for me. Jean had become worried, especially since the three hikers never passed me on the return trip. Returning to our van, I met Jean, who had just returned from his search. I thanked them all for their concern, and Jean got over being upset after hearing my story.

The next morning, we drove north to a small town named Pine Creek, then east to Kakadu National Park. The entrance fee was twenty-five dollars per person, paid to an Aborigine who was probably allowed to keep half or more. In three days, we never were asked to show the pass. The first event was a visit to the Cultural Museum displaying forty thousand years of Aboriginal history. Following that we visited Yellow Water, an animal refuge with wallabies, water birds, and crocodiles. The main feature was a five-hundred-foot-long steel platform that stretched along the marsh. Try as we could, we failed to spot any crocs.

Next we drove to the base of a hill that sported the highest elevation of the park, with a half-kilometer climb to a roofed overlook. The view was disappointing owing to the rather flat landscape, obscured by haze, smoke, and the tall trees, which blocked much of the view. While we were seated, catching our breath, we met a young couple that had climbed up behind us. We had first seen Irene and Nathan at the croc platform. They were French and had met at the university in Sydney. Somehow they had managed to see three crocs.

Just as we reached the parking lot at the bottom of the lookout hill, who pulled up but two of our French friends from Nitmiluk? After advising them that it would be dark before they could reach the top, we broke out the wine and beer for a party. Tibo and Antoine had dropped off the third guy in Katherine to catch a train. One was from Paris, the other from Burgundy, and both were students from Sydney. Jean is from Normandy. Anyway, we swatted thousands of mosquitos before the beer ran out. We kept running into Tibo, Antoine, Irene, and Nathan throughout the rest of the trip.

The next morning, we visited the Nourlangle art site, which contains incredible rock art. The area consists of red sandstone rocks up to three hundred feet high, with eroded caves that provide refreshingly cool shade. Most art depicted hunting scenes and game, but some depicted Lightning Man, the god of electricity. This happens to be an area of extreme electrical storms. The state has gone to great lengths to provide safe and convenient passages between petroglyphs with concrete walkways, steel platforms, and safety railings. They also provide fascinating lectures throughout the day.

We managed to attend a very interesting lecture entitled "A Jigsaw in Time." The lecture hall was a cool, sheltered, rock-art-covered cave with two long wooden benches. Ranger Cristian Diddams and a young female assistant, using a small bag of rocks, nuts, and twigs, were able to describe life at this location for the past forty thousand years. The bag contained specimens from a very careful scientific analysis of a one-meter-deep hole that had been dug twenty feet from where Diddams was sitting. Examined layer by layer, the dig revealed Aborigine development in hunting and cooking skills plus changes in the natural environment, the end of the Ice Age, floods, and drought.

At Jabiru, we visited a very well presented natural history museum displaying local geology, animals, and plants, plus native creations. The leaves of the palm like pandanus plant can be woven and used for clothes, roofs, string, and rope. The most interesting creature exhibit was a fox bat, also known as the flying fox. This giant bat has a foot-long body and a four-foot wingspan. The skull and snout actually does resemble a fox, hence the name.

Thirty kilometers from the village of Jabiru is an area of the park called Ubirr, which is located at the extreme eastern edge of the park. Ubirr consists of red sandstone rocks that rise vertically up to three hundred feet above the level ground. A prominent feature is a three-hundred-foot scarp, which forms a long natural border between the public park and Arnhem Land, which is reserved for the native people. At the foot of the scarp is a brown two-hundred-yard-wide flat strip stretching for miles and covered with magnetic termite mounds. The brown strip fades to rich green vegetation, kept moist by the many branches of the Alligator River—a strange name as there are only crocodiles. Arnhem Land is huge, stretching to the Gulf of Carpentaria and beyond. Most Aborigines prefer the hunter-gatherer lifestyle to modern civilization, though some have elected to become rangers and park workers. The government respects this. They have incorporated one modern bit of technology; they prefer to hunt with the rifle rather than the bow. Ubirr is rich in rock art, and one very interesting overhead depiction shows the arrival of white men in sailing vessels.

Australia is dry and with the exception of continuous burning, has a clear night sky. It was the last night to appreciate the gorgeous southern sky with my thirty-degree-south sky chart. I don't think Indonesia has any observatories, owing to continuous cloud cover. The next morning, we took an eight-kilometer nature walk along the Alligator River, where we found our first croc, a small timid creature who quickly swam away. We also saw a large rare jabiru marsh bird and more rock art.

The next day we washed and returned the camper van. While Jean was helping me carry my stuff to the airport shuttle station, we met Baz, our crewmate from New Caledonia, just walking down the sidewalk. I bought us all a combo breakfast at McDonald's, and we enjoyed a two-hour reunion.

Bidding good-bye to my friends, I caught a bus to the Darwin Museum to kill time before the flight. During the last ice age, ten thousand years ago, the sea was four hundred feet lower than it is now. Early man was able to walk between the Indonesian islands and across the shallow basin to Australia. I watched a ten-minute video of Aborigine life that followed one family cooking, hunting, weaving, painting each other, and just hanging out. Darwin was bombed by the Japanese in early World War II and suffered a 200-mile-per-hour hurricane fifteen years ago, which destroyed much of the city. An entire room was dedicated to the storm's devastation and World War II.

While sitting in the airport shuttle, I met Ana, a twenty-five-year-old German student who had just finished classes in Sydney. She was studying to become an audiology engineer with the intention of designing hearing aids. She told me that if you have severe hearing loss, you should get hearing aids as soon as possible because the tiny muscles of the interior ear can atrophy. I took her advice seriously and now own two of them.

From Darwin, you can fly to anywhere in Australia, but if you want to leave the country, the only destination is Bali. Two airlines compete for the business. The lower cost Chinese airline I picked had no free service or knee room. I arrived in Bali in less than two hours. After paying US $40 for a visa, I converted my Australian cash to Indonesian. The Indonesia rupee is loosely tied to the US dollar, but a hundred rupees equals only a penny: US$1 = 10,000 rupees. If you can mentally remove the two least significant zeros, it becomes easier to compare. The first rule of trade is never pay the asking price. Unlike in the United States, where most things have fixed prices, here everything is bartered. Just think of it as a game; they all do. The taxi drivers wanted two to three hundred thousand rupees for a ride from the airport to downtown Kuda Beach. I negotiated a price for seven dollars (seventy thousand rupees). To keep things in perspective, the average worker here makes about the equivalent of ninety dollars US per month.

My first business was to explore on foot and purchase some food, a charger connection for my depleted camera battery, and a small electric cooker to make coffee or heat soup. While sitting on a corner resting across the street from a small Hindu temple, I observed a strange ritual. The major religion in Bali is Hindu; virtually all the rest of Indonesia is Muslim. Hindus moved to Bali to escape religious oppression from Muslims. A young girl came out of the temple with several small woven containers. In a ritualistic ceremony, which included burning incense, she placed one basket on a shoulder-high shelf at the foot of a statue, one on the sidewalk, and another out in the street.

Apparently, this offering is made to pacify potentially evil spirits. I noticed that there was a teaspoon full of rice and some veggies and crackers inside each of the woven and stapled palm baskets.

That evening while exploring, I went in search of fellow adventure travelers or backpackers. I found seven young male students from South Africa getting ready to have dinner. They introduced me to their favorite restaurant, where for about six or seven dollars, you could buy a great meal and a one-liter local beer. This was a really fun group, all had just received bachelor degrees in business from Cape Town and were here to party and surf. Most had Dutch ancestry, but the kid sitting next to me was 100 percent Norwegian. Sven made a list in my logbook of some of the major attractions, including where to find magic mushrooms. Immediately on finishing dinner, they bid farewell; their mission, as you probably guessed, was to hit the nightclubs and seek female companionship.

I decided to continue exploring and headed down toward the beach, which was about a kilometer distant. After walking about three blocks I came to a long, dark unimproved open space. A small motorbike with two helmeted women pulled up alongside me. The driver was about thirty, and the young woman in back about eighteen. After a smile and a couple of words, the driver grabbed my member. It was kind of a paralyzing experience. If a guy had done it, I would have punched him out. Anyway, she said we could have some fun for ten dollars, and I said no thanks, I was married. She let go, and the eighteen-year-old immediately grabbed me, then jumped off the bike, grabbed my wrist, and attempted to lead me away. She was only about a hundred pounds, and I managed to remove her grip. These two young prostitutes were 100 percent street legal as both were wearing helmets.

It was ten o'clock Saturday morning, and while walking down the street, I heard a percussive gong sound coming from a nearby building. It turned out to be a temple, and some well-dressed men indicated that I should go upstairs to check it out. Approximately twenty children with four instructors were playing a gamelan orchestra, striking over a hundred gongs. The children, all young boys, seemed to be having the time of their lives and really enjoyed having an audience. It was a warm and happy experience; I stayed for about twenty minutes, taking pictures while we both waved and I clapped.

The main attraction at Kuda Beach is the swimming. Imagine a shallow base of fine white sand slowly slanting down under eighty-degree water to a depth of five feet at a distance of seventy-five yards into the Indian Ocean. With waves only two feet high, people were walking their boards way out to the starting line for twenty-five-dollar surfing lessons. It doesn't get much better than this.

Traveling without any Internet devices, I usually purchase an international phone card to call home. But in Indonesia, not only are they not for sale, but they don't even have phone booths. After asking the right questions, I was directed to Sebastian, who ran a small travel agency nearby. With the aid of a computer and printer, he made a setup, and I dialed the phone. At a cost of a dollar a minute, or any part thereof, I could speak directly to Annie. It turned out that this was the cheapest telephone in Indonesia. Other places wanted five dollars a minute; one hotel began charging even before making a connection.

I rented a motor-driven cycle from Sammy and headed south. In the beginning, it was a scary experience, not just because I needed to relearn to lean into the turns but mostly because I felt defenseless. When the locals get behind the wheel of a car, they undergo a Jekyll-and-Hyde transformation from friendly, considerate, polite people to racing drivers sitting on the edge of their seats. The goal is to pass everyone in any manner possible. The roads are set up on the British system, so you pass on the right but only if that lane is clear. The more astute drivers pass on the left or try to intimidate you to move to the shoulder or sidewalk. Once while I was approaching an intersection from the outside slow lane, a driver in the fast lane actually came into my lane and pressed his vehicle against my right elbow. I thought I was going to go down but managed to react and move over slightly. I eventually quit being paranoid and sort of relaxed. Not having witnessed any actual accidents, I figured the other drivers knew what they were doing.

The first destination was Benoa, a tourist harbor town offering Jet Skis, boat rentals, fishing, diving, and parakites. I found a shady spot to relax and managed to make friends with a middle-aged lady taking a break from her job renting boats. Komang Sutres is the third born in her family. The first four names in order are Wayan, Made, Komang, and Icetut. She commutes thirty kilometers each way to work for a salary of eighty dollars and gets only two or three days off per month. I bid her a sympathetic good-bye and walked around the southern tip of Benoa, past half a dozen businesses, a hotel with a tiled pool, two temples, and finally a gas station. I remarked that the sixty-five-cents-per-liter price was very cheap; he said cheap for me but expensive for him, on ninety dollars a month.

After getting lost in a resort area featuring a forty-foot Buddha statue, I managed to reach Ulu Watu, at the southernmost tip of Bali. It was getting late, so I passed up a temple tour for ocean access. After paying a small amount to park, I negotiated the three hundred steps down to a cave-like entrance to the sea. Rolling up my pants and removing my shoes, I went wading through the shallow surf to the opening. It was a spectacular experience with the small waves coming in, the warm water and sand under my feet, and the sunlight reflecting everywhere. While I was enjoying myself, a macho surfer dude couldn't stop laughing at me; he must have thought I looked ridiculous while wading with my pants rolled up in the shallow water. It felt really good to me. I was secure enough to smile, wave and stare him off. From inside the cave, I climbed up thirty concrete steps, then across a short bridge to a small restaurant with a magnificent 180-degree overlook of the Indian Ocean. It was enclosed and had large plate glass windows and even some outside tables. Not wanting to be on the road at night, I had to skip a beer and sandwich, politely refusing service, and made my way back to my room.

On my way to the Totem restaurant, my favorite, a forty-year-old woman came up alongside me and asked whether I could use a massage. When I told her no thanks, she opened a paper bag full of Viagra and Cialis priced at $2.70 each—cheapest in town, she said. Still not finished with her pitch, she said, "Massage have happy ending." A couple of blocks away, I met Sven and a Dutch companion just leaving the Totem, a really great-value place.

My last day in Bali found me riding north to the port of Padang. Riding in the slow lane of a four-lane highway, I was surprised to be waved over by a policeman wearing a bright chartreuse shirt. He requested my driver's license and vehicle registration and then told me to follow him to a pullout off the highway staffed by fifteen bright shirts. Informing me that my crime was driving without an international license, the head cop said I was liable for a twenty-five-dollar fine, but since I was a first offender (how did he know?), he would let me off for ten dollars. It was a smooth, efficient, and paperless transaction. He never wrote my name or provided a receipt, just placed the currency in a cigar box. After returning the key and registration paper, he waved me on and began processing the next offender.

It was a beautiful day, with gorgeous green hills, trees, sea views, and rice paddies. I missed a turn and pulled off the road. While I was attempting to decipher the map, Wayan Kantra pulled off to give me directions and his business card. I would have to return two hundred meters and then drive left for two kilometers to the seaport. I thanked him, and twenty minutes later I arrived at scenic Padang harbor, with a ferry terminal, two ferries, official government buildings, restaurants, fishing and other commercial boats. For $3.50 I could take a four-hour, thirty-mile ride to Lombok, the next island east.

Lombok is separated from Bali by a deep channel, and the separation has been named the Wallace Line. During the Ice Age, when the sea level was four hundred feet lower, Aborigines could walk to Australia from Bali and Java, but they had to build a boat to reach Lombok and islands to the east.

After exploring I found the only place to get a hot meal was inside the terminal. Waring Mama Butet had many choices, allowed me free samples, and gave me the $1.50 local price for a chicken drumstick on rice. Also included were the following choices:

Pave = bitter vegetable
Terong = mushrooms
Mi Hun or Mihun Gerang = glass noodles
Suup = soup (wok cooked carrots, cabbage, and peppers)

The meal was delicious. She really seemed to appreciate my interest, and I took her picture. She didn't have change for my thirty-cent tea, so she asked me to accept a small bag of peanuts.

I returned the motorbike to Sammy. I kind of felt sorry for the guy. He did business on the sidewalk, not able to afford a shop. His customers were referred to him by local businessmen. My ten-dollar, two-day rental was the only income he had for the period. I suggested he put up a sign, but he said the police wouldn't allow it. I felt good that I hadn't chiseled him down to the rock-bottom three-dollar-a-day rate.

While enjoying my last meal at the Totem from a table overlooking the narrow street, I spotted Ana walking by and invited her to sit down. It was also her last night in Bali. Unfortunately, she had a headache and couldn't stay. She sat for a few minutes and told me of her visits to museums, temples, and other cultural things. I snapped her picture, gave her a hug, and wished her a safe trip.

Early the next morning, a taxi driver wanted $6.50 to the airport. Marvin told me about his family and life in Bali during the short ride. He makes only between eighty and ninety dollars a month but enjoys his life. I flew the same Lion China airline as from Darwin—again without knee room or service—to Sulawesi. In Dutch colonial times and up until 1947, Sulawesi was named Celebes. Arriving at noon after a two-hour flight, I picked up my checked bag and placed it on a cart. I hadn't moved more than fifty feet when an official-looking man with a plastic-coated official-looking badge grabbed the other end of my cart and said, "Follow me."

Yacobs Ambalembang and his understudy, Yonaton Patandung, escorted me and my gear to the airport coffee shop. Yacobs explained that they were from the tourist bureau and were there to help me. Silly me—I didn't even know that I needed help. All I wanted to do was get a room and spend the next day and a half exploring the seaport of Makassar. For two hours Jacob tried to sell me a guided tour to Toraja, a village and cultural center eight hours north by bus. He said Toraja has been kept by the government exactly as it was six hundred years ago, when the people were headhunters. The $350 guided trip would have been extremely rushed and expensive for a single person, including a rented car with a driver and all. Since I was on my own theme trip, following the Portuguese and Dutch exploration and expansion, I declined.

The taxi drivers in Makassar have a sort of fair-trade price of twelve dollars from the airport to town (zone 2). The driver let me off at the gate to Chinatown to begin a room search. The Legend Hotel was twenty-five dollars, but next door was the Legend Hostel for only ten dollars a night (it was a backpacker place). Unfortunately, they were full, but for a two-night deposit,

I could spend the following two nights at Legend. She sent me to a real dump 150 yards down the street.

While I was sitting on a couch attempting to determine my whereabouts in the Lonely Planet guidebook, a young couple came down the stairs on the way to town. I asked whether one of them could help me locate myself on the city map. Katrien sat on the armrest next to me and quickly identified our location. They were on the last day of a trip in the north, swimming, diving, studying culture, and so on, and were going to check out the town. I asked to tag along, and they said sure. Katrien and Jens were from Belgium. She had just completed medical school and was ready to intern; Jens was a self-employed environmental engineer. We located Fort Rotterdam, restaurants, and a somewhat-rickety pier extending out into the harbor. It turned out that the pier was over five hundred years old and had been used for loading spices and other cargo on Dutch and Portuguese ships. We were inside the forty-day Ramadan period in a Muslim city, so we couldn't find any beer.

They were traveling with another couple and were to meet for a crab feed at a fancy place. Astrid and Imre had also just completed medical school and met us at the door. So, there I was, swapping stories and hearing about Toraja from Europe's finest, a really great way to spend the first night.

The first thing after moving my gear to the New Legend Hostel was to check out Fort Rotterdam. The tour guide was Abdul, a 23 year-old English major and volunteer docent of Bugis decent. During our short two-day time, together, we became friends. He laughingly told me that six hundred years ago his ancestors were cannibals. With the arrival of the Muslim traders, his ancestors were converted to the following of Mohammed. The fort was built by the Portuguese and completed in 1540 with the labor of three thousand native Makassar people. Makassar, about fifteen hundred miles east of Malacca, is now a large container port and together with Timor formed the major Portuguese East India seaports of the spice trade. The fort, with a canal and a pier, made for easy loading of cargo. The Portuguese enjoyed a trade monopoly for a hundred years until the Dutch arrived with more ships and bigger cannons.

In 1660 the Dutch sank six Portuguese ships in the harbor, captured the fort, and renamed it Fort Rotterdam. The Dutch held on to it except during the Napoleonic Wars, when it temporarily was controlled by the British. Indonesia was known and governed as the Dutch East Indies until the Japanese invaded in 1941. After the war the colony won its independence from the Dutch. Inside the compound are some buildings displaying Japanese architecture, but most are Dutch colonial. Abdul gave me a great museum tour while I took pictures and made notes. The island is populated by three ethnic groups: The Makassar people in the southwest leg, the Toraja immediately to the north, and the Bugis everywhere else.

The next day I toured the container port and then went north toward the naval base. A stern-looking guard hurried to meet me before I could reach the gate, possibly worried about my knapsack. When he realized, I was from the United States, he became friendly and gave me a thumbs-up, a fist bump, a high five, a handshake, and then followed with a salute.

Moving on, I found someone to repair the strap on my knapsack and asked how much. He wrote 200 on his hand. He did an excellent job of hand stitching, completing it in only ten minutes. Fair is fair; I handed him a thousand rupees, which equals a dollar, five times his asking price. Then he became a thief and pretended the job cost two thousand. At that point I should have snatched back the dollar and given him the amount he bid, but I just frowned at him and walked away.

I returned to Fort Rotterdam for a more thorough survey and walked the top of the walls. Following that, I found a shady spot out of the intense heat to sit and rest. Suddenly it was as if I had become a celebrity. Children came up to talk and practice English, and all wanted pictures with me. It was fun and a great ego boost. That evening Abdul took me on his motorcycle to make copies of my historical notes on Prince Henry, Columbus, Magellan, and so on and then showed me where to get a beer. We had a great time together while I gave him a history lesson. He didn't drink any beer.

Next morning, I took a two-hour flight to Ternate with the goal of actually pulling a clove from a tree. In the fifteenth century, the Moluccas were the only source of cloves in the entire world. I negotiated a taxi ride with a guarantee to find cheap lodging. The driver put in a good effort and found a place but then wanted more cash. A deal is a deal; he finally gave up because a new flight was due at the airport.

Beginning to explore Ternate on foot, I discovered the Sultan's Palace, which had been built by the Portuguese but, of course, using local labor. The front portion is now a museum. Inside are three display cases, each containing gifts that were presented to the sultan, who welcomed these before entering any trade agreements or negotiations. The left case contains a gift from the Cheng Ho Chinese visit in 1460. The right case contains a gift from the Dutch in 1618. The center case contains two magnificent suits of armor complete with helmets and shields. These were brought by Magellan's friend Francisco Serrao in 1510. Information regarding Serrao is from the book *Over the Edge of the World* by Laurence Bergreen. Magellan described Serrao's activities to Anthony Pigafetta, the Venetian scribe. Serrao fell in love with the island, married a native girl, and spent the rest of his life on Ternate. What I just described is my first understanding. What really happened, according to Bergman can be found in the chapter on Magellan. He commissioned the palace project, built trading forts and infrastructure, and ran the trading operation. Caught up in some kind of intrigue after residing there for over twenty years, he was mysteriously poisoned.

Below the palace, which is located on a hill, is a long pier extending over three hundred feet into the water. Buildings on the pier contain several small sewing factories, a search-and-rescue office, and a government office at the end. Two small boats engaged in the water taxi business were tied up near the end. I had a eureka moment: my first sight of Ternate cloves. The search-and-rescue operator dries cloves on the pier, the cloves are spread out on large plastic tarps, while waiting for news of any new problems over the radio. The drying operation requires about five days in the tropical sun, and the cloves must be covered during the frequent rains.

I continued back south along the waterfront past a shopping mall—which contained a KFC franchise—many small businesses, and a huge and beautiful mosque that had two tall spires, or minarets. Searching for the tourism office noted on the city map of the Lonely Planet guidebook took me through a huge farmers' market. Unable to find the tourism office, I questioned members of a nearby police station, but they didn't know either. I finally gave up the search. If it still existed, no one could explain where it was.

The next day I returned to the pier with the intent of having a pair of shorts mended. While explaining the job to a tailor who spoke no English, a local man offered to translate. What a lucky break meeting Ibraham Umakamea. Ibraham, like many people on the island, wanted to practice English and asked me to speak with his children, who were studying it in school. Now retired, he used to be an announcer on Voice of America. His house was located nearby on the main island perimeter road. He then asked whether I would speak to one of his young students. I nodded, and he made a short call.

At his home, I met his young daughter, Rahmawati, about 14. His son was not home, but after a few minutes Suratman Dahlan showed up on his motorcycle. Suratman, who prefers the nickname Atman, is a 23-year-old English student at the university and receives some private tutoring from Ibraham. For about an hour we discussed the island, my quest as an amateur historian, and some historical knowledge I had accumulated. The discussion went exceptionally well, and when Ibraham excused himself for a short Ramadan visit across the street to a mosque, Atman volunteered to give me a tour of the island the next day. We parted with Atman, agreeing to meet here tomorrow at nine in the morning. Ibraham requested that I be prompt.

On my way to an early-afternoon lunch, a thirty-year-old man named Amad fell into step alongside me to practice his English. He accompanied me into the local KFC restaurant, where you get chicken with rice instead of mashed potatoes. He would not sit down, because he was fasting for Ramadhan. He told me that he could not afford to eat in a place like this, so, feeling somewhat guilty about eating in front of him and his being poor and all, I had the second piece of chicken and some rice wrapped up by a worker who had been standing alongside him, listening to our discussion. It sure didn't make me feel great, and I wished I had given him the large piece when Amad said it was for his son. These friendly and happy people are absolutely dirt poor, and I was forced to contemplate my blessings.

The next morning, I hurried, not wanting to be late to meet Atman. According to my watch, it was 8:56, but strangely no one was there. I knocked on Ibrahim's door, but nobody answered. I sat on his front porch until nine fifteen, contemplating what to do next, when Ibraham opened the door, asked me why I was late, and said that Atman had gone home. I felt really stupid; Ternate is an hour earlier than Makassar, and I hadn't advanced my watch.

Fortunately, he accepted my apology and called Atman, who lived in a nearby village, and we were on our way by eleven.

Despite my bungled start, this turned out to be the best day of the entire trip. The first stop on Atman's four-speed Suzuki was Fort Tolluco. The fort appeared in good condition. It was constructed with stone blocks and is located several hundred feet above the water. Atman read the sign (no English): designed by Francisco Perro, completed 1540, acquired by the Dutch 1610. A chained monkey was caged near the locked gate at the entrance. Apparently, the owner charged an entrance fee, but because it was wet and slippery, there was to be no tour this morning.

We continued counterclockwise around the island where the perimeter road made a jog around a strange fifty-foot man-made promontory. It was the end of the airport runway, which was capable of accommodating a Boeing 737-400. Continuing on, Atman turned off on a narrow asphalt trail that weaved between six- and seven-foot-high boulders, finally stopping at a small memorial near the shore. Sometime before the arrival of the Portuguese in 1510, the volcano that formed the island had erupted, hurling out these giant boulders, lava, and black sand. In the aftermath over six hundred natives had lost their lives. The memorial sign was created by the hand placement of three different-colored materials. Atman let me take a small souvenir piece of red coral.

Soon we were on the much wetter windward side of the island, where the spice trees thrive. Atman pulled left and off the road toward a small house in Sulama village. Anwar, the nursery man and owner of a tiny nutmeg plantation, agreed to show us around. Nutmeg when ripe is slightly smaller than a tennis ball and has a very hard surface. A week after being picked, it splits open at a longitudinal groove, similar to that found on an apricot or a peach. Inside is the nut or brown seed, encapsulated inside a red mace covering. The red mace, which has a woven, stranded, plastic, artificial look, does not completely cover the nutmeg nut. It is removed, dried, and then sold separately. Anwar's operation reminded me of other typical nursery plantings. Mace-covered seeds are set halfway into dark, fertile soil until they take root. After forming shallow roots, they are transplanted to small plastic pots. After several growing stages, they are ready to become trees. At the time of the

Portuguese arrival, Ternate and the Moluccas were the sole source of cloves, and the Banda Islands were the sole source of nutmeg. Today, as a result of much nursery work, both spices are distributed over a wide area. Dried cloves exported from Ternate fetch five dollars a pound, or twelve dollars a kilo, and nutmeg four dollars a pound. Anwar generously let us pick two nutmegs.

About a kilometer farther down the road but still inside Sulama village, we stopped on the ocean side of the road, where a man on a ladder was picking cloves and stuffing them into a large, deep white canvas bag. Karim came down to greet us and demonstrate his operation. The thin seeds, about a quarter inch, or six centimeters, long, form at the ends of short stems, about five or six to a sprig. They are picked individually and then laid out on tarps to dry in the sun like raisins. I had come to Ternate to pick a clove from a tree. This was my eureka moment, and Karim let me pick a sprig. About this time, I started receiving multiple bites on my ankles. I hurriedly said good-bye to Karim and rushed through the eighteen-inch-tall grass back to the edge of the road. I discovered I was being eaten alive by *Bifii Gunange* ants—real beefeaters, these little critters.

Continuing on, we passed through villages with freely roaming chickens, and goats. Tarps were laid out for drying cloves, nutmeg, and mace, always on the left-hand side of the road, with the shore side reserved for traffic.

In Bentang Kastela village, Atman made a right turn, coming to a stop at a four-sided ten-foot-tall white monument with a three-foot rendition of a red clove on top. The front five-foot-wide side wall depicts the scene of a murder in bas relief. On February 28, 1570, Jorge de Castro stabbed Sultan Khairun in the back of the neck with a stiletto. Circling counterclockwise around the monument are two scenes depicting the retaliation and killing of all Portuguese in Fort Bentang. The final scene dated December 31, 1575 depicts the new sultan ordering all Portuguese to vacate Ternate under penalty of death. Behind the monument was a pastoral scene with a cow grazing on lush green grass in front of the broken walls of the fort. A woman appearing to be a nun waved from a large wooden structure on a small hill to the right. I thought it was a Catholic church or convent not condemned by the sultan. When I returned to Ternate in 2014, I discovered that the wooden building was actually a mosque.

We left the monument and continued 150 yards down the narrow dirt road, passing a bright red search-and-rescue jeep hooked to a speedboat on a trailer. Parallel to the shore and set back a hundred feet is a 200-foot-long by 5-foot-high tan-painted wall sporting a six-scene mural. Painted mostly with black lines, the first scene depicts the arrival of the Portuguese, who are admiring the cloves, their ships in the background. Continuing left to right shows the construction of the fort, trade, the murder, retaliation, and the final panel: the scene of the Portuguese leaving under penalty of death. It amazes me that after all the effort made to reach Ternate and establish a very profitable luxury-goods spice trade, someone could do such a stupid thing as murdering the sultan.

There is no evidence of any 450-year-old pier or wharf construction on the rocky shore. I must guess that there used to be one to smooth loading and help keep the valuable cargo dry. The ships had to anchor on a lee shore, and if the anchors dragged, they were on the rocks. While loading must have been difficult, the source was conveniently close by.

We continued on to our final stop. Bentang Fortress, located at the narrows between Ternate and Tidore Islands. Bentang has been partially restored. When the Portuguese were evicted, they resettled on Tidore, two miles to the south. Atman deciphered a sign for me: Completed in 1540, used until 1575. The Spaniards came in 1609. The Dutch arrived in 1624, then left in 1627. The Spaniards returned in 1663.

The 43-kilometer trip left both of us pretty tired, especially Atman, who was fasting without any food or water. I gave him some small gifts of tea, raisins, and crackers and some cash to refill his tank and for the superb personal tour—my idea, not his request. He asked me whether I would meet with his friends that night for a discussion in English. I told him of course I would.

He picked me up at seven thirty and proceeded to the village where he lived with his parents. After meeting them and many relatives and posing for photos, I went with him to a well-lighted eight-by-ten-foot room with a blackboard on the back wall and a small table supporting a heating pot. Inside were six of his friends, all students studying English at the university. These were the happiest, poorest, sweetest, warmest, friendliest people I have ever met. As a somewhat-macho-type male, I am reluctant to describe full-grown men as sweet, but that is their true personality. These are all Muslim folks, suffering fasting by day but enjoying life in the evening. It is a real shame that Muslims in general have received such a bad rap since 9/11, which was caused by terrorists. Never will I stand for anyone demeaning someone just because he or she is Muslim.

Isone Iwan, twenty-one, and his girlfriend, Hursila Waham, twenty, were an item. Her nickname was Sila. Nineteen-year-olds Icon Gorontalo and his girlfriend, Achy Soamal, were also a couple. She had the same gorgeous Javanese face as had my last manager before I retired. Erwin, nineteen, was a first-year student, Andi, twenty-two, was in his second year. They were all eager to practice their English (which was excellent) and ask me embarrassing questions on rules. My teachers were probably rolling over in their graves. Caught cold, I did the best I could. One question that I remembered was about the difference between "shall" and "will." I was stumped, eventually saying that "shall" is a weak and poetic word while "will" shows strength of commitment. I punctuated by flexing my bicep. OK, teachers, did I pass? They were very curious about me and my quest for knowledge about the Portuguese. I recited what I knew about Columbus, Magellan, Prince Henry, and so on. I hope they had as good a time as I did. The session lasted for two hours but seemed like only fifteen minutes. Atman had me back in my room by ten thirty, and we agreed to meet the next morning.

I am sure that this was one of the most stimulating and rewarding days of my entire life. For sure this gave me the inspiration to write my first book. Now my thoughts were rambling about Prince Henry, his fort at Sagres, and any information regarding the navigation school.

Atman failed to show up at nine, and I impatiently waited a half hour. My mind consumed with curiosity, I rushed down to the waterfront to work out the details for the next leg of the trip. I walked the dock and found only two ships tied up. One was an interisland ferry, and the other a small interisland cargo ship. On Ternate, there is no security fence; I could have just climbed aboard either vessel. Unable to communicate in English at the ticket booth, I made an acquaintance with a woman in the quarantine area. After she inspected my passport, she said I could hop a ship bound for Java. Unfortunately, it would not depart for two days and would cost around $400. At this point I was fired up and ready to go. I stopped at the local airline office. That afternoon they had seats open for a $90 flight to Makassar or $155 to Jakarta. I had plans to study old Batavia in Jakarta, so the decision was a no-brainer.

As I was checking out, the deskman handed me a note from Atman: he had to fix a mechanical problem before meeting me. I responded with a note that I had a great time yesterday, had much sympathy for mechanical problems, was really sorry I couldn't say good-bye in person, and now was committed to fly. This was really sad; Atman had made my entire trip worthwhile and provided the inspiration for this book.

Seven dollars got me a taxi ride to the airport in what turned out to be more like a local bus. Locals, probably friends, hopped on and off without paying. The driver took one woman a mile out of the direct way to the airport to drop her at home. For five dollars, instead of sitting on a backless, crowded hard bench, I stayed in the VIP lounge and received an ice-cold Coke, cookies, and all the hot chocolate, coffee, and tea I could consume, plus a comfortable overstuffed chair. It was worth it as the plane was seventy-five minutes late. Unlike the Chinese airline, this one offered ample knee room, snacks, juice, and a hot meal.

In Jakarta, the cheapest taxi I could negotiate was fifteen dollars for a ride to Jalan Jaska, an area that Lonely Planet said had many cheap rooms. Most places were full, but Bloom Street Home Stay had a room for nine dollars. It was really bad: there was no room to walk alongside the bed, and the bath and restrooms down the hall were ugly. The next morning, I had to step over people sleeping on the floor to check out. They evidently never turned anyone away. Fortunately, next door was a place that was not listed but that rented for the same price, actually a dollar less. The difference was that it had room to walk alongside of the bed, had minimal furniture and a private bath, and was relatively clean.

I had breakfast at the local KFC. In the parking lot a uniformed crew was marching and practicing to the sound of a whistle. They were all keyed up, and their enthusiastic cheers had a military ring. A short while later, they came inside and set up on an out-of-the-way counter next to the wall. Then began a series of time trials, taking and dispensing orders with chanting and much gleeful enthusiasm. They put on an impressive show. The goal, I found out, was to win a contest with a Kuala Lumpur KFC in Malaysia.

Ready to explore, I went inside a store that advertised itself as a worldwide parcel-delivery service but with a name I was unfamiliar with. There were half a dozen young males at the counter, most with nothing to do. Finding one with some grasp of English, I asked him to indicate our location on my map. It was wrong, and I wasted an hour before the map made sense. Jakarta is a city of over ten million, and understanding my location was critical.

My first order of business was to call Annie, whom I hadn't spoken with since Bali. After three kilometers of exploring, I came to the Borobudur Hotel, a $130-per-night five-star palace named after a famous Buddhist temple. They did an airport-type screen on my knapsack and then sent me up three floors to a communications room. The line was busy, so I went below to the garden. What a place: Olympic-size swimming pool, spa, three tennis courts all enclosed with trees, bridges, waterfalls, and a sculptured garden spread over three acres. There was even a bronze model of the Borobudur Temple. A very closely timed seven-minute call was fifteen dollars, but at least the charges were honest.

The next order of business was to replace the small heating pot used for tea, noodles, and so on that I had picked up in Bali for $4.50. It had been fast and efficient at 240 volts, but the element burned out after about twenty cycles. Nowhere could I locate a small-appliance store. Jakarta—at least the area I was roaming—was served by gigantic multistory malls. Inside were fast-food restaurants and a large grocery store but mostly store after store selling clothes and shoes. After an exhaustive one-hour search, I stopped at a shop selling ceramics. When my request in English didn't work, I made a line-drawing sketch of a coffeepot with an electric cord. Bingo, a picture is worth a thousand words. The young lady set down the coffee cup and escorted me to a hardware shop. I graciously thanked her and made a thorough search: nothing.

While I was waiting until ten in the morning for the Golden Truly Mall to open, I decided to grab something local to eat in an alley next door. Now learning to substitute graphics for English, I pointed to a meal a customer was happily enjoying. The lady with the propane-operated food cart understood perfectly. For a dollar I got some soup and a curry chicken dish—excellent. The malls were spaced about three miles apart. The two more I searched were almost identical to one another, and the results were again nothing.

Now I began to search museums for trade history. Museum Bank of Indonesia was free, with some information on early Portuguese and Dutch trading, a drawing of the layout of early Batavia, and bags full of spices. Nearby was Museum Serarah Jakarta, in a plaza guarded with ancient Dutch cannons. It contained a more complete display than the Bank Museum had, with ship models and pictures of old forts. Sunda Kalapa and old VOC Batavia were a mile farther north, but it was too late in the day to explore them.

Now after dark, I began exploring my local Jalan Jaska area and found a small hole-in-the-wall restaurant serving local food. For under $1.50 I got shish kebab chicken, rice, green veggies, and tea. A tiny, very frail old woman came in, begging with a plastic cup. I gave her about fifteen cents' worth of change from the table, and she left. Finishing up a very tasty and filling meal, I took off down the narrow road to see what I could see. There she was again, the frail beggar slowly working her way down the street.

The best dollar I ever spent was buying dinner for that poor woman. I put my hand on her shoulder and brought her back to the restaurant, gave the young owners a dollar, and said to give her whatever she wanted. They wouldn't allow her to sit but packaged a takeout for her. There were smiles all around, and I'll never forget that happy, thankful look on her face.

Continuing on, I saw some ridiculous-looking prostitutes. The first one was about forty-five; she was somewhat chubby but spoke cheerful English and was very friendly. Her outfit was comical, with high heels and a miniskirt; she just seemed really out of place. A couple of blocks later, a young Chinese woman in a white wedding dress with matching heels was walking ahead of me, and she also looked out of place. She stopped while I continued walking. Suddenly she came from behind and rushed by, taking very small shuffling steps, and then stopped inside a drugstore about fifteen feet ahead. She smiled and looked back to see whether I had noticed her. How could I not?

I took the train to Kota, mailed Annie some trip notes, and picked up a used inflatable life jacket before reaching Sunda Kalapa, the site of old Batavia. My estimate is that half a dozen buildings from the old Dutch compound are still standing. Two huge ones are made of brick. An old drawbridge spans the central creek. Maritime Museum Bahari is located inside one of two large wooden VOC warehouses. Full-size dioramas depict Columbus, Magellan, and Portuguese and Dutch traders. There are original wooden cases with the VOC logo stencils clearly visible. I took pictures of the many storyboards, the several layouts of the Batavia trading center, and ship models. There is a watchtower, but nobody was there to allow me inside. It would have been great to view the old harbor from high above.

I walked all around, even inside an adjacent slum, looking for the harbor entrance breakwaters shown in the layouts but never could see them. I walked a kilometer east to the current harbor to complete the maritime tour. It was full of many interesting large and colorful wooden fishing vessels. Then I took the train back to the area where I was staying. This time it was packed with frenzied commuters. I actually had to shout and fight my way off as people pushed and shoved to board. It required a fair amount of strength to disembark. I missed my stop and had to walk back from the next station.

The next day I visited the National Monument, a three-hundred-foot tower rising above an underground museum. It provided a view of the city that was spectacular though clouded by pollution. Inside the history museum below were about fifty dioramas depicting Indonesia from prehistoric times to European settlement and colonization, Japanese occupation, colonial revolt, and finally the development of a new nation.

Half a kilometer away is the National Museum, far too large to see all in one day. I caught a morning tour with Phivan Wright, a very enthusiastic and knowledgeable docent. She was born in Vietnam but lived some years in the United States and spoke excellent English. Her tour encompassed art, jewelry, tools, weapons, and statues representing Hindi and Islamic culture, as well as primitive exhibits and an explanation of headhunting protocol. After the tour that she officially hosted, she gave me a personal tour of a Dutch Batavia room filled with period furniture and even a Portuguese padrao marker. She even offered to get me inside the Indonesian Heritage Society library, a private collection. I offered to take her to lunch to pick her brain, but she had to catch a flight.

I was ready to leave Jakarta, with the goal of a southwest corner national park and a Son of Krakatoa visit. My landlord suggested I take a bus rather than ride the rails. He wanted to shelter me from the train experience. Had I listened to him, I probably would have been able to reach the park, but I am a railroad enthusiast and so opted for the rails. I took a train back to Kota, then another to Tanah Abang station, where it changed from electric to diesel. The crowded but air-conditioned train went halfway to the destination and then required a change to a local. The grungy local, with standing room only, offered a real insight into the other world. A constant parade of beggars, musicians, vendors, and heartbreaking cripples cycled back and forth until the end of the line. My pocket change went quickly. Not wishing to share my live-on cash, I was forced to turn away and ignore them. The scenery was beautiful, green meadows, lush vegetation, rivers, and many rice paddies.

Rankas Bitung was the end of the line, located completely in the middle of nowhere. I hired a motorcycle ride to the bus station, but there was no bus until tomorrow morning. So, I asked Rizal, the motorcycle driver, to take me to a place with cheap rent, and on the second try, I found a clean room with private bath for eight dollars. I asked him to pick me up in time for tomorrow's bus and then, after a nap, began exploring town. Low on rupia, I attempted to change money; all places were closed, and locals wanted far too high a commission. Ronny, a high school English teacher, overheard me asking a restaurant owner whether he would take US dollars, but he failed to comprehend. Ronny agreed to exchange some cash and sat with me while I ate. Brother fish are very tasty, and I gave him one to take home. When he found out my travel plans, he offered to take me to the coast if I would buy gas. He then invited me to go to the beach with his wife, small daughter, nine-year-old son, and cousin.

I paid off Rizal, had breakfast, and went with Ronny's family to the beach at Carita, where we stayed for an hour. Ronny was fasting, but I bought an ice cream for everyone else. It was a warm experience sharing time with the family. There were no buses running from Lebaun terminal at this time, so Ronny negotiated a motorcycle ride to Unjun Kulon National Park for ten dollars. But apparently Liu, the driver, misunderstood. He took me south but not all the way to Unjun Kulon. He took me to Sumur, an expensive golf-type resort where the rooms start at $85 and go to $275. This definitely was not my kind of place. I found out from the hotel staff that there was no ferry from the park

Hendy Suhendy

through Sunda Strait past Krakatoa. Now I had to change plans on the fly, and instead of insisting Liu take me farther south, I gave him ten dollars more to return me to Lebaun. Liu did really well with me, getting paid for a return trip from a much closer destination than contracted. He was a sneaky one; he even thought I would pay for his gas on the way down.

As we were returning to Lebaun, there was a shout of recognition, and Liu pulled off the road to meet Hendy, who was standing in front of his house. Now a real stroke of luck: Hendy, who works as a tour guide and boat operator, had a room available in his house, like a bed-and-breakfast. He introduced me to a restaurant owner a block down the road for a cheap and excellent meal; then I slept like a baby on a comfortable bed in a clean room for ten dollars.

In the morning, I had breakfast with Hendy, his wife, and a son. She is a midwife and herbologist, working mornings at the hospital and in private practice afternoons. I went with Hendy to drop his son off at school. All the children wanted to meet me. A nine-year-old boy with a four-syllable name introduced himself but cracked up laughing after only three. He never could keep a straight face to finish, even after four attempts.

Hendy had the day off after a long tour with some Japanese the day before. When he asked me whether I wanted to see his village, I said sure. It was hidden from the road but very close by. He introduced me to his mother, father, and sister and many more. Then he showed me his three buffalo, which were really water buffalos. The docile creatures were lying down in the shade, and none budged when he leaped on the back of one. I scratched the head of one and felt its horns. These are very tough and rugged animals, but they have great dispositions. His next question was whether I would like to visit a rice paddy operation. Again, I answered sure.

The field is owned as a village commune and located next to a state electricity-generating plant. The plant sits on rice land that had been condemned. The first thing I noticed was a series of foot-wide walking paths, sixteen inches high, for keeping shoes dry and doubling as dikes to keep in irrigation water. At the time of my visit, it was harvest time, with no new planting taking place.

The first operation is to flood the paddy with diverted water from a flume. Next a water buffalo is harnessed, and the section is plowed to remove roots. These animals have sensitive skin, and the farmer constantly flips water on their heads and back from a long half-round bamboo scoop. Buffalos belong to a very strong union; they begin at six in the morning and are off shift by ten. The paddy is then allowed to dry until it is hard enough to walk on but still soft enough to plant. The farmer, using his index finger, punches a series of holes in even rows with columns about a foot apart. Holding a clod with small green sprouts about ten inches long from another planting, he removes a few sprouts and pushes them into the fresh finger hole. After planting, the paddy is re-flooded and is ready to harvest in three or four months, determined by an experienced planter.

Harvesting is done by cutting with a small scythe. The farmer centers himself in front of five stalks. Moving from left to right, he accumulates the cut stalks in his left hand until he has all five. This extremely efficient operation takes only five or six seconds. He then hands off the fresh cuttings to a coworker, re-centers himself, and repeats. His large woven hat helps shield him from the intense sun. The coworker is a go-between from the cutter to the strikers.

Striking is done against the inside of a wooden box that has half-round riffles nailed horizontally and spaced about four inches apart. The box is four feet high, five feet long, and two and a half feet wide. The long side facing the cutter has an opening two feet by two feet from the top to allow easy removal of the grain. With a striker at each end, stalks in each hand, four stalks are processed. Like synchronized machines, the workers take turns striking until all the grain is removed. The grain is put inside white fifty- to sixty-kilogram bags then spread out on tarps for drying, and the cut stalks are spread around for mulch. This incredibly efficient manual operation, honed by thirty centuries of practice, uses no fossil fuel and leaves no carbon footprint.

The state-owned single-stack power plant, completed in 2009, is fired by coal from nearby Sumatra. The air above it looked so clean that I asked Hendy whether it was actually operating. He said it was. We walked to the corner of the razor wire–fenced compound. A guard allowed us inside to wash our feet in the flume. The compound had housing for the workers, a soccer field, two tennis courts, and its own mosque. The mosque was also accessible from the street without the encumbrance of the fence. The state takes excellent care of the power plant workers and shields them from the outside world. There is a long waiting list of job applicants.

That evening Hendy prepared a special meal on a low grill raised up from the ground with bricks. The fuel was dried coconut husks, which produced great coals. On the grill, he placed five ten-inch fish he had picked up from the market earlier today. While the fish were cooking, he sat with a cutting board in his lap and skillfully minced a clove of garlic, then gave a tomato half six quick slices, rotated it, and gave it six more, forming cubes. He was as smooth as a chef. With peppers and oil, it became a superb garnish. The meal was served inside with a delicious succotash, rice, and a fried veggie called *bakwan*.

The next day after breakfast he proof read my rice paddy notes and then dropped me off at the bus station. What a great and hospitable character; I hope to meet him again. In parting I gave him ten dollars in addition to the lodging fee.

A two-hour two-dollar ride got me to Serang; then two hours and two dollars more put me in Merak. Some young girls pointed the way to the ferry terminal and even offered to help an old man with his bag. I refused but graciously thanked them. The reader will have to admit: most of those I meet are really great people.

A dollar thirty covered a ride across the Sunda Strait to Sumatra. Looking south I was unable to see the famous new volcanic island that recently rose from the sea as Son of Krakatoa. The detonation in the late 1800s killed thousands with the blast, debris, and tsunami. This new unstable monster will kill millions someday. The strait was dotted with many small islands. Immediately after we docked, half a dozen young daredevils rushed aboard. Looking for sponsors, they hung from different railings before plunging forty feet to the water alongside.

I lucked out and caught a bus to Bandar Lampung, a hundred kilometers distant, and then fell into a nap as it was now dark and I couldn't see anything. After arriving, I was directed from the large terminal to a small room where an agent sat behind a desk. My goal as a seafarer was to travel by water if possible, ride to Dumai, and then catch a ferry to Malacca. Instead of the prices being displayed above a ticket counter, tickets here were negotiated one at a time with an agent. Sumatra is about four hundred miles long; Dumai is located on the north shore. Forty dollars purchased a ride from

English-speaking Agus but required a ninety-minute wait and a trip into town for me to refuel.

The long overnight ride was like taking the night train except I provided my own sleeping bag. There were only about a dozen passengers, and I stretched out across a rear seat. Passing through villages with porch lights on late into the night gave me the feeling of subsidized electricity. The bus stopped twice so that the males could get out and pee alongside. I guess the three ladies had larger bladders. At six thirty in the morning, nine hours later, we pulled to a stop in a field near a ramshackle building representing itself as a terminal. My ticket said Dumai, the bus sign said Dumai, but we were in Pekanbaru. At seven the open-walled corner building began serving tea and sandwiches. No one spoke English, and I was starting to get a little nervous. Now paying very careful attention and looking for any clues, I noticed someone checking out the bus with the Dumai sign in the window.

The driver let me board without even looking at my ticket. This time I sat near the front to look for any reassuring signs of my desired destination. I was definitely uneasy; it seemed like we were backtracking. There was another bus-company employee seated in front of me who looked at my ticket and indicated everything was OK. For four hours I watched for signs or anything else for reassurance. I never got any. The countryside was lush green, sometimes planted with orchards of tall, thin trees, maybe rubber. We were passed by over half a dozen trucks loaded with tree sections fifteen inches in diameter and twenty inches long. Later I found they were palm tree sections and used to extract palm oil. We passed an oil-refining operation with a gas burn-off flare that looked similar to one I had seen on the previous night, further adding to my distress. A surface pipeline followed the edge of the road, and finally I could see we were near a seaport. As we passed a Chevron refinery, a sign in front indicated it was a joint operation with Indonesia. I was always curious about where the Japanese acquired their oil during World War II. Now I knew at least one source.

The bus terminal was located in a field next to nowhere. I asked the lone taxi driver to take me to the ferry terminal, which he did; it was a large lot designed to process many cars and trucks. I don't know the schedule for the car ferry, but nothing was happening today. We finally found someone who directed us to a building downtown. Bingo, there is a single ferry to Malacca at ten every morning for twenty-six dollars. A van transports you from in front of the ticket office to the inside the very secure terminal. After some effort and after rejecting a room in a dirty building housing at least three prostitutes, I found a nice clean place with a private bath next door to the police station and for less money. Still on a quest to locate a small heating pot, I found one in Dumai. A little more expensive, it was identical to the broken one I had purchased in Bali.

Boarding the ferry required passing through customs and immigration to depart Indonesia. I really wanted to see the harbor, but there was no obvious way from inside the ferry. Fifteen minutes after getting underway, I noticed some young people leaving through an open watertight door past a sign appearing to say "No Admittance." If they could do it, why not me? On the roof were about thirty young Indonesian Seventh Day Adventists.

By now we were well out of the harbor and out into the famous Strait of Malacca, where Magellan once passed; I was in my zone. The day was hot, the sea was calm, and the view was clear. As we sped along at over twenty-five knots, I participated in many photo ops with the young students. Always alert for danger, I advised one of the chaperones to bring some youngsters down from the curved roof over the ship's control bridge. With no safety rails, one slip could mean sudden death. Surprisingly, there were no life rings or any way to directly alert the crew in an emergency. I observed only three ships during the two-hour crossing.

It was a thrill for me, approaching Malacca with an opportunity to walk in Magellan's five-hundred-year-old footsteps. In the distance was a full-size replica of a Portuguese Nao. We passed under a high concrete bridge and docked at the customs quay.

The Malacca River separates the customs dock from the museum area and the places with cheap rooms. I didn't know that there was a connecting footbridge, and a taxi driver convinced me the only way over there was with him, for about twelve dollars. I found a room, dropped off my bag, and went exploring. I skipped the museums and followed the river up to the ruins of a Portuguese fort, then continued upriver to a storyboard with the history of Malacca's name.

Sometime in the thirteenth century, Sultan Parameswara was out hunting with his dog. A white mouse deer kicked his dog into the river, killing it. The sultan then sat under a tree grieving for his dog. The tree was a *Pokok Melaka*. Later the sultan gave the river and the village the name Melaka. The current name is usually spelled Malacca.

Next day, after finding a cheaper room, I hit the museums. The Maritime Museum is located partially inside the replica of a Portuguese Nao. It turned out to be the most interesting of all, especially for me, since I am an amateur marine historian.

Malacca was known as the Venice of the East. Traders brought the following to sell:

Persians:	perfume, glassware, carpets, and medicine
Chinese:	copper, tea, silk, and porcelain
Indians:	embroidered cloth, opium, and pepper
Burmese:	jewelry and precious stones
Siamese:	rice, liquor, and dried fish
Malaysians:	tin, ivory, and rattan
Sumatrans and Javanese:	cloves, nutmeg, mace, rice, Sandalwood and gold

Arab sultans and traders were closemouthed regarding their sources and the winds that propelled their boats. The southwest monsoon blows from April to October, aiding shipping to the Far East. The northeast monsoon blows November to April, aiding ships to India and Malacca. Traders went mostly downwind.

The Portuguese were considered interlopers, dangerous and disruptive. Their reputation preceded them by Arab traders' word of mouth, especially tales of their bloody conquest of Goa, India. The story of Magellan and his heroics in Malacca has two sides. The sultan wanted to maintain the peaceful and profitable status quo. The sultan's plan to lure the Portuguese in with free access to the town and then capture their ships was concocted because of fear and the threat of formidable firepower. The sultan, who had no cannons, relied only on his cunning and wit. By 1511 Malacca was under Portuguese control, and the sultan was forced to flee.

Today Malacca, the old town, is a quaint little tourist village with a mostly silted-up harbor; the container ports are located a hundred miles east and west in Singapore and Kuala Lumpur. The draw is its rich history.

The next day I caught a bus to Kuala Lumpur. I met Matt and Sara, a backpacking couple from San Diego and LA respectively, and asked whether I could tag along downtown. They said OK and then led me to where they had made reservations near Chinatown at the Step Inn. Yost, the manager, arranged a room for me: his. My next order of business was to contact my nephew Mark. Yost kindly offered his phone and deciphered the telephone number I had. To make it work, he removed three digits in front and added a zero at the end. Within two hours I was sipping beer with Mark, his wife, Asa, and my new backpacker friends, Matt and Sara. I spent the next day with my relatives and then caught a special twelve-dollar train to the airport.

Taking a night flight from Kuala Lumpur to Lisbon by way of Abu Dhabi and Frankfurt, by six in the morning I was enjoying a gourmet breakfast on Eritrean Airlines over the Indian Ocean. I had a very tasty omelet with bacon, potatoes, fruit, a sweet roll, orange juice, and coffee served with real silverware, all the while thinking of Vasco da Gama and Magellan making difficult passages five hundred years earlier on the sea below. The crew was splendid and posed for pictures after giving me a souvenir set of silverware.

I arrived in Lisbon and cleared immigration at ten at night. I caught a subway, which whisked me to the city center by eleven. Now for some brutal lessons: One, the youthful competition for hostels and guesthouses make reservations on the Internet. I wing it and choose not to be encumbered with a computer or the net. The second lesson is don't arrive late at night in a strange city without a place to flop. Lesson three is don't go to Europe in August, as 60 percent of the people are on vacation. Bottom line, after I visited five different hostels and hotels, there was absolutely no room at the inn. By two in the morning, completely exhausted, I gave up and walked to the McDonald's at the town square with all the statues. The floor of the men's room was wet, so I set my bag just outside the door. It was gone when I came out. Fortunately, I had some things in my knapsack, including my camera and notebook.

What to do next? The restaurant closed at three, while I was still gathering my thoughts. I decided to head down to the waterfront on the Taugas

River. A very bright and multicolored light turned out to be a projector. With my back to the river, I could watch a five-minute show projected on the wall of a large building. Using digital images, the projection constructed great edifices incorporating Greek columns.

Now with a much lighter load, I headed north along the riverfront, eventually reaching a ten-track railway station. Suddenly it became clear: get the hell out of the city and directly down to Prince Henry the Navigator's realm. The high-speed train departed from another station, and by eight o'clock I was speeding toward Tunes. The ticket agent made it clear that in two hours I had to change trains there to reach Lagos. I am not sure how fast the train went, but a stencil on the trucks rated them at 243 kilometers per hour. The clickity-clack and gentle motion around the banked curves quickly put me to sleep, not to awaken until just after the train left the Tunes station. Arriving in Faro by mistake, I pleaded my case to Maria, who, after a brief period of silence, scribbled something on the ticket allowing me free passage back to Lagos.

The milk train to Lagos arrived about two. Walking toward the station exit, I was approached by an old man named Vannes who offered a room in town for thirty euros a night. Used to paying only ten or fifteen dollars, I initially said no thanks, but a reality check told me to take it.

Lagos is a resort town with a marina, a seaport, beaches, and a rich history. A fort guards the walled entrance to town, which was the location of the first European slave sales. Lagos was the terminal for Prince Henry's expeditions, and a successful voyage would bring in hides, gold, handicrafts, and slaves. It is sad that this beautiful spot was the focus of so much grief.

On securing the third-floor room with a rooftop view, I started asking questions about Prince Henry. Strangely, many local people had no knowledge of him. Walking from shop to shop, I found that his fort and school, or think tank, was located in Sagres, about twenty-five kilometers east, and that a bus was available at eight the next morning.

The countryside was dry and rocky and sported many wind turbines. Finally, there was a breathtaking view of the Atlantic and a strange white-walled structure built to defend Henry's fort. The bus continued for another two kilometers and stopped in the center of town. In the park was a statue of

Infante o Henrique, the man behind the Portuguese explorations. "Infante" is a term used to describe a king's younger son who in all likelihood will never outlive his older brothers to become king himself. A hundred meters from the statue was a magnificent panoramic view of the blue Atlantic with the Sagres peninsula and Cabo de San Vincente just to the north.

Sagres, with a statue and tiny information center, is thankfully non-commercialized. This sleepy town had no restaurants or visible hotels on the main street, and it required some inquiry and legwork to find a place for breakfast, which was well hidden and located inside a residential neighborhood. The search was rewarded with a hearty meal for a reasonable price.

A brisk fifteen-minute walk brought me to the entrance road of the fortress. Elated, I stopped and drank in the view. This is the place that drew me to Europe from my inspired visit to Ternate. A great white wall, fifteen meters high, stretched from left to right for two hundred meters across the Sagres peninsula. The two corners extend to vertical cliffs approximately fifty meters above the sea. Two stubby walls form a V-shaped entrance leading to a single door. Any aggressors would have been subjected to crossfire from archers, crossbowmen, burning oil, and many strategically placed cannons.

Inside the ten-meter-thick front wall is a large open space with a line of buildings set back sixty meters and parallel to the front, terminating with a church on the north end. Beyond the row of buildings is empty rocky terrain stretching to the end of the peninsula. A paved pathway edged with a one-meter stone wall follows the perimeter, protecting visitors from the fifty-meter cliffs that surround the entire grounds. The entire peninsula measures approximately a thousand meters in length, with the narrowest part being the walled entrance. At the tip is a weather station with several small buildings. The fortress is located on a main north-south flyway, and many plastic plaques describe the birds and their migratory habits.

This was Henry's headquarters, the very place where the caravel was designed, and the location of the first navigation school, or at least the first think tank. This is where the expeditions were organized and where the records of wind and current data were analyzed and updated. Where instruments were redesigned and improved for accuracy and ease of use, where the charts were updated and redrawn to incorporate new discoveries, where the first studies of latitude determination at sea were conducted. This was the epicenter, the source of all European expansion in the fifteenth century. To say that I was elated is a gross understatement.

The fortress contained a restaurant and a small bookstore, where I found two very informative books, one in English and one to be deciphered from Portuguese. To the north of the access road is a hundred-meter sandy beach, sheltered by the Sagres peninsula and enjoyed by several hundred visitors. This beach, the only easy access between the steep cliffs, is the place where Columbus came ashore and the path Sir Francis Drake took when he attacked and entered the fort during the Elizabethan wars.

Walking back to town, I caught a bus to Cabo de San Vincente, some three kilometers north of the Sagres penninsula. Cape Saint Vincent is the southwest corner of Portugal and forms a vee with identical fifty-meter cliffs rising from the sea. It is capped with a lighthouse, which encloses a small museum. To the north, the tall cliffs continue as far as the eye can see—another gorgeous site.

Returning to Lagos, I hand-washed a few clothes and sipped a beer on the rooftop. The landlady came up to say hello and invited me for breakfast the next morning. My reading of the Portuguese is that they stay up most of the night and rise late in the morning. The vacationing youngsters on the street below fit this pattern for sure. I waited until nine o'clock the next morning to knock on the owner's door, but no one answered, confirming my generalized observation.

A four-hour bus to Seville took me back through Faro and past my mistaken train station. Arriving in town at two o'clock and out on the street, I introduced myself to a young Eurasian backpacker from Hong Kong. Yuki had an online reservation at a local hostel and let me tag along with her.

Ten euros bought a coed dorm room at the "Spot Central Hostel", located near the bullring and within a kilometer of all the main attractions. The SCH was only two years old and spotless. It included a simple breakfast and free sangria on the rooftop every night preceding a BBQ. It was owned by Anna, who was unable to find work as an architect. I met fellow backpackers and adventure travelers from all over Europe and the United States. This mix and storytelling over a few drinks is always a highlight of the trip.

Next morning, I visited the Museo Naval de Sevilla, located in a three-story watchtower on the bank of the Guadalquivir River. Actually, the river was rerouted, and the museum now sits at the edge of a canal. Both Columbus and Magellan passed through and conducted business at the Torre del Oro, constructed in 1221, before relocating to Huelva and Cádiz Bay respectively prior to their world-changing departures. The museum contains ship models of the *Niña*, *Pinta*, and *Santa Maria*, plus many others. Of special interest are the flags flown by Columbus and Magellan, which depict the symbols of their sponsoring monarchs. Also, there is a large wall mural depicting the Magellan voyage.

Meddy, a tour guide who works for tips, conducted a two-hour walking tour of Seville. It was once the major Spanish west coast seaport, but that function has since shifted to Cádiz, which sports a huge container port and doesn't require a sixty-mile trip up the Guadalquiver river. For me the two buildings of major interest were the Archivo General de Indias and the Santa Iglesia Catedral. The magnificent church contains the body of Columbus inside a raised casket, supported by knights representing the four major territories of Spain. Located just across the street from the church, the Archivo General de Indias contains all the early records of the Indies commerce in the Caribbean. Unfortunately for me, no photos are allowed. On the second floor, on a table with a glass cover, is a document signed by Balboa. This is the first written record of the discovery of the Pacific Ocean.

I took a round-trip bus ride to Huelva, then a local city bus to Palos de la Frontero. Located on the salt estuary at the base of a monastery, this is the exact location where the Columbus expedition prepared for the voyage to the New World. A small lake, carved from the estuary, contains working models of the *Niña*, *Pinta*, and *Santa Maria*. These full-sized replicas actually sailed to the New World and back for the five-hundredth anniversary of Columbus's voyage before becoming lake bound. On the lakeshore are recreations of Native American Indian dwellings that include woven cotton hammocks, one of their inventions. There is a two-story museum that contains many dioramas and period navigation instruments and weapons. A holographic projection depicting Columbus and describing his adventure in selectable languages makes no mention of how he acquired the ephemeris and the Portuguese secret of determining latitude at sea. It is notable that virtually the entire crew of the expedition came from within 25 miles of Palos.

I left Seville for Cádiz. Again, no room at the inn, so I took a bus to La Línea de la Concepción, a small town adjacent to Gibraltar, and managed to walk around the base of the fortress before sunset. Again, no room at the inn, so I attempted to take a night bus to Madrid. The driver required a prepaid ticket, and the station was closed. After a long night, I decided to return to Seville, where I could call my wife and reorganize.

On the return trip, I observed a thousand kiteboards skimming a bay just around the corner from Gibraltar. On the hills were multitudes of wind generators, and in a flat near Cape Trafalgar was a gigantic array of solar panels. The Spanish seem to be serious about energy independence.

Flying to Venice by way of Madrid and Rome revealed that Iberian Airlines gives away nothing to coach passengers, not even water, between Madrid and Rome. Arriving in Venice in the early morning showed me once again there were no rooms to be had. After exploring the canal city on foot and the Grand Canal area all lit up at night, I was unable find any evidence of Marco Polo other than some street names. Finally, I went back to Rome by night train, my favorite way to travel, especially in European August.

I walked around Rome while planning my next move, finally deciding to visit Amsterdam by way of a night train to Munich. When I awoke at six o'clock in the Dolomite Mountains, the view of the gorgeous countryside was splendid. The journey required changing trains with a two-hour stopover in Bolzano/Bozen, a high-country resort town with a ski lift on the closest mountain. By ten I was enjoying the downhill run to Innsbruck, a beautiful trip along the river. I arrived in Munich at two thirty and was on the way to Amsterdam by way of Dusseldorf an hour later.

Entering the Netherlands at Venlo after ten at night turned into an adventure because the signals weren't working on the local line into Amsterdam. A special train was dispatched to Eindhoven, where the railroad company brought the stranded passengers into a room, apologized, and served warm drinks. Eventually, they provided free taxis to town.

Amsterdam in August, like everywhere else, sported no lodging. After a thorough checkout of the local guesthouses, I booked a forty-euro room in distant Ijmuiden with the tourist information center and then visited the nautical Scheepvaartmuseum. While there were interesting displays and ship models, there was little information regarding the VOC and East Indies operations.

Following a one-hour bus ride, I arrived at the delightful town of Ijmuiden. After checking me in at the hotel, the manager advised me of the local delights. The view from the streets shows only a clean well-groomed sleepy little town, but a one-kilometer walk takes you over a dike to the main locks. This is the shortcut shipping entrance to Amsterdam from the North Sea, and all traffic must traverse three locks. As a maritime junkie, I spent at least an hour enjoying the show.

The next day a three-kilometer walk brought me past the seaport to the Nordzee coast and a fine sandy beach, all owned by Holiday Inn. On the dunes overlooking the beach are many concrete bunkers, which had been used to house coastal-defense guns. Back at the seaport, I jumped aboard a water taxi with the idea of visiting Forteiland, a defensive battery of cannons placed to defend the harbor entrance. No shots were ever fired from there in anger during modern times. During the blitzkrieg of September 1939, the Germans simply invaded from Dusseldorf and crossed the bridge. The water taxi stops at Forteiland only on the first Sunday of the month, so they gave me a free round trip to the opposite shore and back. The return trip carried about thirty cyclists.

My decision was to explore Rotterdam the next day. The Maritime Museum was interesting and included an adjacent harbor full of well-maintained boats representing two hundred years of commercial and private vessels. The harbor outlined with old cranes was operational until the eighties, when a container port was constructed. Sadly, I could find little information there either regarding the East Indies or VOC.

Tourist information centers, besides offering free and useful information and local knowledge, also act as agents, receiving commissions from their recommendations. I wanted to go to London by ferry. Evidently the largest commissions were paid by the P & O line, which operates between Rotterdam and Hull, England, far to the north. Following the center's directions, I waited at a nearby bus stop for a ride to the P & O ferry. Either I messed up or the bus didn't show, but I did manage to return to the center shortly before it closed. With the Hull ferry trip now dead, they came up with another plan, the very one I was looking for.

The Stena Line operates virtually straight across the channel to Harwich, England. A local train stopped a short distance from the dock, and I arrived on board with time to kill. For a hundred dollars, I had a double-bunk stateroom all to myself. The facilities all seemed brand new and included a private bathroom with a hot shower. Actually, the cold-water line to the shower wasn't working, so I had to be careful and quick. On the deck below, trucks and cars were efficiently being stowed away. The ship was equipped with a somewhat pricey restaurant but with large picture windows and tasty food. The ship even had a casino and duty-free store.

By nine thirty we were underway, and it was great to be back on the water. The gentle rolling and pitching quickly put me to sleep, not to awaken until five o'clock to watch the trucks being unloaded at Harwich. A fifteen-dollar buffet breakfast (English) could barely be consumed before we passengers were quickly evicted.

Passengers were directed to customs and immigration, then to a prepaid train to London Liverpool station. By nine thirty I was walking the streets of London for the very first time.

The first order of business was to purchase a phone card and call Annie from one of those quaint little red phone booths. The second was to find a room in August. The local information center had a room for twenty-six pounds a day if I could commit to a week. Actually, the trip was winding down, and the flight home was in six days. My roommate, Ivan, was from Spain. Eighty percent of the guests were from Spain, all there to find relief from a failed economy. After check-in and stowing my gear, I was off on the underground to see the sights.

What an efficient transportation system, with most trains running every ten minutes or less and a digital sign displaying the exact wait time. With one or two transfers, you can connect quickly to any place in the city. My impression of London was not that of a giant city but one of a cluster of small towns all nestled together as one. Always drawn to the waterfront, I took a stroll along the Thames and admired London Bridge with all the lights. The lighting gave the bridge a surrealistic appearance, akin to something from a fairy tale. A British cruiser was anchored nearby, adding to the ambiance while providing liberty for the crew. A castle was illuminated with ground lights. The evening was replete with photo ops. What a spectacular place at night.

The next morning was the first opportunity to enjoy breakfast at the hostel. I met Stella, who writes about firsthand observations in China and has published a book. We have since become pen pals. I took a train to the Royal Greenwich Observatory, which contains a museum that houses John Harrison's early chronometers. Using a chronometer to time a precise measurement of the angle of the sun or a star above the horizon, together with the Greenwich-generated almanac, allows precise computation of longitude (and latitude) at sea. The observatory contains a telescope mounted on an east-west horizontal axis directly on the Greenwich Meridian, simultaneously 000:00:00E and 000:00:00W. This transit telescope allows the operator to make precise measurements of the transit time when a star or the sun crosses the meridian. The results are then tabulated in *The Nautical Almanac*, used for positional determination by seafarers. All longitude measurements are referenced to this prime meridian. All longitudes are W, west, or E, east. The maximum is 180 degrees, where east and west meet on the other side of the world in Tonga.

A few hundred meters below the observatory is the National Maritime Museum, worthy of several hours' study. While I was there, a young fellow dressed as an eighteenth-century sailor sang sea chanties to gather visitors for a tour of the facility. Nearby is the famous *Cutty Sark* clipper ship. The next day I visited the British Museum. The place is so large that I could enjoy only about a third of it in an afternoon.

The following day provided the opportunity to board a train to Charring Cross, located below Trafalgar Square. At the front of the square is a bronze statue of Admiral Horatio Nelson located high atop a pedestal. Nelson is England's most revered hero and was the inspirational leader of the Royal Navy in the destruction of the Spanish and French fleets leading to the demise of Napoleon.

From Trafalgar Square, walking parallel to the Thames River, you pass Big Ben, Whitehall financial district, Downing Street, and the Parliament building. To the right are Buckingham Palace and a long mall leading past the Admiralty and back to Trafalgar Square. Located in the rear of the square is the National Art Museum. Most of the art consists of seventeenth- and eighteenth-century Dutch paintings, marking the period when wealthy Holland patrons, fat with profits from East Indies trade, sponsored the Dutch masters. After dinner, I was able to attend a concert at Saint Martin's in the Field; located adjacent to the square and not in some rural field, Saint Martin's is a conservatory of music. That night the opening piece was Handel's Harpsichord Concerto, one of my favorites.

Stella apparently felt sorry for me and my limited wardrobe since I had lost a bag in Lisbon. One morning at breakfast she presented me with a shirt and several pairs of shorts. Imagine this from a woman whose only income is from a small pension—most generous. She even gave me a copy of her new book.

The Royal Air Force Museum had moved from its advertised location, and she informed me of the new site. A train ride to the Colindale station and a three-kilometer walk brought me to the new museum, where many aircraft from 1910 to the present are displayed. Of special interest were World War II German planes and equipment, all in excellent repair. Included was a short film on the Battle of Britain, where England managed to not just survive but win the battle while using a much smaller air force.

I managed to connect with my niece Kristy and her new husband, Sadek. Kristy was writing the thesis for her master's degree, which she received a few weeks later. We were all able to spend an afternoon in Hyde Park plus a lunch and dinner together.

All good things must come to an end. I bid good-bye to Kristy, Sadek, and Stella then took the underground to Heathrow and US Air to Philadelphia and San Francisco. US Air served tasty meals and provided excellent service. I arrived home August 29, 2013, three months after departing, completing one of the finest and most interesting adventures of my life and with the inspiration to write this book.

Adventure Travel, 2014

————

IN 2014 I BEGAN ANOTHER three-month adventure trip with the idea of filling in some blanks. The first stop was Singapore, which I had first visited in 1958. No taxis were needed; an underground railway whisked me to the center of town. To me the city was unrecognizable. Virtually everything had been rebuilt or was brand new. Another thing is that with everything new, it was also very expensive. With that situation and with nothing to reminisce about, I caught a three-hour bus to Malacca, a place I both enjoyed and found affordable.

After revisiting the museums and sights of old Malacca, I caught a two-hour bus to familiar Kuala Lumpur to regroup and arrange a trip to Portuguese Goa, India. India had had some immigration issues and now required a formal visa. For reasons, I didn't understand, a visa was difficult to get locally but easy in Bangkok.

On July 6, six days after leaving home, I arrived in Bangkok. The Lonely Planet guidebook stated that the Khao San district was both interesting and affordable. I had too much stuff—a small backpack and a small suitcase on wheels—so they wouldn't let me on the smoky city bus, and I had to take a three-wheeled taxi (tuk-tuk). The book had it right: Khao San was seedy as hell, and rooms were near my ten-dollar price range.

My plan was to secure a visa on my own, and the next day, I found the Indian embassy, which had moved two miles from the listed address I had. I pulled a number, and settled in for a lengthy bureaucratic wait. I was presented with to-do list wanting detailed information on where I was going to stay and my exact itinerary with dates and locations. This was impossible to complete, because I always wing it and had no knowledge of anything inside the country. I don't travel with a computer, I don't do e-mail, and frankly my computer skills are extremely wanting. After some frustrating hours in a rent-by-the-hour computer room, I gave up and enlisted an agent.

The travel agency that I chose had the best price, $500 cash, which included everything. It is noteworthy that British are charged the most for visas, Americans are charged slightly less, with Asians paying the least. The next morning the agent took me to the embassy on his motorcycle, where I was photographed, fingerprinted, informed it would take a week, and then asked to surrender my passport.

I couldn't wait to leave smoggy and congested Bangkok and took the first train north to check out old Siam. A two-hour ride brought me to a small city named Nakhon Pathom. It was late; I rented a room, got some street food, and then crashed.

Early the next morning, I inserted my debit card into a bank ATM. It was dark; I misunderstood the instructions, received a printed slip noting $300 but received no cash, and to add insult to injury, the ATM rudely swallowed my card. To make matters even worse, the bank was closed on Friday, not to open until Monday. Now what? Extremely low on money, I returned to Khao San and a ten-dollar room.

I had a credit card but had never used the cash advance feature owing to the expense compared to a debit card. Unsure of myself, cashless, and wary of losing my last card, I enlisted the aid of a young British traveler. She had done this before; she deciphered the Thai instructions and walked me through my uneasy transaction. After thanking her profusely and with time to kill until Monday, I began checking out the local delights.

The first stop was the National Museum, which consumed the remainder of Saturday. Two things stand out in my memory. The first is a huge red ornamented horse-drawn carriage on display. This is the vehicle the king and queen ride when leading parades. The second is a crippled and wrinkled old Caucasian man escorted by a gorgeous young Thai woman, immaculately dressed and wearing stiletto high heels. I was curious as to why she was hanging out with him. Was she a hired escort or the wife of a wealthy man?

The Khao San district is tiny, only several square blocks. There are two main streets, parallel to one another, and each is three blocks long. On

Saturday night, there are wall-to-wall people on both streets. To go from one end to the other requires sidestepping BBQ carts and insect carts featuring edible scorpions, cockroaches, and other tasty delights. In addition, there are carts displaying clothes, jewelry, CDs, and so on. Did I forget to mention the many offers from the prostitutes? That night some open-to-the-street bars were displaying the World Cup final soccer match on giant screens. I was able to watch Argentina beat Germany in overtime, 1–0, for the world title, immediately followed by some crying and much dancing in the street.

Monday was a day to remember. I caught an early train back to Nakhon Pathom, where a bank supervisor returned my stolen debit card, credited my account, and held my hand for an ATM cash transaction. I was short only the transaction fee. A bank security guard named Fromtuy spent an hour driving me around town on his motorcycle, looking for a way to complete an international phone call. He wouldn't accept any money for his effort.

An attractive thirty-five-year-old tourist policewoman named Amachita, who sold tickets to the city's ancient mosque, had been giving my driver phone-location advice. Unable to complete a call home, my next idea was to catch the 81 bus to Kanchanaburi on the river Kwai. Carefully interpreting her instructions, I attempted to map out the route to the bus stop. It wasn't working, but she was determined to assist me. At three fifteen, she locked her desk and logged out. She told me to get into her ten-year-old air-conditioned Honda and began a half-hour search for an 81 bus, stop. While we were strangled in commuter traffic, she spotted an 81 bus, going the opposite direction (but toward Kanchanaburi). She evidently had had some police driver training; she made a U-turn and reached speeds of sixty miles per hour before flagging down the bus, in her immaculate uniform with the shiny insignias. I gave her a big thank-you hug before boarding the bus.

In Kanchanaburi, at the Sugar Cane Guesthouse, I managed to secure a nice room on a barge, floating on the Khwae Yai River. This railroad town is the location of the famous "bridge on the river Kwai" featured in the movie. I found a cheap drop-off laundry and had a tasty dinner, then a shower, and good night's sleep on the barge. It is interesting to note that there was no sewer connection to the shore.

The next morning at the station, I caught the train for a thirty-kilometer ride across the bridge to Nam Tok, the end of the line. This narrow-gauge railroad, built with slave labor by the Japanese, was a connection from Siam to Burma, now Thailand and Myanmar. The line was blasted through the mountains, with workers digging twenty-four hours a day, killing many thousands of natives and prisoners of war in the process. After the war the mountain tracks were pulled out, and that part of the route was abandoned. The current ride hauls tourists across a flat plain and then through a scenic area with a fast-moving river to an end-of-the-line restaurant. Alternate trains haul sugarcane and produce.

The next day I wanted to take the train three kilometers from the station to examine the bridge. To my amazement, the ticket price from the station to the bridge was almost as much as yesterday's excursion. Before taking a cheap tuk-tuk ride to the bridge, I did a photo op of several old Japanese railroad relics in a nearby park. In this collection was a strange articulated locomotive. The rear end of the boiler was actually pivoted to the cab.

The river was approximately 150 yards wide and slow moving. The first bridge, constructed during World War II, was wooden but was later replaced with a steel one. A photo depicted a bombed-out section of the steel bridge. I walked across and found a wide trimmed lawn, some memorials, and a souvenir shack. After a thorough inspection, I walked back to the barge.

I wanted to visit northern Thailand. It was half past noon, and the bus north to Chiang Mai didn't leave until seven. With six and a half hours to kill, I thought I could leisurely return to Nakhon Pathom and give some flowers to Amachita. It turned out to be a mad dash. I spotted the mosque from the southbound 81 bus, which stopped for me a half mile later. The route skirted the town on the highway. A motorcycle driver took me to the mosque, and I caught a glimpse of Amachita headed for the lady's room and waved. The driver dropped me at the bank, where Fromtuy, the security guard, was parked on a bench outside. He directed me to a flower shop. The shop lady didn't have packaged bundles of flowers and had to piece together an expensive creation, which seemed to take a lot of time. Fromtuy took me back to the mosque. It was now past three fifteen on Friday, and Amachita had taken off for Bangkok. An associate called her cell phone, and I had a chance to thank her again. He then promised to give her the flowers when she returned. Fromtuy accepted two bags of nuts and dropped me at the 81 bus, stop.

I was the last passenger aboard the eleven-hour Chiang Mai overnight bus. The next morning, I caught a three-hour bus to Chiang Rai and found a reasonable place to stay at Chat House.

After resting, I explored Chiang Rai on foot. My residence was located near a hospital. A young woman at the admittance counter attempted to help me call home from a public phone. It failed and then kept my coins. She felt sorry for me and generously offered her cell phone. I made a short call to Annie, but the woman wouldn't accept any reimbursement.

Continuing my exploration, I found the place to be a railroad town with a cluster of rolling stock in a park and some passenger cars that were partial housing for a public library. As I continued on, the sky suddenly opened up with lightning and a heavy deluge. I sought refuge under the roofed parking area of the Sun and Moon Hotel. Two young ladies let me come inside. It was a slow afternoon, and they were doing beautiful close-stitch embroidery in the lobby to fill in the time. They offered me tea and asked about my travels. Across the street, a young motorcycle rider skidded and fell, bruising and scraping his knee and leg. They spotted the accident and provided minor first aid. These girls were very private and wouldn't allow me to take their picture. You have to like these warm, generous, and thoughtful people of Thailand.

For about sixty dollars, I hired a private taxi to take me to the northern-most part of the country. The driver stopped at a place called Black House along the way. The compound contained at least ten buildings and was nestled against a small lake with acrees of mowed green lawn. Some buildings housed art galleries, one a small restaurant, and another a Buddhist shrine, but two large buildings contained stuffed and mounted animals. Stretched out on long tables were numerous python skins, over twenty feet long, with the heads attached. It was kind of dark and spooky inside.

The driver continued to the archeology site of an ancient city called Chiang Saen. The site was still being excavated, and there was no going inside. On the walls were symbolic lions and dragons in bas relief.

The final stop was the top of the country. Standing on a perch with a bronze statue at my back, I had a magnificent view of the Mae Kong River, sometimes called Mekong. The river is at least half a mile wide, maybe bigger than the Mississippi. It flowed directly south, straight toward me, two hundred feet below, and then made a sharp turn to the east. The source is located inside China, three hundred kilometers to the north. To the north and west is the flat green marsh of Burma, separated from old Siam by a small stream less than two hundred yards from where I was standing. Across the river to the east, inside the bend, is a Laotian city. Rectangular wooden cargo vessels were plying the far side of the river.

The last stop was the Opium Museum, where you can learn everything you ever wanted to know about this dangerous drug. This area, known as the Golden Triangle, was a primary source of beautiful opium poppies and made many dealers wealthy.

After a three-hour bus ride back to Chiang Mai and an overnight train to Bangkok, I was back in Khao San. My visa for India was approved, and several new pages had been inserted into my passport.

Now twenty-one days into the trip, I could finally visit Goa by way of Bombay. Once there, a thirteen-dollar taxi ride brought me at ten o'clock at night to a cheap guesthouse room for thirty dollars. Checkout time was at nine the next morning. It was expensive and not very traveler friendly, but at least I was able to leave my bags behind the counter while I checked out the town. The harbor was in a long sheltered cove connected to the bay. The Portuguese made it a point to find protected water for their trading ships. I walked all along the waterfront looking for signs of the walled trading fort but to no avail. Goa is the capital city of its province and contains a state museum. Inside I viewed a carrier where a wealthy Portuguese could ride in style on a seat supported by four slaves. When I requested information on the location of the sixteenth-century walled fort, a museum employee went upstairs to search. He returned ten minutes later, claiming there were no records.

A twenty-two-kilometer motorcycle ride took me east around the bay, then south to the far-side entrance to the bay. Perched on a cliff three hundred feet above the water is the very substantial Fort Aguada. The fort was constructed in 1630 to fend off the pesky Dutch. The Portuguese maintained a presence in Goa until 1967, when they were forcibly evicted by the Indian army. I had been looking forward to visiting Goa ever since I began studying

Portuguese trading history and was disappointed in the lack of any trace of the trading fort. Other than Fort Aguada, the only trace of the past is the many Portuguese colonial-style buildings.

That evening I was on an overnight train and arrived in Bombay at noon. After visiting the State and Prince of Wales Museums, I took a twenty-four-hour train to Agra, city of the Taj Mahal. Agra has no public transportation and is very spread out. Ride choices are a motorcycle, three-wheeled tuk-tuk, or taxi. It cost 150 rupees to ride to a crummy 500-rupee room. With no restaurants nearby, I was forced to take a 150-rupee tuk-tuk ride to a food shack. The good part: a tasty curry dish was only 100 rupees.

The Taj Mahal is splendid. It is located on the Yamuna River, which forms the rear border of a very substantial walled enclosure. From the entrance, it is completely hidden by a tall red fortress-like enclosure. I walked a hundred yards then made a left turn through a huge arched gate in the side wall. Going from dark too light while passing through the thick wall, suddenly a magic 3-D postcard image flashes into view. The scene is enhanced by two long parallel strips of water placed on either side of the entrance way and by the immaculate garden. The white marble structure is a mausoleum built to house the tomb of the emperor's favorite wife. His tomb is placed alongside. No shoes are allowed. After purchasing a ticket, each person is given a pair of slippers and a bottle of water.

A three-hour train ride brought me to New Delhi. Delhi and Old Delhi railroad stations are only one mile apart. This huge city has excellent transportation, an elevated train system, and many city buses, which are supplemented by bicycle rickshaws, tuk-tuks, and taxis. Best of all, many rooms and restaurants were within walking distance of the station.

An all-day metro pass was only 150 rupees. I took the Badarpur metro line for sightseeing and museums. I observed a nice park from the train and exited at Nehru station. Unfortunately, there was no access within a mile of the station. A strange park was accessible from Okhla station. There was razor wire on top of the park walls but I was able to enter through a broken gate. Inside were many native tropical plants, but all were tangled and unmanaged. There were many pigs, dogs, and sacred cows plus a few homeless people. The whole place had a rather spooky atmosphere. That evening I was waiting for a connecting train in a station infested by many white moths. A lone crow was having a feast, gobbling a moth every thirty seconds.

My plan was to see the Himalaya Mountains, not cities. I booked a sleeper car to Jammu, Kashmir, but needed to kill time during the day. While checking out of my room, I was surprised by a 10 percent surcharge insisted on by the manager. I guess this was to cover the finder's fee from the street hawker who brought me there. Anyway, he did let me store my bags. With another all-day metro pass, I toured the city and museums, had a great curry dinner, and then boarded the train.

Jammu is the end of the line, and the only way into the mountains is by minibus. Several inquiries led me to another part of town where mountain buses are dispatched early every morning. Passage is negotiated at a wide spot in the road at the edge of town.

After a short wait, I scored a 500-rupee ride to Srinagar and was on the way up the mountain before seven in the morning. The mountain trip is not for the faint of heart. First, they drive on the wrong side of the road, at least from my perspective. Second, the drivers all seem to be maniacs. The goal of each driver is to display his racing skills. If a bus has even a tiny bit more horsepower than the bus or truck ahead, the driver will pass it. The road is two lanes and not very wide. Passing on blind curves seems not to be a problem. In the event where two vehicles traveling in opposite directions happen to meet in the same lane, and the passer is blocked from pulling in, they screech to a stop a few feet from each other's bumper. The guilty passer sheepishly waves and then works his way back in behind the vehicle he was attempting to pass. Nobody ever passed my driver, so I guess he was the winner.

The views are spectacular. Steep cliffs rise above fast-moving rivers sometimes thousands of feet below. Snowcapped peaks are everywhere. Twice we passed through tribes of monkeys spaced along both sides of the road.

We reached Srinagar around four o'clock after two rest stops. There were soldiers everywhere. Kashmir and Pakistan have been having a border dispute ever since the line was drawn by Lord Mountbatten in 1947. Pakistan has since initiated two bloody intrusions into India. The border dispute is so intense that each country feels the need to develop nuclear weapons. The Border Security Force (BSF) maintains bases in all populated areas along the border, other areas being too steep. Tanks and armored vehicles seemed to be spaced every two hundred yards. Each soldier I saw packed an automatic weapon.

On exiting the bus, I was offered a room on a houseboat. For 600 rupees, I had a nice room on a wide, slow stream. People were relaxed and friendly along the stream, which provided a shady park-like environment. For 150 rupees, I had a dish called Hong Kong noodles—delicious.

The final trip up into the mountains required a tuk-tuk to Batamold, a minibus to Tangwav, and then another to Gulmarg. Gulmarg, a ski resort, is the end of the line. I am not sure of the altitude, but it was cold and hard to breathe, and it rained periodically. A two-stage cable car led to the summit, where the ninth-highest peak in the entire world could be viewed, inside Pakistan. It was disappointing. I had paid 600 rupees for a ride to the top and found the second stage was not operating, supposedly owing to snow fall at the top. It did not appear to be snowing to me. The view from Gulmarg was unspectacular; the mountains were smooth and rounded with some snow, not nearly as majestic as the California Sierra Nevada peaks.

Back in Srinagar, I went to the airport and found the only way to Spituk, nestled among some peaks near the Nepal border, was a flight from Delhi. That night I found another room on a houseboat and then returned to Delhi the same way I came.

With time running out, I decided to visit the Corbett wild animal park in Ramnagar to view wild tigers in their natural surroundings. I took an overnight train and arriving at four forty-five in the morning, I walked one and a half miles to a bus dispatch area. Nobody could give me directions to the park. Finally, I paid a tuk-tuk driver twenty rupees to take me there. The park entrance was only five hundred yards from where I started. Had I known the location I could easily have walked.

Early in his career, Jim Corbett was a hunter who shot many tigers, often to rid fearful villages of man-eaters. Later, as their numbers began rapidly dwindling, he began a crusade to protect them and created the sanctuary that I was attempting to visit. It had rained the night before, and sadly, the park did not allow vehicles on the wet roads, so it was closed.

My thoughts regarding India are as follows: I was disappointed that there were no records of the trading fort and early city of Goa, that the cable car at Gulmarg didn't run to the top, and that the Corbett tiger park was closed. People were generally friendly, and occasionally a person would offer a seat on the metro, but it was more common to see youngsters hogging the seats reserved for the aged and invalid. I have never seen so many line cutters in my life, mostly young people who generally responded to my stern stares and left. Rude pushing and shoving in lines was common, and I suppose that I wasn't mixing with the educated or gentlefolk. Loud pushy drivers attempt to intimidate pedestrians with horns continuously blowing. The whole place seemed to need a good scrubbing, and people threw trash everywhere. On a more positive note, the government has outlawed thin plastic shopping bags. The rail system was good, and the trains ran on time. The passes through the Kashmir Mountains were magnificent.

After first returning to Delhi, I flew to Jakarta to meet my wife, Annie, who was arriving from the United States by way of Japan. This was her first time in Indonesia, and I wanted her experience to be memorable. I brought her to the seedy Jalan Jaska area that I enjoyed. She wasn't crazy about it. I reserved a room at the Margo Hotel, but the bed was soft and worn out, so I took her across the alley to the Kresna Hostel, where I had been staying. It had a better bed at one-third the price.

We toured several museums at Jakarta Kota. She enjoyed the puppet museum most, which was a new one for me. The next day we visited Sunda Kalapa, the original Dutch trading area with a museum housed in two former VOC warehouses. This is one of my favorite places in Jakarta. This time the watchtower was open, and we climbed to the top. Try as I might, I could see no evidence of the harbor entrance to old Batavia, which had long ago silted up. She especially enjoyed the huge wooden fishing vessels in the "new" harbor, half a mile away. These large fishing boats have unusual lines with very steep bows and are painted with many bright colors.

We caught two trains to Rangkas Bitung, the first one electric and then a diesel for the ride through the gorgeous green country with many rice paddies and open spaces. Somehow my memory of the location of my cheap but good room was flawed. The frustrated driver eventually dropped us at the police station. Our good luck was meeting Sergeant Sigitarian Syah Rivai. This helpful and friendly fellow first took us to two expensive hotels but, following my clues, finally located Hotel Penginapan, the one I had been searching for. It is the first hotel on the right after crossing the river, two blocks before the train station. During the ride in his police car, we learned that he is trying to reach Africa as a soldier on a UN peacekeeping mission.

We stayed over in Rangkas to rest, do laundry, and wait for a Monday-morning bus to Labuan. Things were mostly nonscheduled at the bus station. Some drivers were doing maintenance on their own minibuses while others were waiting to fill theirs before departing for other destinations. I finally negotiated a ride with a taxi driver who managed to intercept a Labuan-bound bus coming from a northern city.

Much to my happy surprise, my friend Hendy had recently opened a small office in the Labuan bus station to promote local tours in the Sunda Strait to both Krakatau and a national park at the southwest corner of Java. I had met Hendy a year earlier, He had given me a tour of his family village with his three water buffalo, a visit to a working rice-harvest operation, and a stay at his home. Hendy took us one at a time on his motorcycle to his house.

Hendy's spouse, Ita Noveta Sari, a midwife herself, had just given birth to a baby girl the day before. Today she was carrying the newborn around the house with apparent ease. Amazing. Things were a little chaotic as the well pump had just failed and there was no water available for washing.

Hendy found us a room, and we bought him dinner while we planned a trip to Krakatau—actually, Son of Krakatau. For $400 we bought a tour out and back to this brand-new island, thirty-five miles away in the middle of the Sunda Strait.

We boarded a speedboat at eight the next morning for a fast, two-hour ride. The crew consisted of the owner-driver, an assistant, and Hendy. It was a beautiful, warm, and slightly overcast day. The boat slid to a smooth stop on a black-sand beach with barely any surf. Just beyond the beach is a sparkling new rain forest with birds, including parrots, and with at least one four-foot green iguana. The volcano, which first broke the surface in 1929, is now three thousand feet high. The rain forest that covers the eastern shore began sprouting in 1990. To us it could have been there forever. For an hour we climbed, to about eight hundred feet up the base of the mountain, which is as far as is allowed. The footing was difficult on the loose red lava chunks, and one slip drew blood. The view was spectacular. A small wisp of smoke emanating from the top, the rain forest below, and two beautiful ex-volcanos, each only two miles distant, with tropical-colored water lapping at their edges. The park service built two wooden tables for our enjoyment, and Hendy brought five delicious box lunches plus two pineapples and a melon. The setting was idyllic.

On the return trip, we cruised within fifty feet of a crescent-shaped island known as Mother of Krakatau. The nearby gray granite cliff, which drops straight down to the sea, was once part of the inside wall of a crater, now with one side blown away. These peaceful surroundings mask the violent danger lurking below. This spot rises directly above the intersection of two major faults. In 1889, so much molten lava tried to squeeze out of Krakatau that it exploded, killing thousands and spreading ash over the whole globe for two years. The same exact thing happened earlier to the island we were cruising past and would be the explosive end of this newest one at some unknown date in the future. It should be noted that several major cities are nearby, including Jakarta, Kuala Lumpur, and Singapore. If the blast and ash doesn't destroy them, then the subsequent tsunami will try.

When we returned to Carita Beach, we took off our shoes and waded the last ten feet to the shore, which was only a hundred yards from our hotel. We all had coffee, thanked Hendy for a fantastic day, and then bid him good-bye.

The next day we caught a minibus north to Merak; then for three dollars each, we took the ferry across the Sunda Strait to Sumatra. It is interesting to note that it was impossible to avoid cigarette smoke on the ferry. Receiving huge contributions from the tobacco industry, the government is making no attempt to curtail smoking in Indonesia. Malaysia, a hundred miles to the north, is making some effort. The two-hour ride was smooth across flat water with an occasional island and no view of Krakatau.

I wanted Annie to get the flavor of Sumatra, so we caught a bus south twenty-eight kilometers to Kalianda. It was another two-kilometer motorcycle ride to town. The guidebook touted the Beringin Hotel, where a room was only eight dollars. There was nothing special about the town; it was definitely not set up to attract tourists. Unable to locate a restaurant, we were attracted by a sign in the window of a small house. The family put together a very tasty meal. All of them spoke English, and the five young children were very inquisitive. We had a fun time, and all engaged in a photo op.

We caught an air-conditioned bus for the return trip, and I negotiated the price down to ten dollars for both of us. Following a search for drugs, the bus, to our surprise, entered the ferry and then took us all the way to Jakarta. Annie wanted to scale up, so we hired a tuk-tuk ride to the Borobudur Hotel, where a room was only $137 per night. The hotel is named after the famous Buddhist temple, which we wished to see but, owing to time constraints and a holiday, were unable to. This hotel, set on four acres, has an Olympic-sized pool, three tennis courts, a spa, and elaborate gardens. There is also a small replica of the famous temple.

Following two nights of luxury and a visit to the central museums, we booked a room and a flight to Bali. There is nothing like swimming in the eighty-degree water of Kuda Beach. It is a fine white-sand beach that descends slowly into the Indian Ocean, so slowly in fact that you are eighty yards from the surf before your head is underwater. What a perfect place to learn surfing.

The next day we hired a taxi to Ulu Watu, the southwest corner of Bali, and toured the grounds of the Hindu Pura Belam temple. The cliffs drop two hundred feet to the sea, and there is much evidence that the walls have been moved farther inland due to erosion. The view is spectacular, especially with some whales swimming below. The place is the home for many thieving monkeys. I lost a plastic water bottle, and a lady nearby lost a camera to them. They study their victims carefully and are very quick to take advantage of a careless moment.

The next stop was Blue Point, one of my favorite places and only a few miles to the north. You climb down steps to a cave-like grotto with sunlight reflecting off the walls and ceiling. The shallow sandy pool ebbs and flows with the surf. Concrete steps lead to a restaurant sixty feet above. There we enjoyed a beer and sandwich with a 180-degree view of the Indian Ocean. Three-quarter-inch clear plastic panels provide shelter from the elements, but there is an outside table with a completely unobstructed view. On the swells below were at least thirty surfers.

Time was becoming a factor, and after only two days we flew to Makassar. Makassar is the major city of Sulawesi (formerly Celebes). This large island is bisected by the equator and is shaped like a dancing man with limbs extending to the east. On arrival, we purchased a plan to visit Toraja, and that night we were on a three-hundred-kilometer bus ride north.

In the morning, we were met by our guide, Marno, who began our tour after allowing us a brief rest. Toraja is located mostly inside the crater of a huge extinct volcano that self-destructed eons ago. All that is left of the crater walls is a steep crescent-shaped ridge to the northeast, which is studded with many spires. The circular area bounding Toraja is about forty kilometers in diameter, and the surface is covered with lush green farmland. To understand the strange Torajan culture and their burial rights requires understanding their creation myth.

In the beginning all the Torajans enjoyed access to and from heaven with a long ladder. Everything was fine and idyllic until someone stole the fire from heaven. God became enraged and removed the ladder. It was cold and dark, and the people became very sad. Two thousand years ago, God lowered a house containing his grandson on two long ropes, one attached to each end. The weight caused the roof to sag. The sagging roof design is incorporated into all Torajan houses and grain-storage buildings. One end of each house incorporates a painting consisting of a black-and-white rooster. They face one another from each corner, and cockfights are used to resolve all serious disputes.

God's grandson mixed with the people, and all village chiefs are his direct descendants. He laid down a list of rules for entry to heaven; one required a blood sacrifice of humans, pigs, and water buffalos. Until seven hundred years ago, all islanders were headhunters. This practice was curtailed with the arrival of the Muslim traders, and human sacrifice became no longer acceptable. Following the arrival of the Portuguese traders, most Torajans accepted Christianity.

Marno gave us a grand tour of the countryside and several villages. All about were lush green rice fields and vegetable crops with plenty of chickens, pigs, and buffalo. Each village had two rows of sagging-roofed buildings comprising two-story houses and equally tall grain-storage sheds. Most buildings were painted and in excellent shape. Each village had a communal grain-storage shed to provide for the less fortunate.

Enabling close relatives' entry to heaven is a prime consideration for all Torajans and can consume tremendous effort and as much as 70 percent of their income. Insured entry can require sacrificing multiple buffalos, a white one costing up to $8,000. Pigs are much cheaper. When all the required animals have been gathered together, they are killed and eaten in a massive ceremony enjoyed by all the villagers.

Following the death of a relative, the body is bled, then injected with formalin, and placed inside a coffin for the long wait to complete the qualification process. Preferred burial is inside solid rock, but less fortunate relatives are interred in wooden buildings. We stopped alongside a thirty-foot-diameter boulder, which two men were hollowing out with hammers and chisels. Progress was only a few inches per day. When completed it would entomb thirty bodies, each stacked on a horizontal wooden shelf.

We attended a party celebrating the opening of a new Catholic church. In front, there was a large tent covering two hundred folding chairs in long rows, serving as a free sit-down restaurant. Bands took turns playing lively music in front of a PA system while a long parade of teenaged children joyfully bounced and swayed hundred-pound pigs trapped in boxlike containers mounted on twin poles for easy carrying.

Finally, Marno took us to his own village and upstairs in his house. He opened a coffin and proudly showed us his ninety-year-old mother, who had died three years earlier. She was very well preserved and would soon be entombed after a giant ceremony and the sacrifice of three buffalos and many pigs.

Back in Makassar I showed Annie Fort Rotterdam, which was captured from the Portuguese by the Dutch. I inquired about my friend Abdul Rahman, whom I had met the previous year. From his mentor, Mohammed Muyazdlala, we learned that after completing final exams as an English teacher, he was performing a community service requirement 150 kilometers distant. In the fall, he would become a full-time teacher.

We arrived at Sultan Babulla Airport and began our tour of Ternate, my favorite island. The first order of business was to meet my friend Suratman through his mentor, Ibraham. I didn't recognize Ibraham's house—he was redoing the front—so I inquired of a neighbor, who set me straight. Ibraham was home and introduced us to his wife, Mulxati, and his two daughters, Nurlita and Rahmawati. While he entertained us on his front porch, we learned that Suratman had also completed his teaching requirements and was doing his community service at a remote location. Ibraham made a call on his cell phone, and Achy Soamole arrived fifteen minutes later.

I had met Achy the previous year when Suratman had invited me to meet his fellow English, students from the university. She agreed to give us a tour of the island and asked whether she could bring her boyfriend, Icon, whom I had also met before. The next day I rented a taxi, and the four of us began a counterclockwise tour of Ternate.

The first stop was fort Benteng Tolluco, commissioned by Magellan's friend Francisco Serrao, who was the first Portuguese ambassador. Suratman had taken me there, last year, but it had been closed due to slippery conditions. This very substantial fort comprised of red lava blocks was set on a cliff two hundred feet above the sea and was completed in 1540. It had provisions for six cannons.

The second stop was Batuangus cemetery, located on the north shore. Before the arrival of the Portuguese, the volcano that had created Ternate erupted, spewing hot ash, lava, and huge ten-foot-diameter boulders. This event killed over six hundred natives; most of them are buried nearby. A marker consisting of small hand-placed chunks of coral, set back one hundred feet from the shore, commemorates the tragic event.

Continuing on, we stopped at Sulamadaha Beach and paid a one-dollar entrance fee. This sheltered black-sand beach with picnic tables provided fun for many children and their families plus an anchorage for small fishing vessels. In the distance was a tiny island.

The next stop was Tolire Lake, three hundred feet below and nestled against the base of the volcano. This beautiful uninhabited lake hides a sad story: when a young girl was molested and killed there by a close relative, the gods, with the threat of an eruption, forced everyone to leave this gorgeous place. For a small price, we enjoyed a hot meal with barbequed corn on the cob and hot tea high above the lake.

Now on Ternate's windward side, which receives over three hundred days of rain every year, Annie saw her first clove tree. It was the end of August, and all the cloves had been picked a month earlier. Only the precious seeds were missing from the forty-foot-high tree shimmering in the breeze. Nearby, close to the road, Annie picked a tennis-ball-sized nutmeg from a tree ready to be harvested. A week after the nutmeg ball falls or is removed from the tree, it splits open, exposing the one-sixteenth-inch red mace covering the nut. The mace is removed from the nut, and both parts are dried in the sun on separate plastic tarps by the side of the road. These are closely watched and must be quickly covered when rain comes.

We continued on, then turned right onto a narrow road, and in a hundred yards stopped in front of a twenty-five-foot-high monument. On the top stood a giant six-foot replica of a red clove. The white five-foot-by-five-foot, four-sided structure proclaimed a story in bas relief pictures and words, each side depicting a scene. The Portuguese traders were welcomed in 1511, but in 1571 Jorge de Castro murdered the sultan in an act of rage, sinking a knife into his neck. The natives responded by killing all the traders in the fort. The final scene depicts the eviction of the Portuguese, all to be gone by year's end 1575, never to return, under penalty of death. The mostly disassembled ruins of fort Benteng Kastela are located behind the monument and was being enjoyed by a cow eating the lush green grass.

The rocky shore two hundred yards beyond the monument was where the ships were loaded with the precious cloves. No signs of any piers or wharfs could be seen, but back toward the interior was a 6-foot-high and 200-foot-long stucco wall that served as a sign board. Six different scenes were painted on the wall depicting the Portuguese trading effort from start to finish.

The final stop was at the fort Benteng Kalamata, which has been mostly restored. It is situated on the shore at the closest point to the island of Tidore, only two miles distant. Following the sultan's murder, the traders moved to Tidore for a short period before being evicted by the Dutch. All the above stops were covered in greater detail in the 2013 trip.

Back in town I tipped the taxi driver, thanked him for a great ride, and then took our friends, Achy and Icon, to dinner.

The government was constructing a new museum adjacent to the Sultan's Palace, but the artifacts were yet to be moved from the palace. My favorite things inside are the two suits of Portuguese armor, a gift to the sultan from

Francisco Serrao in 1511. The custom was to gift the sultan prior to discussing any business. My hope was to hold and examine the pieces and then photograph one of my friends actually wearing a suit. Things like that would be impossible in Europe. Ibraham was to help me but was unable to swing it. He promised "next year."

On my last day in Ternate, a man named Amin asked me to speak to the students at Valiant Club. This private school, with students ranging from primary grades clear up to high school, focuses on teaching English. Rusdi A. Karim, educated in Holland, is the headmaster. The children are very inquisitive and eager to practice English and learn the customs of foreigners. Standing in front of the class, fielding questions from these eager students, was a real ego boost; I felt almost as if I were some sort of celebrity. You can just feel the love. One nine-year-old girl raised her hand fifteen times with questions. After the students were dismissed, I was invited into a back room to eat, drink, and discuss life with Rusdi and his staff. I love Ternate and its wonderful people.

We flew to Kuala Lumpur and then took a two-hour bus ride to Malacca so Annie could experience this historic city. She was especially impressed with the Maritime Museum, whose entrance was located up inside a replica of a Portuguese Nao cargo ship.

Our next stop was Nairobi, Kenya, to assist a PINCC (Prevention International Cervical Cancer) medical team with a mission to eliminate cervical cancer in women. We met Carol Cruickshank, the team leader, then flew to Kisumu, and finally a minivan ride to Muhuroni, where we stayed.

Monday morning, we set up shop in Saint Vincent's Hospital, Muhuroni, and were up and running two hours later with two examination rooms. The goal was to screen local women for cervical cancer. It had been discovered that swabbing a 7 percent solution of ordinary white vinegar on the cervix (the opening to the womb) will provide a simple and reliable test for cancer. After allowing two minutes for the vinegar to react, a skilled doctor, trained midwife, or nurse is able to make a decision. In some cases, a lengthier test using iodine is required. Owing to the remote location and time constraints, the earlier-established procedure of taking a small piece of tissue and sending it out for lab analysis was not practical.

By the second day there were three exam rooms, and Jean, a gynecologist from Boston, had the final word in case of doubt. About 35 percent of the women were HIV positive, a sad commentary on the state of affairs in Africa. Happily, most of the women were cancer-free. An unfortunate few were incurable, but this clinic was able to remove tissue with an electrically heated wire or by using a cryogenic (freezing) method and provide a cure for the luckier ones.

Annie and I were assistants. She assisted in the exam room while I washed and sanitized the silverware (vaginal speculums), interviewed and filled out questionnaire forms, did gopher jobs, and occasionally held hands in the exam rooms.

The team was comprised of very interesting folks. Carol, the team leader and only non-volunteer, made all the reservations and insured that all necessary equipment was on hand. Dr. Jean had the final say on any medical decisions. Her husband, Eric, was a scientist from Woods Hole Institute. Madeline was a nurse practitioner–midwife from Berkeley. Jan was a public defender also from Berkeley. Donna was a retired school teacher from Jackson, California. Ann was a nurse practitioner from Utah. My wife Annie was a retired graphic designer. We all enjoyed rapping in the evenings.

The original plan was to create a second clinic in a slum of Nairobi. Carol determined that the environment there was too dangerous and canceled that week. We now had time to kill and needed to make the most of it. We all returned to Nairobi, where Madeline decided on a safari. Annie and I thought it was a splendid idea and signed up to accompany her.

We flew Safari Link Airlines to a remote airfield located on a grassy ridge. The airport infrastructure consisted of two buildings and a yellow wind sock. One building housed two toilets at the end of a dirt runway. A second tiny building, when the panels were opened, revealed a counter and was where national park fees were collected. The park entrance fee was eighty dollars cash per person per day. At the landing field, we were met by our driver-guide, Tongkai, who explained the operation and began finding animals along the ten-mile drive to the camp. We were introduced to lions, giraffes, cheetahs, Thomson gazelles, and warthogs along the way, all in their natural environment.

The camp, named Masai Mara, is located inside a 270-degree bend in the Talek River. A fence at the open side completes the perimeter of the compound. In the center is an open-walled structure that houses the food preparation area, tables, and chairs for the guests. In the rear are six large white tents. The tents, consisting of two compartments—bedroom and flush-toilet bathroom—are made of substantial material and incorporate a sewn-in floor. Ours had a high-walled outdoor hot-water shower. What a treat to shower in the warm sun. The meals, which included desserts, were all prepared by a chef, and each was delicious. At night, we were guarded by Masai warriors, who wielded heavy seven-foot-long and very sharp steel spears.

At nine in the morning, we piled into the Toyota Land Cruiser and began our second outing. Tongkai, a thirty-five-year-old Masai warrior, had been studying animals since he was five and was the senior guide. We began a long drive to another section of the Talek, where the river was much fuller. This place contained many crocodiles, who waited under water with only their nostrils out or, when full, sunned themselves on muddy islands. Spaced away from the crocs were groups of up to thirty hippos happily eating grass on the river bottom. The land away from the river was extremely dry and littered with the bones of slower creatures.

Lions lay around near the river in small groups, knowing that their prey must eventually seek water. Elephants kept together in large groups under the leadership of a senior female. The biggest attraction was always the baby elephant, who seemed to enjoy the attention of the entire group. Gazelles browsed in large herds, always alert for predators. Occasionally, a herd of wildebeests could be seen following a huge migratory circle that crossed into Tanzania. Giraffes with their long necks could be seen from a mile away while grazing in groups of three to five.

In the early mornings, shortly after sunrise, as many as half a dozen colorful hot-air balloons could be seen taking off with a bright blast of propane. On the ground the buzzard cleanup crew was busy picking the bones from the night's kill. These birds were reluctant to share, and the younger, weaker, and more timid ones had a long wait for breakfast scraps.

On the third day, we managed to observe a cheetah stalking a herd of Thompson gazelles from a distance of about eighty yards. The vehicle didn't seem to distract her, and most of the creatures we observed paid no attention to them. She was observing from behind a five-foot boulder. The gazelles were aware but did not run, and slowly increased their distance while still nervously grazing. It turned out to be a Mexican standoff. The cheetah has a slight speed advantage over the gazelles, who can twist and turn on a dime. To be successful, the cat must start the chase within fifty yards of the prey, and the kill rate is about 50 percent. Cheetahs are thoroughly exhausted after a chase and take many hours to recover. To help insure success, they seek out injured, infirm or younger slower animals.

Tongkai did his best to show us everything there was to see. The rarest animals are the leopard and black rhino. We never glimpsed a leopard but eventually saw a rhino twice, possibly the same one. In the hunt for the elusive rhino, whose numbers keep dwindling from poaching, we crossed many muddy streams. The four-wheel-drive Land Cruiser has a snorkel five feet above ground, and the engine is sealed against brief exposure to water. In his search, he was able to successfully ford every creek and mud hole, even when water came up within a foot of the windows. The black rhino, which is actually dark gray, never fully exposed itself, and we were never to glimpse more than the upper 50 percent of its body.

A final note regarding the camp: President Obama, when he was a senator, brought his family here while introducing them to his Kenyan relatives. He, his wife, and his two daughters each planted a thorny tree (yellow-barked acacia, or fever tree) on the camp grounds, and the area is now known as the Obama Forest.

We flew back to Nairobi, bid good-bye to Madelyn, and visited the Kenya National Museum. On display are over a thousand stuffed birds, a live member from every native reptile family, and mounted animals in their natural settings. The crown jewel of the exhibits is the early-man display inside a fireproof glass vault. Kenya and Tanzania are the countries where the earliest hominoids were discovered, and this is Kenya's finest collection. On display are bones discovered by Richard Leakey; his wife, Mary; and his son. Not included are their specimens from Olduvai Gorge, Tanzania.

With a few days left before our flights, we hired a taxi to Lake Naivasha in the Great Rift Valley, only eighty miles from Nairobi. On the way, we had a spectacular view from the eight-thousand-foot rim to the valley three thousand feet below, with the rift extending far beyond what the eye could see.

Nearby is a national park named Hell's Gate. For my seventy-fifth birthday, I rented a bike to explore the park. The bicycle was a basic model with no springs on either the front forks or the seat. The road through the park's canyon is graded dirt exhibiting tractor tread marks everywhere. I chose a twelve-kilometer loop route, the shortest one. The canyon view was wonderful and contained animals in their natural habitat. I rode past zebras, gazelles, warthogs, and water buffalo. One time, after a fall caused from hitting loose powdery dirt, I rested under a shady tree. Directly across the road, a hundred feet away, was a small herd of buffalos, also enjoying the shade. Apparently, I was the main attraction, and they never took their eyes off me. These are the most dangerous animals in the park, more so than the alleged cheetahs and leopards, which I never saw.

Carefully reviewing the map, I made a left turn at a junction to follow the loop. I found it easier to walk the bike uphill toward the rim. Eventually, I came to a paved road, turned left, and kept riding. The road led to a huge geothermal steam plant with a dozen modular generators all under one roof. This is a huge operation with twelve-inch insulated pipes running for miles. I passed two well-drilling operations on the way, each destined to supply more steam.

At the end of the paved road, on top of a hill, I questioned a worker for directions regarding the loop trail; there were no signs. Following his directions, I came to a gate guarded by two young girls with very bad teeth and minimal English. They had no knowledge of the loop trail and pointed back to a road I had just passed. This road led to a paved road, and unknowingly I ended up backtracking. When I realized what had happened, I located the turnoff where I had entered, and retraced my route. The twelve kilometers became more like twenty, and I fell down at least four times. I was completely exhausted when I returned the bike and called the driver for a ride back to the hotel. While pedaling, I collected three beautiful specimens of sharp black flint, the material of spear points and arrowheads. You never find this rock in California as the native Indians picked it clean eons ago.

On our last day, we picked a trip to Elsamere, ten miles away on the shore of Lake Naivasha. This twenty-acre site is the former home of Joy Adamson, the featured character in the movie *Born Free*. Elsamere is named for Elsa the lioness.

Joy's husband was sent to track down Elsa's mother, who had become dangerous and had killed a native. On hearing of the death of the mother, Joy went to the scene and brought home and raised the two cubs. Joy and Elsa became fast friends. Over time the young lions were returned to the wild, but the most touching part of the story was when Elsa proudly showed off her new cubs to Joy.

Joy was also a gifted portrait artist, and more than two hundred of her works are on display in the National Museum. This site is currently used as an environmental training center with a mission to educate local children. We enjoyed a marvelous lunch served in the living room of Joy's former house after a delightful hike on the grounds.

Annie flew home, but I continued on to South Africa. At Cape Town, I attempted to score a boat ride around the Cape of Good Hope and made a visit the Royal Cape Yacht Club. Unfortunately, I was unable to connect. The clubs premier annual event is the Cape town to Rio race.

From a room on Long Street, I explored the city, the library, and museums. The National Museum houses a huge dinosaur exhibit and planetarium. Many fossils were discovered in the process of mining. Table Mountain rises vertically over eight hundred feet directly behind Cape Town. A tram connects to the top, and I enjoyed a sunny afternoon with an unblocked view of the city, Table Bay, the South Atlantic, and the mountains to the east. The local weather, which can be very gusty, often forms a heavy fog in the morning that dramatically spills over the edge of Table Mountain.

The first Europeans to view the area were the members of the 1488 Dias expedition but apparently, they never made landfall. The first to visit were the crew of Portuguese explorer António da Saldanha in 1503. He named the mountain and the bay after himself and then departed after filling his casks with fresh water. In 1510 Francisco de Almeida also pulled in, obtained water, claimed it for Portugal, and then raised anchor and left. Eighty-one years later British commander James Lancaster pulled in, obtained water, and then left after describing it in his log as a "good baie." In 1620 the British laid claim to Cape Town but never established a fort or permanent buildings. Finally, the Dutch, with the goal of provisioning their fleet, established residence. In 1652 Governor Jan van Rieback built a fort and planted a seventeen-acre garden in what is now the center of town. Under direction of the VOC's Lords Seventeen, he began creating the necessary infrastructure of the present city.

With a yearning to see more and to track the explorers, I rented a car. The first stop was the Cape of Good Hope. The tip of the cape forms a point with two cliffs and is over two hundred feet above the South Atlantic, providing a magnificent panoramic view of water and mountains. From that height, there was no apparent current but considerable wind from the southeast. Points of interest included the lighthouse and a museum with heavy emphasis on shipwrecks. The cape is known for its wild flowers, but I could find only half a dozen.

I continued along the coast for about 100 miles, my next major point of interest being Cape Agulhas. This is the southernmost point of Africa and separates the Indian Ocean from the South Atlantic. The sea is shallow and very rocky, and the apparent four-knot Agulhas current, pushed by southeast winds, beckons any unlucky vessel onto the shore. The museum next to the lighthouse describes over a hundred shipwrecks. Typical causes are engine or steering failure; blown-out sails, halyards, or sheets; emergency anchor failure; being overpowered in a storm; or simply running too close to shore. The cape is patiently awaiting its next victim.

My next stop was a wonderful visit to Mossel Bay. I happen to be a railroad nut and ate and slept aboard a string of parked passenger cars located only two hundred feet from the edge of the bay. The highlight of the trip was a visit to the Dias museum the following morning.

In 1488 Bartolomeu Dias was sailing south down the African coast against the wind and current. On a hunch, he set a course farther to sea and found the going faster and easier. Thirteen days later he steered toward shore to avoid a squall and re-establish the coast. To everyone's surprise there was no land. Proceeding north he found the coast to be running east-west. Dias had made history as the first European to round both capes of Africa. He continued along the coast, searching for water and provisions, and put in at Mossel Bay, where he found both.

To commemorate this event 500 years later, Portugal built a full-sized replica of a caravel and in 1988 sailed it from Lisbon to Mossel Bay. South Africa created a museum, and the *Bartolomeu Dias* was placed inside. What a treat for me to walk the decks and inspect this magnificent re-creation.

The caravel, designed under the influence of Prince Henry the Navigator, was the first ship able to "go to weather," actually sail into the wind. The spars at the top of the two masts can support conventional square sails for running downwind or be rigged to slant forward and create triangular sails to beat into the wind. The excess sail was then gathered parallel to the deck, and later actual triangular sails were cut. This innovative design enabled the Portuguese to become the world's first blue water seafarers.

My curiosity now drove me to explore the interior. That afternoon, after leaving the coast and passing through a town named Rust, the highway entered a magnificent canyon. Over eons the river had carved down through the red rock and left room for only itself and the winding road at the bottom. The sunset illuminating the thousand-foot-high steep red walls provided a dramatic close to one of my most memorable days. Continuing on for two more hours across an immense flatland, I arrived in Beaufort West, in the very center of South Africa.

The next point of interest was the Kimberly diamond mine far to the northeast. Driving almost continually across the dry flatland, similar to the American Southwest, with mountains rising from the plains like islands, I spent the night in Bloemhof. I must have been tired and lost my glasses when I exited the car to rent a room. A sixty-year-old woman signed me in, and I proceeded to unpack. Later, while searching for the missing glasses, I managed to lock myself out of the room. It was around ten at night when I returned to the closed office and met the husband of the lady who checked me in and who by now had retired. Rather than assisting me, he became belligerent and even accused me of being drunk. This obstinate man had obviously been drinking; at least two empty wine bottles were visible on his table. The conversation became heated, and he said that if I didn't leave, he would call the police. Fortunately for me, the noise awakened his wife, who kindly let me back into the room. This obviously unstable man was the only unpleasant person that I encountered on the entire trip.

The next morning, I found the missing glasses on the ground in the dirt where I had first exited the car. They were brightly illuminated from the early-morning sun and, fortunately, were undamaged.

Arriving in Kimberly around two, I followed the signs to "The Big Hole". The Kimberly mine has been shut down since World War II. The grounds are now operated as a concession. There is a small railroad station at the mine, and Rhodes's private car is on display. The tour begins with a movie and is followed with a stop at the rim of the three-quarter-mile-wide hole where millions of dollars' worth of diamonds had been mined.

The round hole is over five thousand feet deep and is now filled with greenish water rising to five hundred feet from the surface. The rock has a light-blue color, and chunks can be examined in steel mining cars nearby. Across from the giant hole, the town of Kimberly begins within three hundred feet of the rim.

It was discovered that diamonds could be found inside the rock of miniature volcanos. The carbon, squeezed under immense pressures and temperatures possible only deep within the bowels of the earth, formed the diamonds, which are the hardest and most beautiful stones on earth, though it is possible to synthesize them in a lab. There are nine mines currently capable of producing diamonds, all under monopolistic control of De Beers.

Following the rim tour, the group is led into a large elevator, which descends extremely slowly to a fake underground tunnel carved to simulate original mining conditions. Recorded sounds are broadcast throughout to create a mine atmosphere. Following that, a door opens into a large museum with displays of interest about the operation. In the center is a huge walk-in vault with copies of large and famous necklaces, brooches, and pins. Alongside are smaller real diamonds, most for sale.

For a final treat, I decided to visit Victoria Falls. I stopped in Potchefstroom to make travel arrangements. Because it was Thursday and I wished to visit the park Friday and Saturday before returning the rental car on Monday morning, I had to pay a premium. For $967 I booked a round-trip flight from Johannesburg to the town of Victoria Falls, Zimbabwe. Included was a room with breakfast and an evening river cruise on the Zambezi River. On a bad hunch, I drove into downtown Johannesburg, looking for cheap lodging. What I found was traffic congestion in a huge unfamiliar city. Two hours later, after dodging hordes of jaywalkers, I cleared the city limits and found the airport. I wasted another two hours searching for a cheap room and ended up paying $75 close to in to the airport.

It was a two-hour flight over very dry and barren country with much evidence of mining. Zimbabwe is tied to US currency, and the local ATMs spit out US dollars. Everything was very rushed. I checked into the hotel at three and squeezed in a quick walk to the Zambezi River gorge before meeting a four o'clock minivan ride to the evening river-cruise entrance. The gorge is two hundred feet deep with fast-moving green water—very scenic. The walls are vertical, and if the river had been higher, this would have been part of the falls. Immediately on my leaving the hotel compound, local hustlers fell in step with me, attempting to sell beautiful hand-carved dark-brown hardwood animal statues. The statues were extremely cheap, but I didn't have time to barter and just barely met my ride.

The three-quarter-mile-wide but very shallow river upstream from the falls gives life to the extremely arid countryside. The slow awning-covered barge with tables and chairs, open on four sides, provided a perfect view. For twenty dollars extra, there were unlimited alcoholic drinks and delicious snacks. Visible animals were the usual zebras, buffalo, warthogs, hippos, and gazelles, but no lions were to be seen. The highlight was watching an elephant cross the river. Most of the way he could stand up, but eventually he had to swim. I didn't know elephants had that ability. He used his trunk as a giant snorkel. Sitting next to me was a man from Arizona named Mike. He had recently published a book using Amazon and offered to give me some tips when I was ready.

Saturday morning had a hectic beginning. At the last minute, I decided to book a thirteen-minute helicopter ride for an aerial view of the falls. The lady who makes reservations didn't show until eight fifteen, fifteen minutes late. Next she had trouble with the credit card reader but found another source, and eventually I reserved a nine thirty flight for $130.

The chopper kept running while discharging the previous group and included me in the next seven passengers. This ride, though expensive, was worth every penny. The view was magnificent and provided a perspective of everything. The river was 75 percent full, and so were the falls. Upstream the wide river tapered and twisted to the horizon and was bounded by the parched earth. Downstream was a powerhouse that stole some of the thunder from one of the scenic wonders of the world. It was a photo op for all and was over much too quickly.

By now it was late morning, and I still hadn't seen the falls up close. Walking quickly, I covered the three-quarter-mile walk to the park entrance in twenty minutes and paid the thirty-dollar entrance fee, and there it was: tons of water pouring down from a two-hundred-foot ledge as far as I could see. I watched it from two more vistas, each better than the last, but the falls were too close and wide for a full panoramic view from any one spot on the ground. I could stay for only half an hour lest I miss the ride to the airport. I happened to be fortunate that this was the dry season. The paradox is that with a full flow from the Zambezi, all you can see is mist.

Hurrying back toward the hotel, I encountered the vendors again. I had promised one a sale and obtained a five animal, hand carved hardwood set, each about five inches long, for fifty dollars. I asked him how long he spent carving them. He said thirty days.

I had hoped to clear customs and exit the airport quickly but hadn't written down the car's parking-place info. Fortunately, I remembered the deck level and that it was located facing out from the edge near one corner. I found it in the third corner with the help of an electronic key but then couldn't exit because the card reader didn't like my ticket stub. Eventually, Freddy, a friendly attendant, made a phone call to let me out. By now it was dark, Saturday night, and the car needed to be at Cape Town, 1,100 kilometers away, on Monday morning.

I was traveling the north-south toll road on the return trip, reasonably fast and straight. If a car makes really good time between toll gates, it can generate an electronic ticket. I didn't have that problem, but after following a slow truck up a hill for ten minutes, I found the only safe spot to pass but had to cross a double line to do it. It was a trap, and a policewoman flagged me down from the center of the road at the bottom of the hill. After I sheepishly listened to her scolding, I was notified the fine was $200. Luckily for me she let me off with just the scolding.

I returned the car on time, caught my flight, and returned home on Air Emirates through Dubai and then across Russia, the North Pole, and down to San Francisco. As I complete the write-up of this adventure, I have no desire to board another airliner for a long time to come; my curiosity has been well satisfied.

The highlight of the trip for me was walking the deck of the Dias. Victoria Falls were magnificent especially from above. I had always been fascinated by early hominids and the state museum in Nairobi contained samples of more than a dozen. It was a thrill to visit "Son of Krakatau" with the brand new rain forest and to slowly cruise by the vertical walls of the blown out crater nearby.

I enjoyed reuniting with Hendy but missed Atman and Abdul. I am looking forward to presenting all my friends with an autographed copy of this book which they inspired. I think they will be proud to read their own names in the acknowledgement.

2017 Wrap-Up

My primary objective for this trip was to obtain permission to use personal photos for this book and to pass out free copies to the persons who inspired me to do this project. The secondary objective was to visit islands Banda Run, Banda Niera and Tidore.

The trip got off to a frustrating start. United Airlines in a matter of self-protection wouldn't allow me to board without a visa or a document showing that I would exit Indonesia inside of 30 days. I always try to wing it so that I have the flexibility for last minute opportunities. I gave in and using my cell phone (didn't bring a computer) called Cheapo air and arranged for a return ticket exactly four weeks later. I had arrived 3 hours early. With me unable to produce a printout and UAL unable to contact Philippine Air prior to the departure cutoff, they issued me a ticket for the next day.

Arriving in Jakarta 3 days later, first day lost, second day stolen by the international date line and the third was actual travel time via Tokyo, I booked a ticket in the future 3 days to Ternate. I then boarded an express bus to Merak. My goal was to link up with Hendy in Lebuan. Merak was a mistake, I should have exited in Serang where a direct route is available. Interestingly nobody in Merak knew how to reach Lebaun including the members of the police station and I obtained the answer by querying each passing bus.

I had mistakenly thought that I could communicate with my smart phone with-out paying extra to AT&T, by using Skype or another mode. I was blocked and couldn't even down load anything. Unable to communicate, I proceeded to Hendy's front door but found nobody home. By checking with his nearby village, I found that he was in Jakarta for the weekend. A friend had his cell number and we arranged to meet the following afternoon. Meanwhile I got a ride to a cheap hotel. While ordering dinner nearby, I met Yudi. Juniardi

Yudi gave me some tips on what to order then we discussed what we were each doing. Now that I can describe myself as a writer, people are eager to rap with me. Yudi is a builder and is in the process of constructing over 500 residential and commercial units all surrounding a lake in Lebaun. He had Sunday off and insisted on picking me up and entertaining me while not allowing me to pay for anything. After hanging out at Carita Beach and feeding me at an expensive restaurant, he dropped me off at Hendy's. In return I gave him an autographed copy of the book.

Hendy put me up in his place, signed a release for his photo then took me to a wedding reception. Next day he showed me the village vegetable garden. We had to cross the highway and walk 300 meters through the forest. It was impressive with about 3 acres of string beans, cucumbers, tomatoes and much more, all under cultivation. Along the way, he picked up a very strange looking fruit. The Indonesian name is snaket. It has the exact look and texture of rough snake skin. Using his knife to cut it in half, it had an interesting sweet flavor. Now with a new awareness, I noticed them for sale several times in the marketplace.

Next, we visited the rice processing plant. After the harvested rice is dried on tarps in the sun, it must undergo the hulling process. It must pass through two identical looking machines. The first loosens the hull and the second removes it. Next it is run through a shaker where full length grains are separated from broken smaller ones. Finally, it is placed in 60 kilo bags. Following the tour and after a big hug, I boarded a bus back to Serang then an express to the Airport.

All of Indonesia is on "Island Time" including the airlines. People live a life of much lower stress then in the U.S. They all get along with each other and don't appear to harbor any anger. The people are friendly and eager to assist any one in difficulty (more on this later dealing with Lion Airlines). I arrived at the airport 4 hours early for a 1:30 am flight to Ternate. It was an all-night wait, finally boarding at 5:30 am.

3 hours later I was at Sultan Babulla airport, Ternate, walking on the tarmac heading for the baggage claim. My backpack displays "CERT" in 3

HASYIM

inch letters which stand for Community Emergency Response Team. This was issued to me by the Marin county disaster department following a 2-day class. It attracted the attention of Amir who thought I might be a safety engineer.

Amir is a mining engineer and is Deputy Director of the NHM gold mine located on the adjacent island of Halmahera. He insisted on giving me a ride into town but first took me to his home for conversation and a delicious meal. Following that and showing much patience we attempted to locate the home of my friend Ibrahim Umakamea. It didn't look the same from the street as in 2014 which looked different than it was in 2013. Later I found it on foot. Next, we attempted to locate rooms I previously had stayed in, one I couldn't find and other with no vacancy. Eventually we found a homestay next to Masjid Muhajirin mosque, just a few hundred meters from the seaport entrance. Amir will receive a copy of the finished book.

This homestay has 16 rooms, is clean and new with air conditioning and a sit-down toilet. It rents for just $13/day. It includes a real breakfast, cooked by the owners-wife, Kartina, in a restaurant downstairs. Both Kartina and her husband Abs were gracious hosts, she making phone calls and even negociated a low priced ride to the airport, he giving me a ride to my friend Rusdi's school, inviting me for a meal at the mosque and showing me where to find maps. Ternate Kota is the only "dry" town I found in Indonesia. He did inform me that there would be "no wine and no women". This couple will also receive a book

Following a nap, I took off on foot seeking Ibrahim Umakamea. The reason I couldn't identify his place from the street was because the front had been completely remodeled. Giant steel roll up doors now concealed a large classroom area located in front of his home, all under one roof.

Ibrahim was home, signed my release and welcomed a photo op with his family. One of his daughters is attending the university. He is now running a formal English school while before it was more like private tutoring. He was unable to provide location details for Suratman Dahlan but did promise to work on it. I stayed and gave a lecture to some of his students. The following day I stopped by to see if he found anything. He had gone to Atman's village but his parents were not home. That night I gave a lecture to a different group of his students.

Abs gave me a ride to Valiant School to reunite with my friend Rusdi Karim. Rusdi, educated in the Netherlands, runs the largest English school on Ternate. I first met him in 2014 when he asked me to meet his class and provide them someone to converse with. Since then the school has been expanded to 1000 students with 25 instructors, all trained by Rusdi himself. Rusdi purchased the building next door to the school and plans to install a tunnel between buildings and increase the enrollment to 2000. Since he is educating the children of the most influential people on the island, I asked if he had any influence with the sultan who controls the Portuguese Armor in the palace museum. Rusdi said he knew the sultan, actually, he is the Crown Prince who will soon replace his deceased father. Rusdi promised to see what he could do.

My secondary objective was to visit the Banda Islands to see for myself, the island that was traded for Manhattan, New York. First I had to fly to Ambon, one hour south. To reach the ferry port which is about 15 km distant, I negociated a price of 100,000 rupia, about $8. The ferry to Banda Neira costs approximately $33 and runs every other day except Friday which is a Muslim religious day. I arrived on a Friday and stayed in a nearby hotel, returning at 7:30 the next morning. A maximum of 16 foreigners are allowed on a single trip and they must purchase special tickets. The departure time was 9:00 am but the start was delayed until 10:30 for the delivery of a casket. Six hours later we arrived at Neira. I managed to obtain a room at the Delfikal guest house, within 250 meters from the ferry landing.

I made friends with a British couple from London who had a room nearby. Alan builds sets for a theater company, Shameen is a pharmacist. Following dinner, Alan showed me where the ATMs were hidden and I tried my luck with an ATM card. I couldn't get any cash until I used a credit card the next morning. Next, he showed me where to catch the boat to Run island. The location is at the south end of the waterfront, 500 meters from the ferry landing.

The next day With the boat to Run not due to depart until 11 am, I managed a tour of the Dutch trading fortress. Constructed in the 1600s, it is pentagon shaped with a single entrance and very thick high walls. Cannons could easily reach to Run Island away from the dock

any spot in the harbor including the volcano, Gunung Api, very close by. At ground level are 12 rooms for trading, administration and security.

The boat is 9 feet wide and about 50 feet long. The diesel engine is directly coupled to the propeller shaft. With no reverse. The boat is polled backwards then it begins moving forward when the engine starts. Ladies and children sit on reeds in the covered forward section. The enclosed engine compartment is located in the center and the helmsman controls the tiller from its roof. Passengers sit wherever they can in the stern. There were no visible life jackets or radios and I hope they had a fire extinguisher. The boat speed was 6 knots and it tracked very well, requiring minimum rudder.

Two and a half hours later we wound through the coral reefs and docked, bow on, to a long wooden wharf. Prior to leaving Neira, the house manager had called ahead to make reservations without asking any questions of me. I had been traveling with Ger, a spry 66year old Irish grandmother and followed her knowing I would at least have someone to converse with. She had been staying at the other Delfikal guest house and her manager had made reservations at Manhattan II.

Immediately after checking in, I climbed 400 feet to the surface and began exploring this magical island. Run is a ½ by 2-mile-long limestone island and is 10 miles from Naira. This is one of the original sources of God's natural nutmeg trees (all are located in the Banda Islands). The north end is lower than the south end, is easier to reach and is under heavy cultivation. I was checking out the less access able south end.

This is the GARDEN OF EDEN. There are no snakes and Adam and Eve didn't show but this fertile soil could grow anything. In this tropical rain forest, everything is lush green. Everywhere the eye can see are ferns, grass, nutmeg and coconut trees all projecting out of the rich black soil. I reached down with my bare hand, no tools, and grabbed a handful of dirt. A child could have done the same thing. It was completely friable and I slowly worked it through my thumb and fingers until it all fell back to the ground. When I was finished, my hand was sticky with some natural miracle growth additive. I was wearing a thin shirt, shorts and a very worn pair of shoes with a hole in one sole and no socks. Walking through the vegetation I encountered no nettles or poisonous leaves but every few feet I did have to unhook a 1/16 diameter vine.

Walking along near the edge which was covered with bushes, I almost stepped out into space and barely managed to avoid a 20-foot fall. I was looking for places Nathanial Courthope would have placed cannons. Nearby was a steel structure capable of holding racks of nutmeg for drying. Apparently no longer in use as a nutmeg factory, it was named El Dorado. Following my initial survey, I had to carefully climb down the limestone cliff, very dangerous for an old timer. I had to toss my light rain jacket ahead and face into the wall carefully securing hand and foot holds.

The next day Ger, a French traveler named Jean and I rented a boat for exploring and snorkeling the 80 degree F water. The north end of the island is connected to a tiny island named Nailaka by a ½ mile partially submerged sandspit. Nailaka is one of the locations Courthope placed cannons for the defense of Run. Slightly to the east is an underwater formation known as the wall which supposedly offers great snorkeling. The water wasn't flat enough that day to enjoy it. In the morning, we had traversed the sandspit but we had to round Nailaka on the way back due to the rising tide. We found that the boat owner was also the local policeman.

After lunch, while walking the frontage path and studying a wall mural, I encountered a man named Mr. Burhan. He had been drying a few pounds of nutmeg and mace in front of his house and turned out to be the owner of the guest house, Nailaka, which my manager had reserved. Burhan was dark skinned but had European features and spoke excellent English. He is the local teacher with classes in the mornings. Because he was the one I was originally scheduled to stay with, I checked out of Manhattan II and into Nailaka.

He showed me the north end of the island with much easier trails and pathways. I asked to see a cinnamon tree. The trunk was 6 or 7 inches in diameter and grey in color, very unremarkable. Had he not pointed it out I would never have known it was there. He grabbed a leaf and rolled it between his thumb and forefinger. The exquisite smell of that leaf left no doubt to its identity. Cinnamon sticks are formed by making vertical cuts in the bark. Burhan claimed the cinnamon tree is very hearty and can thrive in a wide latitude belt. Nearby were some clove trees. This was February and clove seeds are not ripe until June or July. Many times, there are two seasons of cloves, the second harvest in December. Mashing a clove tree leaf left no doubt to its identity. Most open space on this end of the island was cultivated with vegatables.

I only had time to stay on Pulau Rhun or more commonly Banda Run for 2 nights. The first night was at Manhattan II. The food was good and the accommodations were excellent even having mosquito nets over the beds. One feature it had over Nailaka was sit down toilets. Nailaka had the Arab open pit style and the showers were from a dipper. Both guest houses had warm water, heated on the roof during the day. Manhattan II wash water was slightly brown where Nailaka's was clear. Both houses served cubed mangos with every meal. The thing that swayed me in favor of Nailaka, besides the owners excellent English was the exquisite egg-plant Indonesian that was served for dinner. There is a third guest house named Manhattan of which I have no knowledge. All 3 are competitive and charge $13/day. I cannot imagine any other place in the world where a tropical paradise experience could be had for such a bargain.

I boarded the boat for a return to Neira about 8:30 am. This was a different one than the boat I arrived in though the dimensions were about the same. Shortly after getting underway, deadly black diesel smoke began pouring out of the engine room. Apparently, some type of cover had worked loose and the problem was resolved within a few minutes. We encountered a smooth sea and were back to Neira by 11.

That afternoon I had time to visit the Neira museum and found it to be a real treasure. From pictures hung on the wall, I snapped a portrait of Cohn and a Dutch ship under construction. There were many guns, knives, ship models, coins and other artifacts on display. The museum is located directly across the street from my residence and controlled by the manager.

The ferry departed at 9 am and with smooth seas arrived at the harbor 6 hours later. I scored a taxi ride to the airport, made a reservation and found a place to stay directly across the street. The motorcycle group who enjoy providing rides to the city 5 km away were very interested and followed me across the street to the hotel, almost in disbelief.

My flight on Garuda Air was unable to land due to severe weather over Ternate and returned 2 ½ hours later to Ambon. Garuda put me up in a hotel with a complete stranger for a room-mate, which included meals and taxi fare

— Back in Ternate

both ways. My new companion was both amiable and helpful, even attempting to make my cell phone communicate locally. He happened to be a technical representative of Epson with good skills but AT&T had me locked out. Anyway, his English was excellent providing great conversation between us I managed to get my room back and hooked up with Rusdi again. That evening I lectured to a group of his on the Portuguese. Next day I visited the neighbor island of Tidore. The distance is only 2 miles and the ride was less than 50 cents on a work boat.

Abdul?

Tidore is a very laid back place almost wholly dependent on Ternate for supplies but they do grow most of their own food. Like its neighbor, it was created by a volcano so most everything is located in the flatland between it and the sea. A small power plant is located to the east of the harbor. The main city is over 30 km to the south. A three- km walk showed mostly farming punctuated by some mini convenience type stores, political signs advertising candidates for a coming election and a school. I caught a ride back to the dock area on a very unusual vehicle. It was a takeoff of a double wide seat bicycle driven RICKSHAW but it substituted a motorcycle for power. The double wide seat was in the front. For the return trip, I rode inside a speedboat to avoid baking in the tropical sun.

Rusdi came by to inform me that he had arranged a photo-op with Crown Prince Hidayat Mudaffar at 4 pm. It was 3:30 when he told me but we did manage to make it in time. After obtaining a signature allowing his picture to be used in the book, Rusdi and I posed with the Prince in front of a gold, two headed eagle called a Garuda. This Garuda is the symbol of the kingdom which includes the islands of Ternate, Tidore, Moti, and Makian. The Crown Prince will soon become the 49th Sultan of Ternate.

The first Sultan, Sultan Cico, AKA Baab Mansur Malamo, reigned from 1257 to 1277, prior to the coming of the Arab traders circa 1350. The 25th Sultan, Sultan Chaerun AKA Jamil is the one murdered by Castro. He reigned from 1535 to 1570. The Prince replaces his father, Sultan Mudaffar Syah, 1975 to 2015.

It was the third day of my second visit to Ternate and I still had no information regarding Suratman Dahlan. I was scheduled to fly to Makassar at 4 pm. Rusdi agreed to escort me along with Ibrahim Umakamea who knew

who reigned

for a half mile ~ ~~riding with him~~

where Atman's parents lived. Fortunately, they were home and informed us that Atman has completed his Masters in English studies and would be arriving at the airport at 1:30 today.

Rusdi and I met him at the airport where we had a two-hour reunion. Atman plans to continue his studies and obtain a PHD in English. I now had to plan for a 3rd visit to Ternate to catch up with my friend's activities and obtain more signatures.

The next morning, while waiting in Makassar for Fort Rotterdam to open, I took a slow walk to reacquaint myself with the local area. I was actually stalked by a rickshaw cyclist who thought I should not be ~~walking~~? I *Ok* noticed people entering a covered outdoor amphitheater and decided to check it out. Inside was a Lions Club vision event for school children which had yet to begin. The PA system, the best I had ever heard, obviously installed by an audio engineer, was playing "New York, New York".

I found an empty seat on the aisle behind two teenage girls. The one in front began making a sketch. It completely surprised me when the young girl reached back and handed me the drawing. It was her way of introducing herself, wanting to make conversation with me. She had made a sketch on each side of the sheet, the one in front of a young girl holding a rose. She indicated that her nickname was Lidya. It was very touching and for a moment I was at a loss, finally ~~deciding to~~ I decided give her a copy of my book with a note inside. This 15-year old girl possessed a real talent and probably could work for Disney Studios.

A short while later I was inside Fort Rotterdam seeking information regarding my friend Abdul Rahman. Mohammed Muyazdlala who is a licensed tour guide and runs a small but very effective English school at the fort informed me that Abdul was in Monado establishing his 25th English training school. He promised to set me up with a flight there.

I had first met Mohammed who goes by the nickname Lala, meaning light, in 2014. He is the person who mentored Abdul, who was my tour guide to the Fort Rotterdam museum in 2013. Lala works with students from the university, training them as tour guides. Two of his students who are training at the Merchant Marine Academy spoke so well that I could easily have taken them to be Americans. Lala's background in English goes back to 1976. He

This was his 25th school

was escorting A professor from England on a tour of Run Island in the Banda group. The professor asked Lala what his fee was? His reply, Just, spend an hour each day teaching me English. Over time Lala became proficient and his students are the best examples of his success.

Abdul met me at the Monado airport 2-days later. He had leased a 3-story building on the coast, near downtown, to house the classrooms. His team was busy painting and remodeling the building. The plan was to install a coffee shop and business counter on the first floor with classrooms above. It was amazing how Abdul had progressed from a student tour guide and docent to a dynamic businessman in four short years. His goal is to establish new schools far into the future.

I planned to fly direct to Ternate, bypassing Makassar so I arranged with a travel agency to fly Lion Air. The flight was both direct and cheap but was cash only. Securing and printing the ticket kept 3 people busy for 15 minutes and when complete, they requested a photo-op with me. Indonesia is really a friendly place.

On arriving at the airport, the next morning, I found the flight had been cancelled. Lion Air, run by the Chinese, is the armpit of the industry. I knew that seat spacing placed my knees against the back of the seat in front of me and that they didn't even provide free water during flights but I hadn't expected the cancellation. They said I could arrange to find my own room at my cost and take a chance on an early morning flight or request a refund. The cash price for the flight was 500,000 rupia and the refund amounted to 390,000, a loss of about $9. Evidently, they felt no responsibility for the travel agency fee.

The Indonesian employees did their best to remedy the problem and set me up with Nam Air next door. Five people working on my behalf, employees of both companies, assisted with my baggage and walked me through security enabling me to board a plane that had had landed late. I was actually airborne 30 minutes before the cancelled flight was scheduled to depart. These people are really great.

Back in Ternate for the third time, my homestay was full but they helped me book at another place. The next day Atman and I retraced part of the 2013 route in search of Anwar, the gardener/owner of his nutmeg gave me several nutmeg nuts covered with mace —

plantation. Traveling on the perimeter road, we found his place 11 km from town. Anwar was home and happy to see his picture in the book. He only knows a trifle English but is the headmaster of a nearby school. After a brief conversation, he signed off for the book, gave a tour of his current operation then bid us farewell. With the Ternate business concluded, Jakarta was the next stop. *Anwar will rev a copy of this book*

In Jakarta, I had 2 days to enjoy before the return flight to San Francisco. I especially wanted to hook up with a docent from the National Museum. Phivan Wright had given me a special personal tour and had recommended "Nathanial's Nutmeg" as a reference book for my project. Unfortunately, the museum was closed for renovation and I had no way of looking her up.

I wanted to purchase a used inflatable life jacket, virtually impossible in the US. I had bought one in 2013 for about $30 and managed to locate the same store. The previous owner had sold to a shrewd Chinese man who wanted twice my 300,000 rupia offer. This stop was on the way to the Sunda Kalapa Maritime Museum which I had visited twice before. The long walk gave me plenty of time to plan my purchase strategy. After revisiting the museum and watchtower I returned to the store. I hid a 100,000 rupia bill so that my wallet showed only 400,000 rupia plus a few smaller bills. My final offer was 400,000 rupia, about $32. Instead of vocally describing an offer, I have found that displaying the actual bills works best. I showed him the cash and he hesitated. Then I threw out a couple of smaller bills. He returned the smaller bills, we shook hands and I scored the life jacket.

On the final night it rained, not a heavy downpour but a steady drizzle. I personally enjoy the warm tropical rain, put on my old worn shoes and a light waterproof jacket then headed outside. The air was clean and the rain refreshed my face. With no concern of damaging my shoes, I could walk in a straight line, through mud and puddles with all the freedom children enjoy. I was in my zone. I passed 2 carts selling kebob gyros and stopped at the second one. The cart had a flat panel which sheltered the owner from the rain. He sliced and heated the carved lamb on a propane burner then added the fixings. The completed sandwich is placed inside a long narrow box with the owner's business name printed on the outside. How can you beat that, a fresh hot and delicious sandwich while walking in the warm rain.

It was still relatively early and wishing to extend a had delightful evening on the last night, I sat down next to a street girl who patted the seat next to her. The area is called Jalan Jaska and is one of the seedy areas of the city. I personally enjoy this type of neighborhood which is both more interesting and affordable than the sterile hotels downtown. The lady was very attractive with wide set brown eyes and a distinct European look. Obviously, there was a Dutch grandfather in her gene code. Street girls scare the hell out of me as they could be carrying any type of disease, but I was just looking for a little conversation. I shared a quart of beer and asked what she did during the day. She was very evasive on this but did speak excellent English. She kept asking me to rent a room where she would provide a massage with or without a happy ending. Without needing any of her services, I gave her 20,000 rupia for her time and the conversation.

With the benefit of observing Indonesia over a period of four years I have determined that the country is undergoing a rapid transformation. There is a huge enthusiam to learn English. Much new construction is underway both in remote areas like Lebaun and in urban locations. Indonesion Telecom is installing fiber optic cables to connect all the islands. The country is definitly on the road to moderinazation. Too bad the government refuses to curb smoking.

The last two signatures I needed were delivered by email from Julian Roe and Jean Pierron. This brings me to the end. This world is an interesting and exiciting place waiting to be explored and enjoyed by everyone. My advice to any CURIOUS person is to get up off that rocker, turn off the TV, spin the globe, locate a destination, purchase a bus, boat, rail or airline ticket and ENJOY.

ten

Who would have thought:

That a C student in boring WORLD HISTORY would ever be inspired and driven to write a book on the subject?

That a C student in ENGLISH, who panicked at the thought of writing a paper would ever be driven to do a book?

That Prince Henry, born only 70 years after Marco Polo's passing would open the gate of exploration, and 65 years after Henry's Passing, less than a single lifetime, Dias would ROUND the CAPES, Columbus would discover the NEW WORLD and the Magellan expedition would CIRCLE the GLOBE?

That a single company employee would control the entire DUTCH EAST INDIES?

That a single person would rule SPAIN, PORTUGAL, most of NORTH and SOUTH AMERICA, the CARRIBEAN, GUAM and the PHILLIPINES?

That a single country would control most of the WORLD?

That the same country would spark the INDUSTRIAL REVOLUTION?

That following WWII, the two most hated enemies of the USA would become her strongest allies?

A final note;

I happen to be a curious person who was inspired to create this work after visiting Ternate. This culminates three years of effort. The last four months have been especially intense and I will be extremely happy to get my life back. The reader can learn much of what I learned in a few days or a week. For more detail read the sources listed in the bibliography. As soon as I have five hard copies of this book in my hands I will return to Indonesia, insert a personal note and just feel the love when my friends each receive a copy.

Jim
31 DEC, 2016

Returning from Indonesia three months later brings me to the end. I now have all the required signatures and have been reaquainted with my friends and felt their love. My hope is that this work will inspire some youngsters to understand, appreciate and enjoy this fascinating planet and explore it on their own.

\
Jim
30 APR, 2017

BIBLIOGRAPHY

Aldrich, Robert, *Greater France: A History of French Overseas Expansion*, St. Martin's Press, 1996

Bawlf, Samuel, *The Secret Voyage of Sir Francis Drake*, 1577- 1580, Douglas and McIntyre, 2003

Bergreen, Laurence, *Over the Edge of the World: Magellan's Terrifying Circumnavigation of the Globe*, HarperCollins Publishers, 2003

Brown, Stephan R., *Merchant Kings: When Companies Ruled the World, 1600–1900*, St. Martin's Press, 2009

Clark, Leonard, *The Rivers Ran East*, Publishers Group West, 2001

Cohen, J. M., editor and translator, *Christopher Columbus: The Four Voyages*, Penguin Group, 1969

Editore, Giulio Einaudi, *The Travels of Marco Polo*, Orion Press, 1958

Fraser, Rebecca, *The Story of Britain, from the Romans to the Present: A Narrative History*, W. W. Norton and Company, 2003

Herman, Arthur, *To Rule the Waves: How the British Navy Shaped the Modern World*, Harper Perennial, 2005

Humble, Richard, *The Explorers* (The Seafarers, vol. 3), Time-Life Books, 1978

Mann, Charles C., *1493: Uncovering the New World Columbus Created*, Random House, Vintage Books, 2011

Miller, Russel / Editors of Time-Life Books, *The East Indiamen* (The Seafarers), Time-Life Books, 1980

Milton, Giles, *Nathaniel's Nutmeg: or, The True and Incredible Adventures of the Spice Trader Who Changed the Course of History*, Farrar, Straus and Giroux, 1999

Rosen, William, *The Most Powerful Idea in the World: A Story of Steam, Industry and Invention*, Random House, 2010

Rodrigues, Jorge Nascimento / Devezas, Tessaleno, *Pioneers of Globalization: Why the Portuguese Surprised the World*, Centro Atlantico, 2007

Whipple, A. B. C., *Fighting Sail* (The Seafarers), Time-Life Books, 1978

1. Marco Polo by Rustichello

The listed book, *The Travels of Marco Polo*, is my sole source.

P 262 They have gold in the greatest abundance, its source being inexhaustible

P 263 It happened after some time that a north wind began to blow… year 1264

2. Prince Henry the Navigator

05 third son of Portuguese King Joao: Jorge Nascimento Rodrigues and Tessaleno Devezas, *Pioneers of Globalization. Why the Portuguese Surprised the World* (Centro Atlantico, 2007), 87.

05 at fourteen Henry became a duke: Rodrigues and Devezas, *Globalization*, 87.

05 wore a rough hair shirt: Richard Humble, *The Explorers* (Time-Life Books, 1978), 28.

05 copy of Rustichello's *Il Millione*: Rodrigues and Devezas, *Globalization*, 85.

05 discovery of the Madeira Islands: Humble, *Explorers*, 28.

05 lived in strict celibacy: Humble, *Explorers*, 28.

06 grand master of: Humble, *Explorers*, 28.

06 successor to the Knights Templar: Humble, *Explorers*, 27.

06 Pope Callixtus II granted: Rodrigues and Devezas, *Globalization*, 89.

06 a number of rent-seeking positions: Rodrigues and Devezas, *Globalization*, 88.

07 quadrant and astrolabe were converted: Rodrigues and Devezas, *Globalization*, 129–30.

07 *Regiment of the Astrolabe and Quadrant*: Rodriguez/Devezas, *Globalization*, 139.

08 introduced the *caravel*: Rodrigues and Devezas, *Globalization*, 130.

08 first expedition with a profit: Humble, *Explorers*, 30.

08 first year slaves were captured: Humble, *Explorers*, 30.

09 "The Desire to do Good": Humble, *Explorers*, 30.

09 unifying the royal family: Humble, *Explorers*, 36.

09 padrao marker at Cape Cross: Humble, *Explorers*, 37.

09 safe anchorage in Walvis Bay: Humble, *Explorers*, 38.
09 holed up for five days: Humble, *Explorers*, 39.
09 mouth of the Orange River: Humble, *Explorers*, 39.
10 thirteen days later: Humble, *Explorers*, 39.
10 no land loomed on the eastern horizon: Humble, *Explorers*, 39.
10 had the crew not threatened mutiny: Humble, *Explorers*, 41.
10 flanked by Table Mountain: Humble, *Explorers*, 42.

3. The Rise and Fall of the Portuguese Empire

13 Portuguese spy named Pêro da Covilhã: Richard Humble, *The Explorers* (Time-Life Books, 1978), 89.
13 Covilhã spent his final days: Humble, *Explorers*, 89.
13 with two naos, a caravel: Humble, *Explorers*, 91.
13 Mozambique was one of: Humble, *Explorers*, 99.
13 In Malindi, a Hindu port: Humble, *Explorers*, 100.
14 took three excruciating months: Humble, *Explorers*, 102.
15 Pedro Alvares Cabral led: Humble, *Explorers*, 104.
15 claiming Brazil for his country: Humble, *Explorers*, 104.
15 cargo of half a dozen elephants: Humble, *Explorers*, 105.
15 mob of 3,000 resentful Muslims stormed the depot: Humble, *Explorers*, 105.
15 combination trading post: Humble, *Explorers*, 105.
15 he sacked and destroyed Mombasa: Humble, *Explorers*, 106.
15 a young noble, Ferdinand Magellan: Humble, *Explorers*, 106.
15 he began fortifying a series of harbors: Humble, *Explorers*, 106.
16 looting and burning their ships: Humble, *Explorers*, 106.
16 population numbering 450 settlers: Humble, *Explorers*, 106.
17 5 percent of face value: Jorge Nascimento Rodrigues and Tessaleno Devezas, *Pioneers of Globalization: Why the Portuguese Surprised the World* (Centro Atlantico, 2007), 116.
17 the significant sum of 350,000 cruzados: Rodrigues and Devezas, *Globalization*, 117.
17 in the sands of Alcácer Quibir: Rodrigues and Devezas, *Globalization*, 121.

17 February 28, 1570, Jorge de Castro: Personal observation, monument in Ternate.

18 aggressive religious proselytisms: Rodrigues and Devezas, *Globalization*, 126.

4. COLUMBUS

19 "At a very tender age I entered": Richard Humble, *The Explorers* (Time-Life Books, 1978), 55.

19 north all the way to Iceland: J. M. Cohen, *Christopher Columbus: The Four Voyages* (Penguin Books, 1969), 13.

19 a Portuguese cannon wounded him: Humble, *Explorers*, 55.

19 he headed north to Lisbon: Humble, *Explorers*, 55.

19 the art of cartography: Humble, *Explorers*, 55.

19 acquire…latitude determination: My personal deduction. It existed only in Lisbon.

19 read and write and converse in three languages: Humble, *Explorers*, 54.

20 acquired an impressive library: Humble, *Explorers*, 55.

20 discovered three books: Humble, *Explorers*, 56.

20 Rustichello's *Il Millione*: Humble, *Explorers*, 56.

20 Ptolemy's *Geographia*: Humble, *Explorers*, 56.

21 *Imagio Mundi* by Pierre d'Ailly: Humble, *Explorers*, 56.

21 "The Atlantic is not so great": Humble, *Explorers*, 56.

21 "big talker and full of fancy and imagination": Humble, *Explorers*, 56.

22 introduction to Queen Isabella: Cohen, *Columbus*, 34.

22 relationship with Luis de Santangel: Humble, *Explorers*, 60.

22 the crown's only obligation was to pay the wages of the crew: Humble, *Explorers*, 60.

22 the crown gave Columbus everything he bargained for: Humble, *Explorers*, 61.

23 destination was the Canary Islands: Cohen, *Columbus*, 39.

23 September 6 left Gomera with fresh supply of stores: Cohen, *Columbus*, 40.

23 Polaris…moved in a circle: Cohen, *Columbus*, 15.

23 believed the earth was pear shaped: Cohen, *Columbus*, 15.

23 believed … he sometimes sailed uphill: Cohen, *Columbus*, 15.
23 Columbus spotted candle-like flames: Cohen, *Columbus*, 52.
23 Rodrigo de Triano spotted land: Cohen, *Columbus*, 52.
23 Triano's reward was pocketed by Columbus: Cohen, *Columbus*, 52.
24 believed we came from the sky: Cohen, *Columbus*, 58.
24 began repeating the words of Columbus: Cohen, *Columbus*, 56.
24 he figured they would be easy to convert: Cohen, *Columbus*, 56.
24 The Indians traded balls of cotton: Cohen, *Columbus*, 55.
24 Their most important use of cotton was to make hammocks: Cohen, *Columbus*, 80.
24 island the Indians called Colba (Cuba): Cohen, *Columbus*, 75.
24 found tobacco, a bark-less dog: Cohen, *Columbus*, 75.
24 Pinzon took off on his own: Cohen, *Columbus*, 82.
24 Columbus befriended the king: Cohen, *Columbus*, 88.
24 Santa Maria drifted onto a reef: Cohen, *Columbus*,
24 instead of assisting, made for the Niña: Cohen, *Columbus*, 91.
24 sent a boat to assist: Cohen, *Columbus*, 91.
24 the cacique took ownership: Cohen, *Columbus*, 92.
25 named this site Navidad: Cohen, *Columbus*, 93.
25 weighed anchor January 4, 1493, headed back toward Spain: Cohen, *Columbus*, 95.
25 reunited with the Pinta: Cohen, *Columbus*, 96.
25 secret pact with the crew to split fifty-fifty: Cohen, *Columbus*, 97.
25 Golfo de las Flechas: Cohen, *Columbus*, 100.
25 the two ships became separated: Cohen, *Columbus*, 101.
25 anchored off Santa Maria Island: Cohen, *Columbus*, 104.
25 The shore party was imprisoned: Cohen, *Columbus*, 105.
25 managed to negotiate the return of his boat and crew: Cohen, *Columbus*, 109.
25 on March 3 they encountered the most severe North Atlantic storm: Cohen, *Columbus*, 109.
25 anchored in the Taugas River: Cohen, *Columbus*, 110.
25 he risked a meeting with King Joao II: Cohen, *Columbus*, 112.
25 curious about whether the latitude was below: Cohen, *Columbus*, 112.
25 Columbus arrived back in Palos March 14: Cohen, *Columbus*, 113.

26 Pinzon…rebuffed by the crown, died within a month: Cohen, *Columbus*, 114.

26 the crown commissioned him to raise a new fleet: Cohen, *Columbus*,

26 Returning to La Navidad…all the colonists had been killed: Cohen, *Columbus*, 146.

26 sent Columbus home in chains: Humble, *Explorers*, 77.

26 landfall in Panama: Humble, *Explorers*, 77.

27 governor waited seven months: Humble, *Explorers*, 77.

27 eclipse began February 28: Humble, *Explorers*, 77.

27 died a wealthy but unhappy man: Humble, *Explorers*, 77.

5. MAGELLAN

28 Anthony Pigafetta was the chief chronicler: Laurence Bergreen, *Over the Edge of the World: Magellan's Terrifying Circumnavigation of the Globe* (HarperCollins, 2003), 416.

28 at age twelve he became a page: Richard Humble, *The Explorers* (Time-Life Books, 1978), 120.

28 and backed the wrong candidate: Bergreen, *Over the Edge*, 18.

29 sensed a trick: Humble, *Explorers*, 119.

29 managed to rescue forty: Humble, *Explorers*, 120.

29 stay aboard with them as a placating hostage: Humble, *Explorers*, 121.

29 accused of selling them for a personal profit: Humble, *Explorers*, 121.

29 or absent without leave: Humble, *Explorers*, 121.

29 "For all I care you can sell your services elsewhere": Humble, *Explorers*, 121.

29 possessed a letter from his close friend Francisco Serrao: Bergreen, *Over the Edge*, 30.

30 he was poisoned with betel leaves: Bergreen, *Over the Edge*, 346.

30 a shortcut route to the Spice Islands: Humble, *Explorers*, 122.

30 Magellan's group met Diogo Barbosa: Humble, *Explorers*, 122.

31 Juan de Aranda proposed: Humble, *Explorers*, 122.

31 Young King Charles V signed a contract: Humble, *Explorers*, 123.

31 given the title of captain general: Humble, *Explorers*, 123.

31 King Manuel, had employed a spy: Humble, *Explorers*, 123.

32 reached an enraged King Charles: Bergreen, *Over the Edge*, 41.

32 had Faleiro removed from the expedition: Humble, *Explorers*, 124.

32 Fonseca…he managed to install his illegitimate son, Juan: Bergreen, *Over the Edge*, 55.

32 All three Spanish captains were jealous and resentful: Bergreen, *Over the Edge*, 55.

32 The Armada of the Moluccas composition was as follows: Bergreen, *Over the Edge*, xiii–xiv.

33 September 29 1519, five ships and 260 sailors were underway: Bergreen, *Over the Edge*, 72.

33 they were treated to a display of Saint Elmo's fire: Bergreen, *Over the Edge*, 89.

34 *San Antonio* refused to salute: Bergreen, *Over the Edge*, 92.

34 brought all the captains aboard: Bergreen, *Over the Edge*, 93.

34 Magellan, acting as judge and jury sentenced him to death: Bergreen, *Over the Edge*, 93.

34 Cartagena stated he would no longer take orders: Bergreen, *Over the Edge*, 94.

34 placed the insolent Cartagena under arrest: Bergreen, *Over the Edge*,

34 On November 29, they arrived at Cape Saint Augustine: Bergreen, *Over the Edge*, 96.

34 made Rio de Janeiro on December 13: Bergreen, *Over the Edge*, 96.

34 Orgies and dancing took place ashore every night: Bergreen, *Over the Edge*, 101.

35 Two days after Christmas…weighed anchor and headed south: Bergreen, *Over the Edge*, 104.

35 On March 31 at 49.5 degrees…anchored…Port Saint Julian: Humble, *Explorers*, 129.

35 new home until southern spring: Humble, *Explorers*,

35 he was murdered by Quesada: Humble, *Explorers*, 131.

35 with mutinous Spaniards now in control of three ships: Humble, *Explorers*, 131.

35 on boarding, stabbed Mendoza in the throat: Humble, *Explorers*, 132.

35 Magellan now with a three-to-two advantage: Humble, *Explorers*, 132.

35 At long last Magellan's fleet was under the control: Humble, *Explorers*, 132.

36 Grateful of receiving a pardon: Humble, *Explorers*, 132.

36 sentenced to be marooned ashore: Bergreen, *Over the Edge*, 153.

36 The expedition anchored at Puerto Santa Cruz until October: Bergreen, *Over the Edge*, 174.

36 They named it the Cape of Eleven Thousand Virgins: Bergreen, *Over the Edge*, 175.

36 The fleet passed through the inlet into a deep straight: Bergreen, *Over the Edge*, 178.

36 Eventually they came to a fork: Bergreen, *Over the Edge*, 190.

36 they had found the Pacific Ocean: Bergreen, *Over the Edge*, 190.

37 On November 28, the *Trinidad*, the *Conception*, and the *Victoria* entered the Pacific: Bergreen, *Over the Edge*, 200.

37 On December 22…left sight of land: Humble, *Explorers*, 147.

37 they were able to fish for sharks: Bergreen, *Over the Edge*, 219.

37 On March 6 they reached Guam: Bergreen, *Over the Edge*, 222.

37 natives stole his ships boat: Bergreen, *Over the Edge*, 225.

37 making landfall at Homohon Island: Bergreen, *Over the Edge*, 239.

37 Limasawa…began exchanges with the local ruler: Bergreen, *Over the Edge*, 244.

37 Magellan became a blood brother of the rajah: Bergreen, *Over the Edge*, 245.

37 Was very impressed with Magellan's theatrics: Bergreen, *Over the Edge*, 246.

38 had told Humadon that…same group that conquered Malacca: Bergreen, *Over the Edge*, 258.

38 Magellan was looked upon as a miracle-working prophet: Bergreen, *Over the Edge*, 274.

38 assist him in removing Chief Lapulapu from power: Bergreen, *Over the Edge*, 276.

38 Magellan led a party of fifty warriors: Bergreen, *Over the Edge*, 279.

38 Magellan responded by burning their huts: Bergreen, *Over the Edge*, 280.

38 The natives focused on the captain general: Bergreen, *Over the Edge*, 281.

39 On May 6, 1571…the *San Antonio* docked in Seville: Bergreen, *Over the Edge*, 297.

39 Enrique…developed a plan of revenge: Bergreen, *Over the Edge*, 294.

39 All in the shore party but Enrique were massacred: Bergreen, *Over the Edge*, 295.

39 The *Conception* was stripped and burned: Bergreen, *Over the Edge*, 314.

39 useful items were split between the *Victoria* and the *Trinidad*: Bergreen, *Over the Edge*, 314.

39 Indecisively they meandered...for six months: Humble. *Explorers*, 157.

39 Their luck changed when they discovered Palawan: Humble, *Explorers*, 157.

40 Carvello...abandoned the five crewmen...kidnapped crew members: Humble, *Explorers*, 158.

40 reached Tidore Island: Humble, *Explorers*, 158.

40 the Trinidad sprung a large leak: Humble, *Explorers*, 158.

40 Elcano decided he could wait no longer...he headed back to Spain: Humble, *Explorers*, 159.

40 On September 6, 1522, the *Victoria* reached Barra San Lucar: Humble, *Explorers*, 161.

41 Magellan's name was cleared: Humble, *Explorers*, 162.

41 The *Trinidad* took three months to repair: Humble, *Explorers*, 161.

41 enslaved to construct a fort on Ternate: Humble, *Explorers*, 161.

41 Espinosa and three crewmen survived: Humble, *Explorers*, 161.

6. Spain

42 Isabel, their oldest daughter: Jorge Nascimento Rodrigues and Tessaleno Devezas, *Pioneers of Globalization. Why the Portuguese Surprised the World* (Centro Atlantico, 2007), 87.

42 Catherine was wed to Henry VII's son Arthur: Rebecca Fraser, *The Story of Britain, from the Romans to the Present: A Narrative History* (W. W. Norton and Company, 2005), 250.

42 in the Treaty of Tordesillas: Richard Humble, *The Explorers*, (Time-Life Books, 1978), 91.

43 Balboa...they became the first Europeans to view the Pacific Ocean: Charles C. Mann, *1493: Uncovering the New World Columbus Created* (Random House, 2011), 442.

43 Hernán Cortés arrived in Mexico: Mann, *1493*, 361.

43 aided by massive die-offs from smallpox: Mann, *1493*, 362.

43 the potato…from high up in the Andes Mountains: Mann, *1493*, 263.

43 an enormous silver strike: Mann, *1493*, 179.

43 massive source of mercury: Mann, *1493*, 180.

44 Seven Cities of Cibola: Leonard F. Clark, *The Rivers Ran East* (Travelers Tales, 2001), 297.

44 swapping silver for silk and porcelain: Mann, *1493*, 197.

45 "The Reformation": Fraser, *Britain*, 253.

45 wed his second cousin Queen Mary: Fraser, *Britain*, 281.

46 died still foolishly fighting the Crusades: Rodrigues and Devezas, *Globalization*, 121.

46 he launched the ill-fated Spanish Armada: Fraser, *Britain*, 302.

47 Louisiana Purchase: Mann, *1493*, 469.

48 language has always been the companion of empire: Humble, *Explorers*, 53.

7. DUTCH EMPIRE

49 Madre de Deus: Russell Miller, *The East Indiamen*, (Time-Life Books, 1980), 8.

49 Jan Huygen van Linschoten published: Miller, *Indiamen*, 15.

49 "tolerated" by the sultans: Miller, *Indiamen*, 15.

49 finance expensive expeditions: Stephen R. Bown, *Merchant Kings* (St. Martin's Press, 2009).

50 construct ships four times faster: Miller, *Indiamen*, 64.

50 eliminate Portuguese competition: Brown, *Merchant Kings*, 28.

50 power to wage war: Brown, *Merchant Kings*, 28.

50 "We cannot carry on trade without war, nor war without trade": Brown, *Merchant Kings*, 38.

51 happily surrendered their island to the English: Giles Milton, *Nathaniel's Nutmeg, or The True and Incredible Adventures of the Spice Trader Who Changed the Course of History* (Farrar, Straus and Giroux, 1999), 272.

51 first and only East Indies territorial acquisition: Milton, Nutmeg, 272.

52 He was finally killed while attempting to obtain supplies: Milton, *Nutmeg*, 308.

52 Jourdain commented on 26-year old Coen's peach-fuzz beard: Brown, *Merchant Kings*, 35.

52 three thousand cannons were fired, no ships were actually sunk: Milton, *Nutmeg*, 299.

53 when he raised the white flag, he was shot and killed: Milton, *Nutmeg*, 302.

53 reducing the population of the Bandas from approximately fifteen thousand down to one thousand: Brown, *Merchant Kings*, 46.

54 as a reward for securing a complete monopoly: Brown, *Merchant Kings*, 46.

54 "beware of suspicious English activity": Brown, *Merchant Kings*, 47.

54 snuck back to Batavia with his new bride three years later: Brown, *Merchant Kings*, 50.

54 he found his twelve-year-old foster daughter: Brown, *Merchant Kings*, 31.

56 anchored near the present-day site of Coney Island: Brown, *Merchant Kings*, 68.

56 in 1621 the Dutch West India Company was chartered: Brown, *Merchant Kings*, 72.

56 Peter Stuyvesant was selected: Brown, *Merchant Kings*, 79. : Brown, *Merchant Kings*, 28.

56 Adrian van der Donck preceded the governor: Brown, *Merchant Kings*, 88.

57 an eighty-three-page document known as *The Remonstrance*: Brown, *Merchant Kings*, 94.

57 Colonel Richard Nicolls arrived: Brown, *Merchant Kings*, 98.

58 Nicolls proclaimed that New Amsterdam be renamed New York: Brown, *Merchant Kings*, 98.

58 both sides signed the 1674 Breda Treaty: Milton, *Nutmeg*, 363.

8. THE FRENCH EMPIRE

59 Napoleon III ... sent 14 ships and 2,500 troops: Robert Aldrich, *GREATER FRANCE, A History of French Overseas Expansion* (St. Martin's Press, 1996), 76

59 they occupied the port of Saigon: Aldrich, *Greater France, 77*.

60 1863 Cambodian King Norodom...opted for French alliance: Aldrich, *Greater France*, 79.

60 France took possession of New Caledonia: Aldrich, *Greater France*, 71.

60 French Polynesia… is a protectorate: Aldrich, Greater France, 70

60 France installed Maximilian I as Emperor: Aldrich, *Greater France, 134*

9. THE RISE AND FALL OF THE BRITISH EMPIRE

61 he prompted his daughter Margaret to marry James Stuart: Rebecca Fraser, *The Story of Britain, from the Romans to the present: A Narrative History* (W. W. Norton and Company, 2003), 250.

61 he prompted his son Arthur… to marry Princess Catherine of Aragon: Fraser, *Britain*, 250.

61 the new Prince of Wales became Henry VIII: Fraser, *Britain*, 252.

61 Henry created the Protestant Church of England: Fraser, *Britain*, 264.

61 he married his new sweetheart, Anne Boleyn: Fraser, *Britain*, 266.

61 Anne was accused of adultery, a treasonous offense, and beheaded: Fraser, *Britain*, 271.

61 Jayne Seymour, Henry's third wife…produced male heir…King Edward VI: Fraser, *Britain*, 271.

62 He increased the capital ship count from twelve to eighty-four: Arthur Herman, *To Rule the Waves: How the British Navy Shaped the Modern World* (HarperCollins Publishers, 2005), 40.

62 had to defend against a thirty-thousand-man invasion from France: Herman, *Waves*, 41.

62 Edward VI…made a hasty peace with France: Herman, *Waves*, 42.

62 known as Bloody Mary. She attempted to reinstall the Catholic Church: Fraser, *Britain*, 280.

62 She married her cousin, Prince Phillip of Spain, …to become King Phillip II: Fraser, *Britain*, 281.

63 *Foxe's Book of Martyrs* became the most widely read book in England: Herman, *Waves*, 47.

63 Elizabeth embarked on an undeclared cold war with Phillip II: Herman, *Waves*, 50.

63 waging for-profit economic war: Herman, *Waves*, 52.

63 John Hawkins was a second-generation privateer: Herman, *Waves*, 2.

63 they snuck into the safe harbor of San Juan de Ulloa: Herman, *Waves*, 10.

63 the Spanish, in an act of treachery, attacked the English: Bawlf, *Secret Voyage, 14*

64 The two cousins now had a personal vendetta against...Phillip II: Herman, *Waves*, 20.

64 he hatched up a plan to capture a mule train: Bawlf, *Secret Voyage, 32.*

64 In 1576 Martin Frobisher: Herman, *Waves*, 66.

64 England's first attempt at colonization was made in Ireland: Herman, *Waves*, 71.

64 They were considered savages: Herman, *Waves*, 71.

64 the Scots and the Spanish were needed to be kept away: Herman, *Waves*, 71.

64 Establishing colonies required driving out the existing property owners: Herman, *Waves*, 71.

65 The first uprising was led by James Fitzgerald: Herman, *Waves*, 71.

65 authorized Humphry Gilbert...to respond with any means necessary: Herman, *Waves*, 71.

65 to crawl between two rows of severed heads: Herman, *Waves*, 72.

65 to take the Scottish fortress on Rathlin Island: Herman, *Waves*, 72.

65 In 1578 Drake departed England...secret orders...access the South Sea: Herman, *Waves*, 78.

65 Thomas Doughty...began to claim authority: Herman, *Waves*, 83.

66 Drake captured the...*Nuestra Señora de la Conception*: Herman, *Waves*, 88.

66 eventually reaching his namesake Drake's Bay: Herman, *Waves*, 90.

67 "Is the queen alive and well?": Herman, *Waves*, 94.

67 he was knighted and became Sir Francis Drake: Herman, *Waves*, 94.

67 In 1580, Portugal...was annexed by Phillip II: Herman, *Waves*, 97.

67 Elizabeth dispatched a preemptive strike with sixteen ships: Herman, *Waves*, 113.

67 Dodging fire ships, his squadron became disorganized: Herman, *Waves*, 126.

68 he decided to return to Spain by way of Ireland...half the fleet was lost: Herman, *Waves*, 129.

68 With no Tudor heirs, the throne passed to her cousin, James Stuart, King James VI: Fraser, *Britain*, 313.

68 he wrote the King James Version of the Bible: Fraser, *Britain*, 319.

68 In 1607 the London Company set up a colony...called Jamestown: Herman, *Waves*, 154.

68 In 1620, they set up a second colony at Plymouth: Herman, *Waves*, 154.

68 The colonies quickly became a profitable business: Herman, *Waves*, 159.

68 Charles agreed to attack Cádiz: Herman, *Waves*, 164.

68 Charles, in defense of his friend, dissolved Parliament: Herman, *Waves*, 165.

69 Buckingham was stabbed to death: Herman, *Waves*, 166.

69 The result of the civil war...the Royalists lost...Charles was beheaded: Fraser, *Britain*, 349.

69 Oliver Cromwell became lord protector and leader of the country: Fraser, *Britain*, 355.

69 England was declared to be a commonwealth: Fraser, *Britain*, 351.

69 Both Scotland and Ireland had thrown off English rule: Fraser, *Britain*, 351.

69 Cromwell...proceeded to Ireland and laid siege to the largest garrisons: Fraser, *Britain*, 352.

70 the conquered land was redistributed to Cromwell's soldiers: Fraser, *Britain*, 352.

70 Cromwell managed to defeat Charles at Worcester: Fraser, *Britain*, 352.

70 Cromwell...regained rule over both Scotland and Ireland: Fraser, *Britain*, 352.

70 decreed Parliament... decide issues of importance...England should be governed by a king: Fraser, *Britain*, 360.

70 The fear was that if Holland were defeated, Louis would invade England: Fraser, *Britain*, 398.

70 the French were defeated, twenty-three thousand French soldiers killed: Fraser, *Britain*, 399.

70 England, Scotland, and Wales became Great Britain...UK: Fraser, *Britain*, 402.

71 claimed it was taxation without representation: Fraser, *Britain*, 455.

71 The colonists...finally overran the fort at Yorktown: Fraser, *Britain*, 463.

72 "I had ambition not only to go farther than any man... man to go": Herman, *Waves*, 293.

72 accompanying Cook were scientists Sir Joseph Banks… Solendar: Herman, *Waves*, 301.

72 the worlds' first scientific expedition…precursor to Darwin's: Herman, *Waves*, 302.

72 Cook proved…consumption of pickled cabbage would prevent scurvy: Herman, *Waves*, 301.

72 equipped with a brand-new chronometer: Herman, *Waves*, 304.

73 search for a Northwest Passage: Herman, *Waves*, 305.

73 He was killed in Hawaii on February 14, 1779: Herman, *Waves*, 305.

73 attacked by the VOC, its occupants tortured and murdered: Stephen R. Bown, *Merchant Kings* (St. Martin's Press, 2009),

73 initially the stockholder company wanted to set up trade: Bown, *Merchant Kings*,

73 charter giving the trading company many of the powers of a nation: Bown, *Merchant Kings*,

74 the Mughal emperor died…leaving India without any centralized control: Bown, *Merchant Kings*,

74 Robert Clive, leading a small party, managed to escape: Bown, *Merchant Kings*,

74 Clive, now a captain, led a group: Bown, *Merchant Kings*,

74 Clive led a force consisting of five Royal Navy vessels: Bown, *Merchant Kings*,

75 Clive…won the battle at Plassey Field using bluff and treachery: Bown, *Merchant Kings*,

75 a private company with the power to collect taxes and govern a country: Bown, *Merchant Kings*,

75 the unintended consequences…was a revolutionary dictatorship: Herman, *Waves*, 331.

76 In 1798, Nelson…managed to locate Napoleon's invasion fleet: A. B. C. Whipple, *Fighting Sail* (Time-Life Books, 1978), 74.

76 captains to take initiative if the opportunity were to arise: Whipple, *Fighting Sail*, 72.

76 Captain Thomas Foley…took the initiative…attack from the shore: Whipple, *Fighting Sail*, 78.

77 The goal was to exclude England from any trade: Whipple, *Fighting Sail*, 99.

77 the Danes presumed he would, signed a truce: Whipple, *Fighting Sail*, 105.

77 Nelson chased them back to Cádiz keep them blockaded: Whipple, *Fighting Sail*, 119.

77 Nelson attacked with two columns: Whipple, *Fighting Sail*, 146.

77 *Redoubtable* managed to grapple...allowed a sharpshooter to kill Nelson: Whipple, *Fighting Sail*, 153.

78 the combined French-Spanish fleet was utterly destroyed: Whipple, *Fighting Sail*, 165.

78 Villanueva stated that "all the captains were Nelsons": Herman, *Waves*, 395.

78 gave cause for the United States to declare the War of 1812: Herman, *Waves*, 410.

78 In 1815 General Wellington...defeated his army at Waterloo, Belgium: Fraser, *Britain*, 506.

78 Napoleon...imprisoned on the island of Saint Helena: Fraser, *Britain*, 506.

78 Britain had abolished its own slave trade in 1807: Herman, *Waves*, 419.

78 By 1833 it was abolished in all British possessions: Herman, *Waves*, 422.

79 Lincoln...in 1862... allowed search of US-flagged slave vessels: Herman, *Waves*, 422.

78 the Royal Navy acquired an altruistic humanitarian gloss: Herman, *Waves*, 423.

79 In 1662 the Royal Society was chartered: William Rosen, *The Most Powerful Idea in the World* (Random House, 2010), 16.

79 This elite group helped spark the Industrial Revolution: Rosen, *Idea*, 17.

79 combined with the concept and security of intellectual property rights: Rosen, *Idea*, 324.

79 The biggest mechanical need was pumps to dewater its many mines: Rosen, *Idea*, 23.

79 Thomas Savery...produced the first working steam pump: Rosen, *Idea*, 23.

79 Savery and his heirs...were able,... to extract royalty payments: Rosen, *Idea*, 52.

79 India, the original source of cheap cotton...became one of the largest markets: Fraser, *Britain*, 600.

80 Potatoes, first cultivated by the Inca Indians: Charles C. Mann, *1493: Uncovering the New World Columbus Created* (Random House, 2011), 263.

80 The Irish cultivated this single variety: Mann, *1493*, 269.

80 By 1845 it was all over Europe: Mann, *1493*, 286.

80 Forty percent of the population ate nothing else: Mann, *1493*, 289.

80 Mass migration to the United States and Canada was the result with heavy: Mann, *1493*, 289.

80 Opium Wars...Chinese officials attempted to stop the immoral trade: Herman, *Waves*, 461.

81 strong-armed into giving the company rights to trade from Hong Kong: Herman, *Waves*, 460.

81 enforcement of this policy against Boers would eventually lead to war: Fraser, *Britain*, 589.

81 sixteen-year-old Cecil Rhodes journeyed to South Africa in 1871: Stephen R. Bown, *Merchant Kings* (St. Martin's Press, 2009), 242.

82 with a new partner, he began purchasing shares in the De Beers mine: Bown, *Merchant Kings*, 251.

82 able to build roads, railroads...to the benefit of his companies: Bown, *Merchant Kings*, 254.

82 he "allowed" the colony to be named Rhodesia: Bown, *Merchant Kings*, 268.

82 "Madam, I have added two new provinces to your possessions": Bown, *Merchant Kings*, 279.

82 his negative legacy...left the native blacks without any vote or power: Bown, *Merchant Kings*, 280.

82 positive legacy...He established the Rhodes scholarship program: Bown, *Merchant Kings*, 280.

88 Mountbatten divided the country into three parts: Fraser, *Britain*, 732.

88 Palestine contained four hundred thousand Jews prior to World War II: Fraser, *Britain*, 732.

88 Britain pulled out of Palestine May 14, 1948: Fraser, *Britain*, 733.

88 Jews declared...the State of Israel to be located inside Palestine: Fraser, *Britain*, 733.

INDEX

Salomon, Antonio, 33, 34, 35
Saltpeter (potassium nitrate), 73, 81
Sanlucar de Barramenda, 33, 40
San Antonio, 33, 34, 35, 36, 39
San Josef, 76
San Nicolas, 76
San Juan de Ulloa, 63, 64
San Martin, Andres de, 33
San Diego, 48
Santa Cruz, Admiral, 67
Santa Domingo, 26
Santa Hermandad, 22
Santa Iglesia Catedral of Seville, 27
Santa Maria, 23, 24
Santa Maria Island, 25
Santangel, Luis de, 22
Sandwich Islands, 73
Sandwich, Lord, 73
Santiago, Cuba, 47
Santiago, 33, 35
Saragossa Treaty, 41
Sargasso weed, 23
Sargasso Sea, 25
Savery, Thomas, 79
Saw mills, wind and water powered, 49
Scottish, 62, 64, 65, 70
Scottish Civil War, 69
Scotland, 61, 68, 69, 70
Scurvy, 14, 72
Sebastio, King, 17, 46, 67
Sequeira, Diogo Lopes de, 28, 29
Serapis, 71
Serrano, Juan Rodriguez, 33, 36, 39

Serrao, Francisco, 29, 30, 31
Seven Year's War, 75
Seville, 17, 30, 33, 39, 40, 41, 44
Seymour, Jayne, 61
Shakespeare, William, 61
Shanghai, 83
Ship construction, 4 times faster, 50
Shio Money Tax, 69
Siamese, 37
Sicily, 86
Sidney, Sir Henry, 65
Sidonia, Admiral Medina, 67
Sierra Leone, 89
Silk, 44, 73
Silva, Nuno de, 65
Silver, 43, 44, 46, 49, 63, 64, 80
Simon Bolivar, 47
Singapore, 86, 89
Siraj ud-Dowlah, 74, 75
Slave(s), 8, 16, 30, 40, 43, 55, 63, 64, 78
Smallpox, 43
Smith, John, 68
Sofala, 15
Solendar, Daniel, 72
Sonar, 85
Sonoma, 48
South Africa, 10, 89
South America, 45, 47
South Atlantic, 15
South China Sea, 2
Spain, 17, 18, 22, 23, 30, 31, 35, 40, 41, 42, 43, 44, 45, 46, 47, 48, 49, 61, 63, 68, 76

Proof

Made in the USA
Columbia, SC
11 May 2017